Herbert Hoover, Unemployment, and the Public Sphere

A Conceptual History, 1919–1933

Vincent Gaddis

University Press of America,® Inc.
Lanham · Boulder · New York · Toronto · Oxford

University Press of America,® Inc.
4501 Forbes Boulevard
Suite 200
Lanham, Maryland 20706
UPA Acquisitions Department (301) 459-3366

PO Box 317
Oxford
OX2 9RU, UK

Printed in the United States of America
British Library Cataloging in Publication Information Available

Library of Congress Control Number: 2005926745
ISBN 0-7618-3234-3 (cloth : alk. ppr.)
ISBN 0-7618-3235-1 (paperback : alk. ppr.)
ISBN: 978-0-7618-3234-8

∞™ The paper used in this publication meets the minimum requirements of American National Standard for Information Sciences—Permanence of Paper for Printed Library Materials, ANSI Z39.48—1984

For Cathy and Mary

Contents

Foreword

Vincent Gaddis has written a very good book that gives us perspective on a neglected aspect of policy history—not only *how*, but more important, *why* Herbert Hoover coped with the vexing problem of unemployment as he did. The 2004 political campaign reminded Americans that George W. Bush was at that time the first American president since Herbert Hoover to preside over a net loss of U. S. jobs. As the unfolding saga of globalization moves millions of U. S. manufacturing and data processing jobs to developing countries, we have been forcefully reminded that no issue in public policy or public philosophy is more important or complicated than the issue of unemployment and the location of responsibility for it. Gaddis's innovative approach to the way Herbert Hoover answered these questions skillfully interweaves political history and political economy with *conceptual* history.

Drawing upon theoretical work by Quentin Skinner, Jurgen Habermas, and James Farr, Gaddis illuminates the ways in which language and the meanings of constitutive categories such as unemployment suggested—and precluded—specific political responses. Gaddis begins from the premise that political action is based not merely on a calculus of interests, but on meanings, shared at times, and at other times the basis for conflict and division. Contradictions between expectations and reality may engender conceptual change—or herculean efforts to change reality without compromising fundamental values. To understand party programs and public opinion, Gaddis posits, it is just as important to "follow the ideas" and "listen to the language" as it is to "follow the money." He does this, as he explores how Hoover and his closest collaborators defined this loaded category, *unemployment*, what they thought caused it and might cure it, how certain kinds of state responses to it threatened enduring political and moral values, and what seemed best—if those values were to be protected—by way of political action. Gaddis opens a bright, clear vista on the processes of political learning that gave Hoover early successes in his decade-long struggle with employment, and on how these early lessons finally brought him down.

Herbert Hoover was not the only one to wrestle with the meaning of unemployment. From the beginning, and long before Americans settled even on what to call it, they had a hard time coming to terms with the problem. During the American Revolution there were already artisanal wage workers who attempted to push the independence movement in a more radical direction, partly for ideological reasons but also to save themselves from the ravages of wage labor. The republican ideology that gave political meaning to the revolution taught that survival of the new republic depended on virtuous citizens, and civic virtue was linked in the popular mind with "free labor." Fear abounded that expansion of commerce would breed unrepublican luxury among the monied classes. Concern that the mass of Americans might be degraded to a permanent wage status that would reduce them to dependency provided a rationale for Jefferson's "extension of the sphere" through the Louisiana Purchase. Playing upon this dread of dependency, the Southern apology for slavery framed by George Fitzhugh and Henry Hughes charged that Northern "hireling labor" had no defense against losing their livelihoods in periods of slack work and in old age.

The most desperate skirmishes in the rising class war of the Gilded Age broke out when recurrent depressions in trade and business produced wage cuts and urban mass unemployment. No matter how industrial workers organized, their most universal and deeply felt goal was a system that would guarantee accumulation of a *competence*, savings enough to live in old age without being haunted by the specter of want. Conceived as a right of citizenship and a central part of the economic and social basis of citizenship, this was understood to include claims not only to decent and continuous wages but also to a property of some sort in a job. The workers' moral economy connected mass unemployment to a lack of virtue in the emerging forms of industrial capitalism and in a state that tolerated economic oppression.

For capitalists and social and economic writers, unemployment also loomed as a worrisome issue. Settlement house workers and social investigators discovered it anew in the Gilded Age as something close to the core of urban poverty. It began to be separated from the older categories of pauperism, and from the analyses, rooted in Protestant moralism and bourgeois culture, that laid blame for it on individual failings. Glimmerings of insight into structural causes began to appear, as when Massachusetts Labor Statistics Bureau Commissioner Carroll D. Wright pointed out that only a small increase in utilization of productive capacity in the textile industry could have soaked up all the unemployed in Fall River in the depression of the 1870s. Before long Yale's Arthur Hadley, a pro-corporate specialist in railroad economics, began noting that unemployment had worsened as manufacturing relied on rapidly increasing amounts of fixed capital. He connected unemployment to a rudimentary modernization theory in which the U. S. was a 19th century version of an undeveloped country. Most investment was in primary production, which was intensely cyclical. Most of the non-agricultural jobs were in manufacturing or extractive industries, which were highly cyclical and prone to over-production. Most workers had relatively simple consumption habits that did not produce enough pressure for economic diversification. Relief from savage downturns in employment would come from a shift in consumer tastes, rising consumption of more diversified goods that would produce upward pressure on wages, and a shift from primary to secondary and tertiary production, which would expand the middling classes of people earning salaries rather than day wages.

But many who studied the problem were not inclined to wait for it to be solved by evolution. Instead, diagnosing and dealing with unemployment became a pressing aspect of the "social question," which set in motion the movement to define a New Liberalism as a way of dealing with the consequences of market failure. Some Gilded Age and Progressive Era new liberals became passionate critics of laissez faire who rejected the assumption in classical economics that "government interference" was almost invariably harmful to the public good. Forming one wing of the Progressive Movement, these statist liberals called for political reforms to protect male, female, and child workers from overwork and occupational hazards, promote unions, and ensure a greater economic security. Because of structural features in the U. S. electoral system and cultural divisions in the highly diverse U. S. working class, a class-based political party did not turn out to be the most expedient method for winning these protections. American workers proved to be much more effectively conscious of class interests at the point of production than they were in politics, so labor reformers attacked the problems piecemeal, mostly at the city and state level. Theories arose showing how capitalists treated many human costs of production as variable costs that could simply be eliminated by firing workers when demand fell. These costs, which included continued subsistence—adequate food, decent shelter—for workers families, did not disappear; they were shifted to the community. Mobilizing new publics, statist liberals resisted biased legal interpretations such as "freedom of contract" that were used by the courts to nullify protective legislation, and they pushed for extending social protection to include insurance against a broad range of hazards, including old age, disability, and unemployment. These features of statist liberal discourse—the indictment of the courts as agents of capitalist employers and a growing sense of social responsibility for reasonably full employment and a fairer distribution of income and wealth—were advanced during World War I, when war mobilization required enlisting the support of workers. Both the National War Labor Board and activist judges on the side of labor forced adoption of minimum wage and maximum hours provisions and insisted on recognition of unions.

This was where Herbert Hoover came in. And it is something of why he moved so aggressively, as Vincent Gaddis's powerful narrative shows, against a continuation, or even worse an acceleration, of the trend toward revising laissez faire liberalism in the direction of greater government interference, in which key decisions in the management of the economy might be permanently transferred from the realm of private to public determination. Among the many contributions of Gaddis's study, one of the most important is his determination not to treat Hoover as "the villain of the piece," a tool of capitalist domination, a bureaucratic aggrandizer of Commerce Department turf, or a headline figure of a "broken decade" in between two "progressive" ones. Rather, he approaches Hoover as something of an intellectual and a morally serious thinker who pondered deeply how to sustain what he saw as the values that made the American experiment historically remarkable and valuable. This accounts for Hoover's—and Gaddis's—preoccupation with liberty and virtue. Gaddis takes Hoover's reverence for these core values as genuine, not hypocritical, rooted not merely in his own biography, which recorded a rise from poverty to affluence, but also in his conception of republican virtue. Ironically, both Hoover's biography and his values might have linked him culturally to producerist-republican memories that had mobilized much of American labor in the 19th century, before its "turn" toward the somewhat contradictory goals of voluntarism and industrial democracy in the early decades of the 20th. That it did not so link him we can attribute—again as Gaddis perceptively shows—to the way his constructions of those two concepts, liberty and virtue, differed from the way they were constructed by labor leaders and by statist liberals.

For Hoover, these were initially private virtues. By no means, as Ellis Hawley has made crystal clear, was Hoover a believer in laissez faire. That hoary myth of 1920s economic policy has been put to rest. Surely believers in something close to a classical liberal vision remained, at Treasury, certainly in Congress, in the National Association of Manufacturers, and abroad in the land. But—and this is where Gaddis's skillful analysis of conceptual change comes so handy—Hoover had expanded on the idea of virtue so that it was not only an essential attribute of individuals in a successful capitalist economy but also a structural element of the economy, the society, and the state. The virtuous economy must be one in which private control of the investment and managerial functions was protected, though production and pricing decisions at the level of the firm could be aided by an informational climate enriched by the state, turning them into a coordinated, cooperative pattern that beneficially shaped the economy and moderated its swings. The virtuous society must be one in which associations and actions, most important among them contract, were voluntary, not coerced. The negative pole for Hoover, as for Woodrow Wilson, was a command economy as they imagined it developing in the Soviet Union, a lesser version of which could be discerned in schemes for redistributing of income and wealth being hatched on the socialist left and on the statist-leaning side of the liberal center. The virtuous state must be one that, in the hands of visionaries like Hoover himself, could mobilize energies in society to create a voluntary corporate commonwealth, and this state must then be willing to "wither away." To avoid entrenching *within* the state regulatory and advisory capacities that might be needed temporarily, Hoover's preference was to incarnate these capacities in the numerous philanthropically-supported advisory committees, conferences, and research teams that he called into being as Commerce Secretary and president. Hoover had scant respect for politics. By maintaining this separation, he believed, politics could not corrupt business.

As Gaddis ably dissects the meanings that virtue and liberty had for Hoover, he attends carefully as well to Hoover's cultivation of what he refers to as "essential publics." Groups that Hoover nurtured were also essentially "counterpublics," to the extent that he intended they would neutralize the publics of female reformers, laborist activists, social investigators, social workers, public housers, sociologists and political economists in the tradition of H. C. Adams, Richard Ely, John R. Commons, and Paul Douglas, and Rexford Tugwell, left progressives in the Theodore Roosevelt tradition, and social democratic public intellectuals such as John Dewey. All of these actors had won considerable standing in the prewar decades, pressing Wilson toward a laundry list of more statist reforms in 1916 than he had espoused in 1912. They were particularly strident in the twenties in calling for government intervention to stabilize "sick" industries such as coal. Hoover's publics, conversely, promoted employee representation instead of collective bargaining with independent national unions and economic growth, as against redistribution. Organized effectively and foundation funded, they could gather information on social and economic trends, study the business cycle, and promote industrial relations programs that provided alternatives to statist methods.

Promoting virtue in these ways and protecting liberty required by definition that nothing be done to promote dependency. Easiest when times were good, this grew increasingly difficult in the two periods Gaddis explores in depth—the short, sharp post-World War I depression and the early years of the Great Depression, over both of which Hoover effectively presided. Unlike earlier corporate liberals whose efforts to achieve social stabilization through cross-class cooperation orchestrated by the National Civic Federation had developed little short of anti-trust reform in the way of a program economic stabilization, Hoover came out of the culture of U. S. engineering. This and his experiences during World War I had convinced him that the answer was greater efficiency, to be achieved by elimination of waste, and by higher levels of production, to be sustained without government direction by voluntary measures to better coordinate production and consumption, leading to higher wages and industrial peace.

But as the polity was constituted in 1920s, Hoover was not the front line in the war on mass unemployment. Always, since the convergence of manufacturing in major urban centers, the front lines in this battle had run through the cities. Poverty, chronic labor surplus, and inadequately-waged employment went together, transforming the cities in the industrial era. Before the New Deal, the national government took virtually no responsibility for urban poverty, the urban housing and sanitation crisis, or mass unemployment. Indeed, national level policies were often at the root of urban crisis, as pro-corporate policies encouraged consolidation of production in big cities, virtually unrestricted immigration flooded the labor market, and monetary policies frequently depressed wages. When needs for relief multiplied and the resources of charities were overrun, the burden had typically fallen upon big city mayors. They had met it in various ways in previous decades, sometimes opening the jails to the homeless, heading inmigrating vagrants out of town, and cranking up city employment on an ad hoc basis. Calls had been rising before the war for putting the scheduling of public works on a more scientific basis so that they could be automatically mobilized counter-cyclically, and for income maintaining measures. Thus Hoover had good reason to fear that the postwar depression would lead to a continuation of the prewar statist turn in U. S. liberalism.

Pressures of this kind would have sent the mayors to Washington if Washington had not come to them. But Hoover did come to them when he convened the Unemployment Conference in 1921. Hoover incorporated the big city mayors—represented in Gaddis's closely textured tale by the Midwestern mayors of Milwaukee, Chicago, and Detroit—into his vision of how to address unemployment without corrupting virtue or endangering liberty. Hoover placed the mayors squarely between Washington's pressure to sustain voluntarism by retaining charitable aid and local public works as the major weapons against unemployment and demands coming from more autonomous, "subaltern" local publics including socialists, local statists in the municipal reform tradition, and African Americans, who in these cities following the Great Migration were the hardest hit by job loss. At the level of social thought, there was national opposition to Hoover's voluntarism rising as well at the national level that connected with these movements for government relief, among social investigators such as Charles Johnson of the National Urban League, who was documenting employment discrimination that made black workers lose their jobs first. As Kathleen Donohue has recently argued in *Freedom from Want: American Liberalism and The Idea of the Consumer* (2003), an alternative vision was rising also among consumption-oriented political economists and public intellectuals in the tradition of Thorstein Veblen, who saw capitalists as perennially willing to sabotage production in order to sustain prices and profits. Another strand of reform thought in the tradition of Simon Patten saw provisions for maintaining consumption as the best way to address the persistent problem of overproduction, sustain demand, and move toward greater economic justice. On the opposite end of the ideological spectrum, within the administration itself, there was Treasury Secretary Andrew Mellon, whose counsel when the bottom fell out of the economy was always, "Liquidate the farms, liquidate the factories, liquidate labor, and the economy will right itself."

Therefore, not only the mayors but also in a sense Hoover himself was in the middle, as in the same sense corporate liberals more generally had been from the moment they conceived their project back at the turn of the century, against a rising tide of democratic statism. Hoover orchestrated a successful balancing act, more or less, in the postwar recession, from which, as Gaddis tellingly explains, he learned some dangerous lessons. He attempted to replicate these moves in the worsening years between 1929 and 1932. This time, although mayors across the ideological spectrum from Socialist to Republican tried to stick with the voluntarist program, pressures to move in a more statist direction rose locally, when need outran resources. They arose nationally as well, as voluntarism weakened and failed, and as a statist block in Congress began to cohere behind proposals for moving responsibility for mass unemployment to the national level through public works funding, public as opposed to employer or union based unemployment insurance, and even the dreaded dole. State governors were erecting statist experiments that not only hired people but had the appearance of far greater compassion that Hoover seemed capable of, as his minions forcefully evicted bonus marchers from where they squatted near the capitol.

The remarkable thing, in worsening circumstances that must have sorely tried his soul, was how steadfast Hoover remained in defense of liberty and virtue as he understood them. The novelty of the situation—a depression this bad and this long—can hardly explain it. We must find our answers in the realm of discourse.

There, Gaddis draws our attention to conceptions of virtue and processes of political learning that may have seemed "wrong" in the context of the Great Depression, but returned like the repressed in the 1950s, survived the Great Society moment, and deeply informed the Reagan revolution, the "return of the market," devolution, and the end of "welfare as we knew it." Who can say that neoconservatives in academia, in think-tanks such as the Heritage Foundation and the American Enterprise Institute, in the dozens of foundations with "Liberty" featured prominently in their titles, and in recent presidential administrations who have justified the conservative counter-revolution in the name of liberty and virtue have not taken a page from Hoover's book? The chapters that await the reader make it possible to address these questions with new tools, leading to powerful new insights about persistence and change in our conceptual history.

Mary O. Furner
Professor of History
University of California, Santa Barbara

Acknowledgment

Writing a book is never a solitary enterprise. I would like to thank all those who assisted me in this project. The archivists and librarians from the Herbert Hoover Presidential Library, Chicago Public Library, Chicago Historical Society, Milwaukee County Historical Society, Walter Reuther Library, Detroit Public Library and Northern Illinois University Libraries exhibited incredible skill and patience with me and I owe them a profound debt of gratitude. They often helped me to refine my thinking and led me to sources that I otherwise may have neglected.

In addition I would like to recognize Clarisa Gomez who served as an editor, technical wizard and prepared the manuscript to the publisher's specifications, and Reiden Dentzer who assisted with the preparation of the index and other assorted editing duties.

This project is dedicated to the people most responsible for its completion. First, my mentor and friend Dr. Mary Furner of University of California Santa Barbara, who first spurred my curiosity in the direction of an analysis of language, its contestedness and the need for an historical analysis of the impact of conceptual frameworks in which policy is developed. Second, my wife Cathy whose encouragement, thoughtfulness and tolerance of many days spent at the computer or out of town enabled me to give the work the attention it deserved. To all of these and all others who have assisted, I owe my deepest gratitude. The assistance of those mentioned only enhanced the quality of this work, all of the errors and faults contained herein are exclusively my own.

Introduction
Herbert Hoover, Unemployment, and the Public Sphere: A Conceptual History, 1919-1933

Appointed to the post of Secretary of Commerce by President Warren G. Harding in 1921, Herbert Clark Hoover organized several national conferences during his tenure in that post and later as president. One of the first, the Unemployment Conference of September 1921, was called to address not only unemployment, but also the generally poor economic conditions in the United States. After World War I, the government relaxed the grip it had maintained on industry during the war, disputes between capital and labor grew, inflation increased, farmers lost markets in the face of European devastation and world depression, and the domestic economy began to decline into a serious depression in which between three and five million workers went unemployed. To solve these problems, Herbert Hoover embarked upon a program of which the Unemployment Conference was the cornerstone.[1]

This conference was significant for several reasons. It was the first conference on unemployment ever called by the federal government. It attracted leaders from all areas of industry, labor and academe, such as John L. Lewis, President of the United Mine Workers of America; Samuel Gompers, President of the American Federation of Labor; Charles M. Schwab, Chairman of the Bethlehem Steel Corporation; Clarence Hicks, assistant to the presidents of both Standard Oil and Colorado Fuel & Iron Company; and Wesley Mitchell, economist at Columbia University. Its cooperative public/private approach to solving problems was innovative at the time and was to be one of its lasting legacies. Also, it furthered the emergence of unemployment as a category requiring definition and a social policy issue requiring solution.[2]

Herbert Hoover called the conference and organized it in this cooperative way for several reasons, all of which reveal something of his conceptions of liberty and virtue, and what it meant to protect them. Along with other influences, these assumptions about liberty and virtue combined to shape his understanding of unemployment and how to address it. This dissertation explores the relationship between Hoover's political philosophy, where liberty and virtue are matters of concern, and his political behavior, as expressed in the Unemployment Conference of 1921 and in his subsequent activities as Secretary of Commerce and President. How did Hoover view the unemployed? How did his views change over the 1919-1933 period? How did his views conflict with those of other participants in the ongoing discussion of unemployment and the role of the state in "curing" it? As a national policy emerged, what was the nature of the conflict between the architects of that policy and big city mayors, some of whom opposed the voluntarist policies favored by Hoover? Was the mayors' opposition the result of their conceptions of the unemployed, of machine politics, or of other social and institutional factors? How were the Unemployment Conference and Hoover's policies related to social investigation in the academic community, the emerging "think tanks," and other policy-relevant bodies? What conceptual conflicts existed among academics concerning the unemployed, and how did their various conceptions of liberty and virtue differ from Hoover's?

This work is significant for two reasons. First, no writer has examined Hoover's political behavior as an expression of his philosophical beliefs. Most historians have focused primarily on Hoover's political actions instead, as seen in his efforts to reorganize the Commerce Department and the politics surrounding his handling of domestic economic problems. Yet, as presidents go, Hoover was a relatively deep thinker who confronted philosophical questions in formal writings and speeches and remained largely faithful to his self-consciously adopted ideological positions throughout his life. His works, *American Individualism* (1923) and *A Challenge to Liberty* (1935), reveal these beliefs and attest to their consistency throughout his career as both commerce secretary and president. Second, despite the growing attention among historians to the construction of meaning, no previous study has attempted to explain how Hoover assigned meaning to keywords in his political discourse. This work attempts to show how Hoover in his context constructed virtue, liberty, and unemployment, and how those constructions translated into action. Knowledge of how meaning became assigned to such terms as unemployment and how that meaning changed over time is crucial to an understanding of why certain social policies developed.

There is a large body of work on Herbert Hoover and the decade of the 1920s. Contemporary historians generally saw the country as entering a new, more technological, yet more democratic era. The progressive historian Charles Beard argued in *The Rise of American Civilization* (1927) that the political decision-makers of the1920s offered solutions to class conflict that arose from a middle ground between classical economic theory on the right and socialism and Marxism on the left. The expanding knowledge of the "machine age," as Beard called it, along with a government committed to organizing and rationalizing the economic and social institutions of the country, put the United States at the "dawn, not the dusk, of the gods."[3] Another survey of the United States during the 1920s, James Malin's *The United States After the World War* (1930), described the decade as one of great economic change, the result being government and industry joining in new organizational and policy strategies. Asserting that the political climate had changed since the Progressive Era, Malin argued that the drive for government regulation had ended, and therefore statist liberals who supported strict government regulation after the war had fallen into decline. At the same time, the conservative push for a return to laissez-faire economic policy was not strong enough to dictate policy either. This situation made possible a new strategy of cooperation among government, industry, labor, and agriculture to generate economic self-government, a strategy that would promote social developments that government intervention could not, and so expand democracy, while voluntarism enhanced individual liberty. [4]

For Malin, the person most responsible for these developing changes was Herbert Hoover as Secretary of Commerce. Malin asserted that it was Hoover who allowed, in fact created, this new method of organization, which relied on new breakthroughs in science and the belief that the best path to the economic self-regulation of industry was the redirection of government away from legislative and bureaucratic controls and toward persuasion and assistance through a new structure of functionally specialized bureaus. Malin saw Hoover as inventing a new political theory that was liberal, reform-minded, and socially responsible, but not statist.

Beard and Malin largely ignored unemployment and other social ills, and many of their assertions were not critically analyzed. Yet, unlike the historians of the 1930s and 40s, they did recognize the importance of this new institutional order, which provided a foundation for policy that would extend (with varying authority) throughout the century. The crash of 1929 and the ensuing depression shaped the views of the historians of the 1930s and 40s, who generally understood the length and depth of the depression as a consequence not of the New Deal policies of Franklin D. Roosevelt, but of the faulty policies of the 1920s, which for them interrupted the progressive tradition that began at the turn of the century and resumed with Roosevelt. These historians, such as Fredrick Allen in *Only Yesterday* (1931), concentrated on the moral deficiencies and political corruption of the period. New Deal era monographs portrayed Hoover as the unimaginative, politically inept puppet of the rich and the special interests, and they gave most other politicians of the twenties the same or worse treatment. From the Tea Pot Dome scandal of 1923 through the stock market crash of 1929, they saw only blundering and corruption. Hoover's time as Secretary of Commerce appeared in such works merely as a holding position in anticipation of his presidency; his organizational and managerial skills and his attempt to restructure government went unremarked.

One of the influential works of the 1940s was Richard Hofstadter's *The American Political Tradition and the Men Who Made It* (1949). Like most historians to that time, Hofstadter focused primarily on Hoover as president. He argued that Hoover's cabinet position served as merely a "stepping stone to the Presidency," and paid scant attention to Hoover's work to promote economic self-government, to correct problems in the coal and agricultural industries, or to alleviate unemployment. Hofstadter dismissed Hoover's social philosophy as biased by his training as an engineer: "Economy and efficiency became ends in themselves," Hofstadter claims. He did not suggest, as this dissertation will, that

Hoover could have seen efficiency in government and industry as the best means to the protection of liberty in a democratic society. [5]

No serious study of Hoover as Secretary of Commerce appeared until well into the 1950s. Still, most historians, like Arthur Schlesinger Jr. in *Crisis of the Old Order* (1957), viewed the 1920s and Herbert Hoover as outside the main developments of the twentieth century, an aberration in the progressive tradition. However, in the 1960s, new perceptions of the 1920s began arise. Some historians working on the progressive movement, such as Robert K. Murray in *The Harding Era* (1969), saw the twenties not as an anomaly, but as a time of significant reform. Murray argued that the Harding Administration was indeed progressive and attempted reform, but through voluntarism rather than overpowering regulatory bureaucracies.

In the late 1960s and 70s, another group of historians, the New Left, brought a powerful critical perspective to historical scholarship. Using a neo-Marxist approach, these historians emphasized the struggle of the American working class to become class conscious and the efforts of capitalists and political elites to promote class harmony and sustained economic growth without statism. From this perspective, the aim of the politicians of the 1920s was to promote imperialist policies and stabilize advanced capitalism on the one hand, and to encourage voluntarism and cooperation on the other. The New Left historians saw these politicians as much more sophisticated than those who came after them. [6]

Another group of recent historians reinterpreted the events of the 1920s from a conservative point of view. Murray Rothbard claimed that Hoover undercut the conservative values of laissez- faire and promoted statist policies. Hoover, Rothbard argued, worked not for open competition and individual liberty, but for the corporatist social structure that was further developed during the New Deal. [7]

With the opening of the Hoover Presidential Library in 1963 and the Harding Papers in 1964, a new revisionist tradition developed which has proved Hoover to have been a more important leader than he was supposed in the 1930s and 1940s, and a more reformist leader than he was supposed in the 1950s. Several rich biographies from this group of revisionists depict Hoover as a deeply philosophical and intelligent innovator. Debates among this group generally concern which events shaped Hoover's life most: his Quaker upbringing, his training as an engineer, or his experiences during the Great War. [8]

In the 1970s historians such as Ellis Hawley, Robert Cuff and Joan Hoff Wilson extended their revision of Hoover to his role as Secretary of Commerce. Generally, they saw that Hoover believed neither in the laissez-faire ideology of the late 19th century nor in the large regulatory state. Hoover attempted as Secretary of Commerce to stabilize the American economy and social structure. Melvyn Leffler described Hoover as "a twentieth-century enlightened manager and scientific reformer . . . involved in promoting harmony between capital and labor." For these historians, Hoover served as a transitional figure between the laissez-faire of the late 19th century, the rapidly changing policies of the

Progressive Era, and the bureaucratic, regulatory, democratic statist government which came about during the New Deal. [9]

The revisionists, then, have aligned themselves more closely with the historians of the 1920s than with those of the 1930s, 40s, and 50s. Yet they continue to debate how Hoover achieved his goals and the consequences of his policies. One revisionist theory, that of Hoover as an architect of the "associative state," forms one of the central categories of this work. Forcefully argued by Ellis Hawley, this theory claims that Hoover saw in the advancing industrialism of the early 20th century the evolution of an associational order. Since the 1890s, a new system had been taking shape, characterized by a "commitment to science and productivity, and the mutuality of interests that would connect such structures into instruments of social progress." In the face of the strife following the Great War and such disruptive events as the steel strike of 1919 and the depression of 1920-21, Hoover saw that this system needed to develop more quickly. He envisaged "an associative state, tied to, cooperating with, and helping to develop and guide the new associational order." Hoover reorganized the Commerce Department and initiated policies according to which economic and social issues could be decided through voluntary associations. The state, in Hoover's opinion, was to promote efficiency and cooperation and not to function as a "trader, investor, or detailed regulator." This associational order would assist the institutions of capital, labor, agriculture and government in achieving not only economic self-regulation but labor peace and a higher standard of living for all Americans. [10]

The Unemployment Conference of 1921 was the beginning of Hoover's political, or institutional, construction of the associative state. This dissertation builds upon Hawley's theory, but goes further in establishing the centrality of the business cycle and unemployment in Hoover's thinking, and in assessing his effectiveness in mobilizing intellectual and institutional resources to promote a full employment economy without subverting liberty. I intend to go beyond the early stages of the formation of Hoover's unemployment policy to examine his responses to challenges from various quarters to the policies of the associative state and to asses the impact of those challenges on his actions after 1929.

To provide context for Hoover's vision, we move to a background section on unemployment in general. One of most the significant works on the poor and poor relief is Michael Katz's *In the Shadow of the Poorhouse: A Social History of Welfare in America* (1986), which outlines the transformation of social policy from the establishment of poorhouses in the 18th century through the development of the welfare state through the early 1980s. Katz asserts that voluntarism alone could not provide for the needs of the poor, and that government can and should take an active role. He does not, however, devote much time to the twenties, or to the Unemployment Conference in particular. Another work, Walter Trattner's *From Poor Law to Welfare State* (1989), traces in broad outline the history of welfare and the professionalization of the social worker. Trattner's analysis of the twenties provides insight into the attitudes of social workers towards the poor, but does not discuss the conference or its significance. Neither does James T. Patterson's *America's Struggle Against Poverty 1900-1985* (1986). Udo Sautter's *Three Cheers for the Unemployed: Government and Unemployment Before the New Deal* (1991) does address the conference to some degree and gives an excellent overview of unemployment policy in the twenties. Sautter's primary contribution is an analysis of the United States Employment Service (USES). This service, originally created during continued to function afterwards and, as a result of recommendations from the Unemployment Conference, became a vital part of the cooperative effort Hoover was promoting. A rousing criticism of the conference and the voluntarist approach as inept and cruel appears in Franklin Folsom's *Impatient Armies of the Poor: The Story of Collective Action By the Unemployed 1808-1942* (1991). In general, however, historians of unemployment have neglected the 1920s, which they portray as a time when unemployment policy was subsumed in larger discussions of corporate welfare systems, industrial relations, and the open vs. closed shop. One reason for this is the low unemployment rate after the recovery in 1923. [11]

The methodology used in this dissertation is designed to allow for a sophisticated analysis not only of the links between Hoover's political philosophy, unemployment policy, and city machine politics, but also of unemployment as an emerging and transforming political concept. Analysis of the Unemployment Conference and unemployment may on the one hand reveal the process by which keywords develop meaning in political discourse, and on the other deepen our understanding of the policies that did emerge, and of the associative state in general.

A new paradigm and a related historiography have recently appeared within intellectual history, dealing in various ways with the history and analysis of discourse. At issue is how political actors develop meanings for particular words and phrases, how they help to construct discourses in which these meanings are shared, and how the terms of particular discourses affect the implementation of particular programs or ideas. In studying Hoover, one must give careful attention to the evolving meanings of words in his political vocabulary and to the underlying values and theoretical propositions behind the main components of his language. Scholarly work on Hoover to this point has been primarily political history; I hope to bring a fresh perspective to the study of this central political actor of the early 20th century. [12]

To reconstruct Hoover's understanding of liberty and virtue I will summarize Hoover's conceptual history of the words *unemployment*, *liberty,* and *virtue*, and determine whether Hoover constructed a definition of unemployment and proposed solutions to unemployment that were consistent with his possibly changing conceptions of liberty and virtue. Two connected approaches make analysis of these issues possible, both drawn from important works in political philosophy and political theory pertaining to conceptual history and the development of the "public sphere."

The works of Quentin Skinner and James Farr in Farr's co-edited work, *Political Innovation and Political Change* (1989) provide an excellent model for the writing of conceptual history. Skinner identifies three requirements for understanding keywords and the concepts they signify. First, one "must know the nature and range of criteria in which a word is employed." That is, one must identify the specific qualities of a word's reference. For example, when one asks what it means to be unemployed, the response will be a list of adjectives, or criteria, that distinguish a word like *unemployment* from other words in the language. In Hoover's case, the range of criteria used to define unemployment was shaped by the qualities of the words *liberty* and *virtue*. Such analysis will reveal the general social beliefs embedded in these two keywords. [13] Second, one must identify the range of reference which determines the circumstances under which employment of the word conforms to the previously agreed upon nature of the word. Identifying its range of reference allows one to relate a keyword to the world in general, taking into account the social perceptions of that word and its meaning. Third, one must identify the range of attitudes a word expresses; this will reveal the word's social value.

I will identify these qualities in the words *virtue* and *liberty* and their relation to *unemployment*, and thereby highlight the conflicts between groups and individual thinkers who assigned different criteria to these words and had conflicting attitudes toward what they mean, and therefore toward how unemployment should be dealt with as a national concern. For example, though being unemployed is simply being "out of work," conflict may arise over the range that criterion covers. Does being out of work refer to those who were previously employed and lost said employment within the last 30 days? Does it refer to any time frame at all? Are women and children included when counting the unemployed? Are those who strike and lose their jobs considered unemployed? What of those who have never worked?

Such conceptual conflicts have significant historical effects. For example, they shaped the debate over one of the primary recommendations of the Unemployment Conference of 1921, one which reflected Hoover's conception of the meaning and history of unemployment. The conference concluded that unemployment was a local problem the responsibility for which lay at the mayoral level. This recommendation reflected one extreme of the range of attitudes toward solutions to unemployment, the other extreme of which led to a call for strong federal involvement. Hoover adhered to this extreme because he viewed any statist solution as an assault on liberty.

Skinner's model of conceptual history has been refined by James Farr. While Skinner identifies the criteria for establishing meaning, he analyzes words at one moment in time. In his work "Understanding Conceptual Change Politically," Farr claims that to understand conceptual change one has to consider not only at Skinner's criteria, but also the "emergence, transformation and sometimes demise" of a political concept over time. Farr argues that conceptual change is "one consequence of political actors criticizing and attempting to resolve the contradictions they discover or generate in their beliefs, actions or practices as they try to understand the world around them." Clearly, the Unemployment Conference was an attempt to resolve contradictions about the concept of unemployment. Several critical questions about the keyword show its contestedness, concerning such issues as government's role in addressing the problem and the supposed moral deficiency of the unemployed. [14]

The concept of unemployment as a political category emerged not during the 1920s but, according to Alexander Keyssar, in his social history *Out of Work: The First Century of Unemployment in Massachusetts* (1986), during the 1880s. The Unemployment Conference and its extension in policy throughout the 1920s reflects the transformation of the concept from a proof of a moral deficiency to a result of the economic system and therefore a major economic, social and political issue, a transformation which in turn led in the 1930s to a call for such statist, interventionist policies as giving money to the unemployed. In incorporating the methodology of conceptual history, this work will have not only to address the specific keywords at issue, but also to place them into a historical context and show where conflicts over meaning occurred and how they were resolved.

The conceptual analysis of unemployment, virtue, and liberty as discussed above must also be contained in a wider model—that of the public sphere. Broadly defined by Jurgen Habermas in his landmark work, *The Structural Transformation of the Public Sphere* (1962), the public is the arena of rational-critical debate outside of government, among private individuals, and distributed by the press and other institutions for serious, critical assessment of policy. In this sphere, people "engage the state on public matters of commodity exchange and social labor." Here is where public opinion takes form and actions by the state come into an open forum for criticism. To be sure, Habermas claims the public sphere came to an end in the early 20th century; but one of the purposes of the dissertation will be to examine this point. Hoover attempted to reconstruct the public sphere after the war. Like previous conferences, such as the Commission on Industrial Relations and the First and Second Industrial Conferences, Hoover organized the Unemployment Conference outside the legislative process and brought influential people from the private realm (business, labor, academia) to discuss a problem relating to the common good. In other words, Hoover attempted to organize the corporatist structures of society and direct them towards finding solutions for social problems. To assist these corporatist units he also organized government agencies and publications, such as the National Bureau of Economic Research, and the publications *Recent Social Trends Recent Economic Changes* and *Recent Social Trends*. This helped to foster the movement of social investigation. After the conference, and throughout the 1920s, he used public opinion as a tool to influence the corporatist institutions of society as well as policy. In all this, Hoover attempted to re-create the public sphere and to use it to bring corporatist groups to adhere to their agreements while simultaneously minimizing the amount of government legislative intervention 16.

Habermas regarded the development of consumer culture as one of the primary causes of the transformation of the public sphere. This led to a dependency upon "administrated" debate, which replaced the rational-critical debate of the salon. As "rational-critical debate had a tendency to be replaced by consumption . . . public communication unraveled into acts of individuated reception." In other words, consumer culture did not stop the development of the cultural marketplace (plays, books, theater, etc.), but the forms of that market replaced public debate. Also, the rise of consumer culture violated the autonomy previously assured by property ownership (for Habermas the primary unit of autonomy) by bringing "new relations of dependence." The public sphere became an individualized arena where others carried on debate through co-opted mass media and mass advertising. The coinciding growth of the state also corrupted of the public sphere. Habermas argued that an enlarged, more active state tended to control the terms in which rational-critical debate could occur and limited the range of people who could participate in debate over state policy.[16] For Habermas, Hoover's attempt to reconstruct the public sphere would likely have been undermined by his belief in ever-expanding consumption as one solution to unemployment, which led him to improve the information about markets available to capitalists.

Habermas' examination of the public sphere and its implication for democratic theory are useful, but several scholars have found limitations in the original work and two of those critiques bear examination here. Nancy Fraser has argued that the rational debate of the public sphere, though supposedly open to all, merely reflected the language of the white male-dominated public and bracketed the discourse of woman and blacks. As she argues, "discursive interaction within the bourgeoisie public sphere was governed by protocols of style and decorum that were themselves correlates and markers of status inequality." Although formal boundaries to political participation were removed by 1921, when women were given suffrage and (in the north) formal structures to prevent blacks from voting were not in place, these two publics were not able to participate with the same impact as the primary publics Hoover gave attention to. Women and blacks did have a small and growing voice in the discussion of aid and unemployment at the municipal level, but that voice was overshadowed by those of corporate and labor leaders, and even of white male leaders of charitable organizations in the cities. Thus, when discussing differing publics competing for space in the discussion of relief, two levels of publics must be understood 17.

Hoover clearly saw the following publics as essential to the corporatist vision: corporate leaders, both individually and collectively through employer associations; labor, expressed through primarily the American Federation of Labor (AFL) and, secondarily and specifically in the area of coal, the United Mine Workers (UMW); municipal leaders; and, finally, those academics in the area of social investigation who studied the issue of unemployment and the role of the state in relief. These groups formed Hoover's essential publics. To carry out his policies and maintain the associative state, Hoover had to be able to manipulate these four publics. Early in the decade, at the Unemployment Conference, Hoover was able to bring all four to endorse his vision, implicitly or explicitly, and thereby temporarily solidified a meaning for unemployment, liberty and the virtuous state. The publics Hoover ignored or opposed may have raised voices of opposition, but they were not able, early in the decade, to affect the conceptual debate.

The other, or as Geoff Ely argues, subaltern publics not only competed for legitimacy with the dominant publics, but also applied pressure to them. Ely speaks primarily of the eighteenth and nineteenth centuries, yet in the 1920s women and minorities did operate as "part of an historical emancipatory impulse." In the early twentieth century both women and blacks asserted themselves politically and, importantly, in the conceptual debate over relief and the state, particularly at the municipal level. However, in his construction of the associative state, these publics did not significantly impact Hoover, particularly early in the decade 18.

During the depression these subaltern groups made a much more significant impact as economic conditions created a political dynamic that challenged Hoover's conception of liberty and the state from the halls of the national legislature to the demonstrations of the unemployed in the streets. The conceptual battle lines shifted as those publics Hoover saw as critical to holding a grip on public opinion and preventing legislation he viewed as threatening began to abandon the primary tenets of his philosophy and thereby create a shift not only in policy, but in the range and meaning of virtue and liberty.

In summary, the writing of the conceptual history of virtue and liberty as they relate to unemployment will proceed on two levels. First, Skinner's and Farr's models for writing the particular histories of these keywords will shed light on the general conflicts regarding the concept of unemployment. Second, the public sphere as an ideal type will provide a mechanism for interpreting the political actions Hoover took as a result of his attempts to influence the continuing emergence and transformation of the concept of unemployment.

In examining conceptual history and unemployment, I will concentrate on three cities, Chicago, Detroit, and Milwaukee, which met two important criteria: availability of primary documents, and population. All three have several significant collections and all were among the 20 largest cities in the country in 1920. I will examine machine politics and unemployment conditions in each, the relationship of its mayor to Arthur Woods, who was to organize mayors to implement the recommendations of the Unemployment Conference. I will also examine discourse in the cities concerning unemployment. Mayors, left as the front line of relief in the voluntarist model, were closest to the dissenting voices who advocated more statist policy; their discourse suggests how and to what degree shifts in the conceptual framework of voluntarism changed over time.

By looking at the politics of the cities, we can see who supported Hoover's recommendations and who did not. We can then focus on what solutions those who opposed the conference's recommendations implemented. Farr and Skinner's methodology allows us to determine whether these opponents had their own conceptions of the meaning of virtue and liberty and if so, what those conceptions were.

Finally, analysis of city politics will show the impact of opponents and supporters of the recommendations. Were any of the conference recommendations actually implemented? If so, how well did they work? If they did not work, why not? Did alternative solutions work? Did conceptions of race influence particular programs? To what degree did blacks' participation in patronage politics influence their ability to take advantage of available assistance? These types of questions shed light on the overall conceptual framework mayors maneuvered within and how those maneuvers fit within the broader conceptual history of unemployment during the period.

The argument will then shift to the academic community, to the theorists and social investigators, in order to determine their positions on the conference and within the larger debate over conceptual meaning and the relation of liberty and virtue to unemployment as a construct. Here, the collections of those who provided analysis through social investigation conducted by universities and think tanks should shed further light on that publics' reaction to the issue of unemployment and the recommendations of the conference. This group includes, but is not limited to, William Liserson, John Commons, Mary VanKleek, Paul Douglas, Wesley Mitchell, Thorsten Veblen, and Leo Wolman.

A concluding discussion will pull together all the arguments relevant to the public sphere—the various publics' view of the role of the state, and social attitudes toward and theories of the unemployed—in order to determine whether Hoover corrupted or enhanced that sphere. The various, interrelated elements of the book should provide evidence for this conclusion.

Notes

1 Ells Hawley, The Great War and the Search for Modern Order: A History of the American People and Their Institutions. 1917-1933 (New York: St. Martins Press, 1979), 58-77.

2 Carolyn Grin, "The Unemployment Conference of 1921: An Experiment in National Cooperative Planning," Mid-America 55 (April 1973): 86.

3 Charles A. Beard and Mary Beard, The Rise of American Civilization vol. 2 (New York: The Macmillan Co., 1927) p. 254.

4 James C. Malin, The United States After the World War (New York: The Macmillan Co., 1930).

5 Richard Hofstadter, The American Political Tradition and the Men Who Made It (New York: Alfred A. Knopf, 1949), 287, 292.

6 Robert K. Murray, "Herbert Hoover and the Harding Cabinet," in Hawley, ed. Herbert Hoover 1921-1928 (Iowa City: University of Iowa Press, 1981), 17-43; Arthur Link, "What happened to the Progressive Movement in the 1920's?" American Historical Review 64 (July 1959), 833-51; Irwin Unger, "The New Left and American History,"

American Historical Review 72 (July 1967), 1237-63; William A. Williams, The Contours of American History (Cleveland: World Publishing Co., 1961).

7 Murray Rothbard, "Herbert Clark Hoover," New Individualist Review 64 (Winter 1966) 3-12; Willmoore Kendall and George Carey, The Basic Symbols of the American Political Tradition (Baton Rouge: Louisiana State University Press, 1970).

8 George H. Nash, The Life of Herbert Hoover vols. 152 (New York: W.W. Norton & Company, 1988); Nash, Herbert Hoover and Stanford University (Stanford: Hoover Institute Press, 1988); Joan Hoff Wilson, Herbert Hoover: Forgotten Progressive (Boston: Little, Brown & Company, 1975).

9 Joan Hoff Wilson, American Business and Foreign Policy. 1920-1933 (Lexington: University Press of Kentucky, 1971); Ellis Hawley, "Herbert Hoover, the Commerce Secretariat and the Vision of an Associative State," Journal of American History 61 (June 1974) 116-40; Robert Cuff, "Herbert Hoover, the Ideology of Voluntarism, and War Organization During the Great War," Journal of American History 64 (September 1977) 358-72, . Melvyn P. Leffler, "Herbert Hoover, the 'New Era' and American Foreign Policy," in Hawley, Herbert Hoover. 1921-1928, 149-50.

10 Hawley, "Herbert Hoover, the Commerce Secretariat and the Vision of an Associative State," 118, 126-140.

11 Edward Berkowitz and Kim McQuaid, Creating the Welfare State: The Political Economy of Twentieth Century Reform (New York: Praeger Publications, 1988); Robert E. Goodin, Reasons for Welfare: The Political Theory of the Welfare State (Princeton: Princeton University Press, 1988); Francis Fox Piven, Regulating the Poor: The Functions of Public Welfare (New York: Pantheon

12 By discourse I mean that particular historical actors engage in discussion with some degree of shared meaning of key concepts. An element of discourse is the analysis of the challenges to established concepts recognizing that "language and its figurative character is a material force that shapes lived experience . . . and based on "the assumption that ideology is determined by the primal text (language) rather than the material world." Quote from Alun Munslow, Discourse and Culture: The Creation of America. 1870-1920 (London: Routledge, 1992) 3-5; see also, Paul A. Bove, Mastering Discourse: The Politics of Intellectual Culture (Durham: Duke University Press, 1992), Bryan D. Palmer, Descent into Discourse: The Reification of Language and the Writing of Social History (Philadelphia: Temple University Press, 1990) and Martha Cooper, Analyzing Public Discourse (Prospect Heights: Waveland Press, 1989).

13 Quentin Skinner, "Language and Conceptual Change," in James Farr, ed. Political Innovation and Conceptual Change (Cambridge: Cambridge University Press, 1989) 9-11.

14 James Farr, "Understanding Conceptual Change Politically," in Farr et. al., 25, 37.

15 Jurgan Habermas, The Structural Transformation of the Public Sphere: An Inquiry into a Category of Bourgeois Society (Cambridge: MIT Press, 1992) 150, 23, 161, 168.

16 Ibid., 160-68.

17 Nancy Fraser, "Rethinking the Public Sphere: A Contribution to the Critique of Actually Existing Democracy," in Craig Calhoun, ed. *Habermas and the Public Sphere* (Cambridge: MIT Press, 1993) 109-143, quote on page 119.1143, quote on page 119.

18 Geoff Eley, "Nations, Publics, and Political Cultures: Placing Habermas in the Nineteenth Century," in Calhoun, *Habermas and the Public Sphere,* 289-340, quote on page 306.

Chapter 1
Herbert Hoover and the Unemployment Conference of 1921

What our people wish is the opportunity to earn their daily bread, and surely in a country with its warehouses bursting with surpluses of food, of clothing, with its mines capable of indefinite production of fuel . . . we possess the intelligence to find solutions. Without it our whole system is open to serious charges of failure.

Opening Speech to the President's Conference on Unemployment by Herbert Hoover, September 26, 1921

The President's Conference on Unemployment attempted to find solutions to the economic depression caused by industrial dislocation after the Great War. Herbert Hoover, then Secretary of Commerce, convinced President Harding, who had ignored the problem for the previous two years, to call the conference in 1921. How did Hoover attain such influence? He was a popular figure during the war as the Director of American Relief in Europe, but he had no political constituency nor was he a long time policy-maker in Washington. Yet, at a time of serious social upheaval, when middle-class Americans were fearful of both domestic and foreign radicalism, Hoover's answer to the country's economic, political and social ills seemed attractive.

Though many Americans were still accustomed to a powerful wartime state, Hoover wished to promote a cooperative social order capable of achieving sustained prosperity, social mobility, and social justice largely through nongovernmetal means. His position, between the laissez-faire economics of the 19th century and the statism of Theodore Roosevelt, was at the time philosophically and theoretically undeveloped, though not without precedent in the American process of continually redefining liberalism. In the following years, Hoover was to inject his own discourse of efficiency and cooperation, his political language and policy analysis, into the political discourse of postwar America.

The first three sections of this chapter focus on the political actions Hoover took to bring his ideas to the attention of the various publics engaged in postwar planning: his participation in the Second Industrial Conference of 1919, his testimony before the Senate Special Committee on Reconstruction and Production of 1920, and finally, his leadership of the Unemployment

Conference of 1921. During these years Hoover began the process of defining his position and persuading leaders of several groups, such as labor, management, and finance to share his vision and participate in programs likely to promote it. The final section concentrates on two key ideas of Hoover's political and social vision: liberty and virtue. It explores how Hoover defined these words and set their range in political terms in his discussion of cooperation and associationalism, how he came to redefine what the two words meant and thereby ultimately to shape New Era public discourse.[1]

As the Unites States entered the 1920s, it confronted severe economic, political and social problems, as it attempted to reconvert and reconstruct its industrial base following the Great War. Things were not supposed to be this way. The forces of freedom had triumphed in Europe and the United States had emerged victorious, having suffered no physical destruction and willing to supply the world with products and foodstuffs. President Wilson predicted the postwar period would provide "greater opportunity and greater prosperity for the average mass of struggling men and women." He was wrong. His administration failed to prepare adequately for postwar readjustment, and the ensuing national crisis did not stimulate any concerted, planned attempt at recovery until the Unemployment Conference of 1921.[2]

During the war, several temporary government agencies were created to rationalize production, wages, and prices in various areas. These bodies, the War Industries Board, the War Labor Conference Board, the Shipbuilding Labor Adjustment Board, and the Board of Railroad Wages and Working Conditions, all of which seemed useful during the war, were quickly abandoned at its close, but without any rational or orderly transfer of control back to the private sector. Meanwhile, government contracts went unfilled, industries tooled for war production were idled, and soldiers returning from Europe had to be reabsorbed into the economy.[3] From the late summer of 1919 through May 1920 the economy did pick up, primarily because of high government spending and loans to Europe. Simultaneously, however, inflation soared disastrously, price controls having been abandoned. Then in May 1920, a depression with a major deflationary episode swept through the country. The Federal Reserve Board tightened credit, but the damage had already been done. Unemployment and layoffs increased and farm prices plummeted.

Meanwhile, violent labor strikes and the infamous "Red Scare" exacerbated the effects of the depression.[4] The Russian Revolution, just a few years old, led to fears a similar revolution in the United States. Strikes therefore appeared to many in the middle class not as a search for justice, but as a prelude to revolution. Unions were weakened by government repression of strikers, such as Attorney General A. Mitchell Palmer's injunctions against coal miners in October 1919 and Massachusetts Governor Calvin Coolidge's direct intervention in the Boston Police Strike of that year. In the political arena, socialists increased their activities and were elected to more local and state offices than ever before. Labor unions were increasingly infiltrated by members of the Communist Party. These movements and the backlash against them created a powder keg ready to explode. Then, in the heat of communist paranoia, as the economy was poised for a collapse, Hoover pulled together an analysis of the economy's troubles and a program that he hoped would put the country upon solid footing in the coming decade.[5]

Before the Second Industrial Conference of 1919, Hoover had begun to piece together an economic strategy for the new era of large-scale manufacturing, increasing urbanization, increasingly powerful trusts, and unions struggling for recognition and higher wages. This relied on voluntarism and cooperation, since Hoover believed that an effective strategy could not be dictated by Washington, but had to be entered into voluntarily by those elements involved in economic policy, each with a commitment to the overall health of the industrial system. As early as 1917, Hoover was troubled by legislation regarding price controls. There was a "necessity of cooperation (by employers) with the labor element of the community in certain important matters," he told Samuel Gompers. Further, Hoover recognized that not only labor but industry as a whole would need balanced representation from all sides in questions of wages and production if there were to be industrial peace during the war.[6]

Upon his return from Europe in 1919, Hoover was deeply troubled by conditions in the United States. In August of that year, Hoover asked Julius Barnes, the President of the Food Administration Grain Corporation, to alert Wilson that although there was a grain surplus to meet the world's needs for the coming winter, "margins are sufficiently narrow to create great danger of speculation and profiteering." Since the Grain Corporation was concluding its operations, there would be no agency in place to thwart the profiteering Hoover saw as imminent. Reinforcing his concern, John Burns, Assistant Secretary of the American Mining Congress, a group of professional engineers, told Hoover in November of 1919 that the country's mounting problems had primarily industrial causes. The increasing labor strife and social unrest warranted some type of national program of action, otherwise, Burns argued, reflecting Hoover's own mounting sense of urgency, "the entire nation" would be "in danger."[7]

Hoover responded to this national crisis by helping to organize the Second Industrial Conference in December 1919. Before the conference met, Hoover outlined his analysis of the economic situation in an article for the *Saturday Evening Post*. There were two main industrial problems, Hoover argued, first, under-consumption of goods and second, under-production of goods. Both of these problems required "combined and coordinated action of effort, intelligence and skill of all elements in production, whether workers, tools or management." For Hoover, the basic institutions of labor and capital were working at cross-purposes, which led to waste of time and energy, and contributed to social and political strife. By contrast, cooperation between labor and capital would allow for the "moral and intellectual welfare of the producer as to hours, conditions of labor, opportunities of education, and so forth."[8]

For Hoover, one way to address the "labor/capital" conflict was to argue that the distinction was a foolish creation of "false class consciousness" which, if not handled properly, could lead to the a revolutionary labor movement as in Russia or to very radical labor unions as in Britain and France. In other words, Hoover saw the American industrial situation as "building for us the very same kind of foundations upon which Europe rocks today." For Hoover, all workers, whether manual or managerial, were laborers, with a common status that should allow them to make joint decisions affecting them all. In explaining this position, Hoover revealed the essence of his thought on cooperation. He reasoned that "there is no quarrel with capital itself [the savings of the nation represented by the tools of production]; the quarrel is over the distribution of its ownership and the profits that rise from it." Cooperation would, at its heart, be redistributive: all members of the community would benefit from a concerted effort to raise living standards for all. Sustained growth with higher wages would lessen tension between classes by raising the standard of living for all. According to this logic, what would be the role of the unions and how would cooperation be controlled? Hoover would have to answer this if his theory of cooperation was to bear fruit.[9]

Hoover envisioned cooperation between groups, and therefore recognized the right of unions to exist as a safeguard for employees. Further, Hoover saw collective bargaining as a rational and just way of settling disputes. Yet, though he understood workers' need to strike for their own protection, he thought that cooperation between enlightened leaders could settle disputes with compulsory arbitration rather than strikes or lockouts. To strike or lock workers out would be "at once a violation of community rights." Hoover proposed that unions be held liable for contracts left unfulfilled after the parties reached an agreement, a proposal would be tenable only if corporations also cooperated. Hoover saw nothing wrong with the combination of capital for larger production and distribution. Yet he did recognize that once the corporation begins to dominate "wages or prices of production, or to prevent the growth of competition, they are in flagrant violation of the principle of equal opportunity".[10]

Another threat Hoover recognized to equality of opportunity, was the threat to competition raised by the specter of the ever more powerful trusts, Hoover viewed the Sherman Antitrust law and the Interstate Commerce Commission as effective deterrents. He applauded the 1911 Standard Oil decision because it had given birth to four regional concerns and hundreds of wildcat drillers, and thereby opened the industry to a fierce competition which led to new product development and lower gasoline prices. However, he preferred the rule of reason and public debate over what was or was not a violation of the Sherman Act to over-aggressive prosecution of trusts. Hoover wanted a center-of-the- road approach. Over-aggressive prosecution would violate private ownership; yet, if combinations became too dominant, "they must be held in control by the Government to see they serve the community and do not violate the fundamental principles of equality." The mediating role of the state, as facilitator and regulator, was fundamental to the idea of cooperation. For Hoover, this role should involve neither the minute and invasive supervision of Theodore Roosevelt's "New Nationalism" nor the unsophisticated "New Freedom" of Wilson. To understand better Hoover's positioning of the state, employers, and employees, we must place Hoover in relation to the corporate liberal tradition which had been developing in the United States since the 1880s.[11]

Hoover was attracted to cooperation and associationalism because he wanted to preserve the tradition of private property, even in an era of large corporations, and to retain the incentives it provided to small businessmen, within the framework of a self-governing system that kept corporations from dominating society. This had to be done without big government, which in Hoover's view could also be an instrument of tyranny. Hoover did not see the state as the appropriate tool for protecting the legitimate interests of either employers or employees, although coming out of World War I some argued that it should be. Hoover firmly believed the market should determine outcomes. However, in an increasingly complex market, some limited form of regulation appeared necessary to keep an appropriate balance of large and small concerns.[12]

Hoover's faith in voluntarism stemmed in part from the success of his experiments promoting voluntary cooperation in WWI food relief efforts. Hoover's development of the Belgian Relief Commission, and later his work as head of the U.S. Food Administration, were based on voluntarism. Building the Belgian Relief effort into a successful campaign to feed and clothe millions of refugees, he secured the cooperation of governments, armies and navies, and staffed and controlled the entire operation without any means of coercion.[13] The success of any voluntarist effort depended, Hoover thought, on the power of public opinion. During the war, this forced Germany to keep relief coming to occupied lands as well as to raise that capital necessary for the relief effort. Hoover returned to the United States assured that voluntarism, when applied to a just cause, was the way to attack problems. Shortly before the Second Industrial Conference, he observed that public opinion could serve as "a corrective at times more potent that a policeman and always more constructive." Coupled with public opinion to pressure employees and/or employers, perhaps orchestrated but not dominated by government, a voluntary effort to promote cooperation would be preferable to one group or another dictating answers.[14]

By November of 1919, Herbert Hoover had defined a method for bringing the country out of its postwar dislocations and putting it on the road to prosperity, which relied on swift resolution of the conflicts not only between small businesses and large corporations, but also between employers and employees, all through cooperation. Government could not dictate the terms of this solution, but Hoover hoped that it could stir public opinion to urge these groups to enter voluntary agreements. The next step for Hoover was to publicize his proposal and find backing for it.

Hoover's first opportunity to unveil his proposal came at the Second Industrial Conference in December of 1919. The conference considered a range of solutions to the conflict between employers and employees. Hoover, as vice-chairman of the conference, put himself in a position to influence the conference significantly. The report of the conference contained primarily Hoover's analysis.[15] In this report and his statements afterward, he pinpointed what he saw as the proper relationship of labor and capital and the remedies to the conflict between them.

The evidence of Hoover's public statements and correspondence in the late 1919 to early 1920 period indicates that he then shifted his analysis to employer-worker relations. Hoover recognized that there was little personal contact between employers and workers in contemporary industry. Workers on ever more intricate assembly lines performed repetitive functions in which they could take little creative interest. This alienation, and the growing aggregation of capital, put the worker in an inferior bargaining position. The Industrial Conference took up a number of questions related to these problems. How could employees achieve a relative equality at the bargaining table? What role, if any, could the state play in achieving negotiated settlements to lessen violent conflict in industry?[16]

In the late 1910s and early 1920s, one model for solving industrial disputes was provided by the Kansas Industrial Court Act, which called for judicial settlements. Hoover strongly opposed this model on the grounds that a court could use "legal repression under drastic penalties of the right to strike and lockout, determination of minimum wage . . . and consideration of a fair profit to the employer." If no other solution could be reached, the act allowed the state to take over the particular industry or company involved. Hoover did not directly oppose the act, as it could serve as one possible solution. However, after analyzing the long-standing system of industrial wage boards and compulsory arbitration in Australia, he concluded that it could not work in the United States for several reasons.[17]

First, the industrial court could raise wages during industrial growth, but in times of depression a court decision to lower wages would force workers to strike. In poor economic times, the court would have to harshly penalize a labor movement that did not accept its rulings. Hoover drew the inference that the state would be an agent of industrial repression against workers by eliminating the workers' right to strike, a right that was "an absolute fundamental to their protection." In addition, workers could not bargain for themselves directly, but would be dependent on the government for protection.[18]

Another difficulty Hoover saw with judicial action involved minimum wages. Hoover believed that each industry, or the companies within a particular industry, would claim a different minimum, while any judicial measures would have to keep a uniform standard across industry. Such a standard, Hoover believed, would undermine the competitive basis upon which industry established itself. In Australia, this attempt at uniform minimum wages led to economic dislocations and a tendency for all wage-earners' salaries to stay at the minimum, which stifled the initiative and productivity of the better workers.[19]

An industrial court would also have to regulate profits, and therefore address the question of exactly what a "fair" profit was, a question which, Hoover reasoned, remained undetermined by "theoretical economics, legislation, or courts" in a competitive industrial nation. In the case of monopoly, the court might determine a maximum profit, but even this, in some cases, "may deliver large burdens to people." Employers accepting some arbitrary minimum profit might maintain it during an economic downturn by lowering wages. To accept the Kansas plan with these, in Hoover's view, inherent problems, would "in the long run and in a logical extreme, substitute government control of industry for competition." The Kansas plan served as the perfect straw man to be knocked down with his own recommendations.[20]

At the Industrial Conference, where various models for industrial relations were under review, Hoover promoted a less intrusive role for government in the settlement of labor disputes. He insisted that the best method of securing meaningful collective bargaining lay not in "legal repression," but in governmental pressure that ultimately resulted in voluntary entry into collective bargaining. A regional chair or a central board in Washington, or both, would monitor conflicts, evaluate the bargaining positions of both sides, and recommend solutions. Although Hoover did not want to force compliance and made it clear that either party could refuse the government's advice, he warned that a failure to comply would result in the advisory group's stimulating of public opinion to force a negotiated settlement. Participation in the process was of course voluntary, and Hoover adamantly reiterated that the government would not act as an arbitrator of disputes. He hoped that if the proper machinery of assistance were in place, labor and capital would begin to see their mutual interest in higher living standards and increased production and would voluntarily find solutions satisfactory to both parties.[21] Hoover believed this non-legislated, assistive government action promoting the voluntary cooperation of labor and capital would stimulate "self-government in industry," without, like the Kansas plan, "imposing the compulsion of the courts, injunctions, fines or jails."[22]

The Second Industrial Conference failed to carry out Hoover's recommendations. Such international events as the League of Nations debate and the negotiation of the peace shifted the spotlight from domestic industrial problems. Nonetheless the conference gave Hoover the opportunity to work out and make public the skeleton of his economic plan. He was therefore well prepared in July 1920 for the Senate Special Committee on Reconstruction and Production which was called after the depression had hit, the election campaign of 1920 had begun to heat up, and international problems had given way to postwar economic dislocation. The Senate Special Committee on Reconstruction and Production, led by William Calder, held hearings on proposed legislation to bring an end to the depression of 1920. The committee sought ways to promote, among other things, home construction, efficient transportation, and savings for investment capital.

Although several proposals aimed to expand the postal savings bank system and provide tax credits for mortgages, none ultimately passed. The committee called Hoover to testify in September 1920, and he took this as another opportunity to ring the bell for higher production and investment, and for cooperation between capital and labor. He also took on another issue---waste in government and industry.[23]

Hoover found one glaring example of waste in the construction industry, which faced two damaging conditions. First, production of war materials had diverted much needed capital and labor away from the industry. Second, the absence of uniform building codes prevented the industry from becoming more efficient, and so limited its potential for expansion. The return of veterans and normal population growth caused a shortage estimated at more than one million homes. The committee did not propose any legislation specifically to solve the housing problem, but the deficiency of housing stock would become one of the main issues at the Unemployment Conference the following year.[24]

Hoover also found waste in rail transportation. A shortage of rail cars had severely limited transport of coal and other material to consumer markets. Compounding the problem, rail operators and some industrial shippers continued to place the fulfillment of lucrative government contracts made during the war before the transport of goods and materials needed in the postwar domestic market, such as building materials, textiles, and coal. The lack of a transitional program returning industry to non-war production contributed to greater waste. By waste, Hoover meant not only inefficient production, but also a "producing capacity for things that were not vital." For Hoover, the production of non-essentials, the filling of unnecessary government contracts, and the loss of savings, which curtailed investment, were the "worst results of the war."[25]

To remedy the situation, Hoover suggested national conferences in areas such as construction. He also suggested a specific reconstruction program, "covering not only matters of finance," which the Senate Committee had focused on, but also matters of labor, a review of government waste, and a streamlining of the departments within the governmental structure. This was a time for Hoover to stress that his recommendations and theories for long-term growth as well as stability across industries did not rest on a large regulatory state imposing unnecessary burdens on business, but rather on a smaller government providing industry with information and assistance in reaching stability and achieving sustained growth. The members of the Senate Committee, however, were leaning toward solutions requiring more, not less, governmental control. Senator Eugene Meyer, Jr., captured the essence of the statist argument for reconstruction. Meyer stressed the fact that although there "was a great reaction after the armistice to get free from government control," the country was not psychologically "in a frame of mind" to support a severely limited policy with limited regulation because the country faced problems "of such universal popular interest that only the government [can] carry out the programs of reconstruction in a comprehensive way." Despite continued government control by the people, only a government-directed market and relief program could solve the technical issues of readjustment of labor policy and social welfare measures.[26]

Hoover flatly disagreed with this position. He advocated a program whose "enforcement only need be educational, together with the indirect pressure that can be brought to bear upon it." The continued intrusion of "government restriction" would not be necessary if government could establish a clear goal and put mechanisms in place for voluntary conformity. None of Hoover's plans for national conferences would prove effective if government processes such as the Senate hearings continued to give credibility to statist solutions. Realizing this, Hoover next moved to organize the engineering community to outline a specific plan for a voluntarist stabilization strategy.[27]

In November of 1920, Herbert Hoover became President of the Federated American Engineering Societies, and as such urged the increasing number of professional engineers to address problems of waste and reconstruct their industry. Disillusioned with the outcome of the Industrial Conference and the Senate hearings, Hoover thought the experts truly qualified to find nonpartisan solutions were engineers. Skilled in problem solving and dedicated to social advancement, engineers were uniquely qualified to meet the task of postwar readjustment and clear the road toward progress.

Hoover led the charge by attacking what he saw as one of the fundamental problems—labor/management conflict. On the 17th of November 1920, he discussed labor issues with the executive council meeting of the AFL. He made clear the position of the engineers with respect to collective bargaining. The question for them was not "should there be collective bargaining?" but "what is the proper method to arrive at an equitable agreement?" The problem with the Industrial Conference and other solutions proposed up to that time, according to Hoover, was that none provided for representation by an independent party. Most were either legally or legislatively conceived and did not put labor and management on equal terms at the negotiating table. Also, although Hoover had made recommendations, to that point none had been carried out. In the meeting, Hoover stressed that only a plan that called for voluntary action could produce the proper negotiating climate.

In addition to collective bargaining, labor conflict was compounded by production problems.[28] Like a long line of employers and engineers since the turn of the century, Hoover accused organized labor of curtailing production. If "every atom of production was realized" Hoover argued, it would eliminate a large measure of unemployment, which he argued was the greatest threat to labor. The higher the unemployment rate, the fewer the opportunities to bargain for higher wages and job security. Since there was no uniform minimum wage, lower demand for employment would drive wages lower and further weaken the labor movement. If labor would "put its back into increased production," a large number of men would become employed and, for purposes of collective bargaining, labor could "not do more to raise itself in the esteem of the American people than to give its cooperation to solve that particular question." This admonition to labor would become crucial, since public opinion figured as the primary enforcement mechanism of a voluntary program for settling disputes. But it met with criticism by Gompers and the other labor leaders present at the meeting.[29]

Daniel Tobin, one of the members of the executive committee, argued that labor was more productive than ever before and accused the press of a propaganda campaign discrediting the labor movement. Furthermore, he argued, the actions of some employers, in operating part-time or closing plants altogether, which the *New York Times* called "little more than a social crime," was the main cause of unemployment. Labor leaders such as Tobin and Samuel Gompers also voiced concern over cooperation with institutions such as the Chamber of Commerce. As Gompers pointed out, the Chamber's embrace of the open shop system was a direct "attack [on] the United trade unions of the country." The open shop system had destroyed earlier attempts at cooperation and, as far as Gompers was concerned, made it"exceedingly difficult" for the AFL to "make any kind of approach to the United States Chamber of Commerce."[30] Disagreements with management about shop councils and minimum or tiered wages led the labor movement the regard cooperation as unlikely. Nevertheless, at the conclusion of the meeting, Gompers suggested that if a solution were possible, Hoover might arrange a conference among employers, engineers, and representatives of the Chamber of Commerce and the A.F. of L. Hoover agreed to try to use labor's desire for a resolution as a tool to bring the two sides together.[31]

The following day Hoover contacted John R. Dunlap, the editor of *Industrial Management*, urging that in housing construction in particular, labor and management stop "arguing over spilt milk" and come together. Government had the power to serve as a catalyst for this cooperative effort. In the following months, Hoover commissioned a committee of engineers from the Federated American Engineering Society to investigate the issue of waste in industry, of which unemployment was the greatest.[32]

In February of 1921, a large segment of the engineering profession came together to solve the nation's ills. Hoover gave the keynote address of the Federated American Engineering Society's convention in Syracuse, New York. In this address and in the preliminary survey of waste in industry by the executive committee, of which he was a member, Hoover's aims were clear. In his testimony before the Senate Committee the summer before, he had identified the problem, but had not yet formulated a clear solution in such areas as construction, agriculture, and the coal industry. Not until the convention in Syracuse did Hoover have an analytical structure in place that allowed him to order problems and thereby treat more critical areas, such as production and unemployment, without being pinned down in narrow debates. In his address, Hoover for the first time clearly stated that he saw the economy not as the sum of narrow problems like collective bargaining or a shortage of rail cars, but "as a single industrial organism." Hoover, and the engineers working with him, could determine the goal of this "organism"—maximum production—and then judge what the deficiencies in the broad system were. These deficiencies, in his opinion, fell under the category of industrial waste.[33]

In Hoover's Syracuse address, the problems of the country loomed larger than in his previous work. The public had blamed not only labor, but the "poor coordination between industries . . . failures in transportation, coal and other supplies . . . mismanagement and a hundred other [problems]." The public saw both industry and government as culprits in the social, political, and economic malaise that had over taken the country.[34]

Though one of the few specific results of this meeting of engineers was the establishment of a committee to examine industrial waste, it did much to help convince groups of the need for cooperation and of the feasibility of a self-governing economic system that could provide the order and stability needed to end the crisis. The message of cooperation had penetrated the political conversation and was picking up momentum. Several news agencies supported Hoover's analysis and called for cooperation; the engineers were poised to make their analysis and propose their solutions; Hoover now needed only the federal government's leadership to bring groups together and facilitate action. He thought the report on industrial waste might provide a catalyst for effective leadership, but grew increasingly convinced that he would have to put himself in a position inside government to provide the leadership he desired.[35]

Following the election of Warren Harding in November 1920, the President-elect went on an extended vacation to select his cabinet. Impressed by Hoover's relief efforts during the war, Harding offered Hoover his choice of the secretaryship either of the Interior or of Commerce, despite strong opposition within the Republican Party to the appointment of Hoover to any cabinet level position. Senators Knox, Smoot, and Hiram Johnson argued Hoover was too liberal in his stance on the League of Nations and too internationally minded for either position. Several senators and Harry New, one of Harding's advisors, wished to omit Hoover from the selection process. Nonetheless, Harding offered him the Commerce Department job on February 12, 1921. Hoover did not wish to enter any public office; however, as he said, "under the circumstances of our nation's difficulties . . . I have no right to refuse your wish." He accepted Harding's offer on the condition he could enlarge the Commerce Department and have a free hand in its operation. [36] Hoover needed a department large, efficient, and powerful enough to persuade the different elements in the private sector to embrace his plans.[37]

As part of his demands, he gave Harding a four-point plan. First, he wanted not only the direction of various bureaus, but also a strong hand in "the field of foreign commerce in which are involved the entire political policies of the government in their reflex upon our economic life." In other words, Hoover wanted to control or at least influence the country's foreign policy, especially in areas concerned with trade. He therefore asked that the State Department cooperate with him and that the merchant marine be brought under his department.[38] Second, he demanded the authority to carry out a voluntary standardization program for manufactured products, which would be backed by legislation only "when constructive results and experience had been obtained." Third, he asked that the Department of Labor assist him in reducing labor friction.[39] Last, he requested the authority to "call for voluntary services of men and committees of inquiry [to discuss] social and industrial currents." It was in this voluntarist spirit that President Harding called the Unemployment Conference. Hoover believed that if his conditions could be met, the conference would solve the country's problems in a manner equitable to all groups concerned.[40] Hoover's appointment as Secretary of Commerce put him in a position to have his ideas regarding reconstruction finally not only heard but acted upon. His programs, largely ignored in the aftermath of the Second Industrial Conference and the Senate Committee on Reconstruction and Production, could now take center stage; he could now begin to define the language and set the tone for New Era political discourse.

In June 1921, the long awaited "Waste in Industry" report prepared by Edward Eyre Hunt, Hoover's secretary and himself a progressive Republican, became available. Hunt showed that poor management accounted for more than 50% of the waste in industry, inefficient labor or strikes for less than 25%. Management's chief problems came from "faulty control of material, design, production lack of research and defective sales policies." Of these problems, design caused the largest percentage of waste because of the lack of standardization within industries. For example, in 1920 there were 216 different sizes of tires. This caused excess inventory at the dealer's shop and eventually, shortages and higher prices for consumers. After the "Waste in Industry" report, tire manufacturers agreed to reduce the number of tire sizes to ten.[41]

Yet the report did not entirely absolve labor. It found most of the waste attributable to labor resulted from union rules which made work less, instead of more, efficient. Some painter's unions, for example, insisted on a four-and-one-half-inch limit on the size of brushes even though a larger brush would be more economical. Requirements for lathers dropped to twelve bundles per eight-hour shift when "formerly output was sixteen bundles." In other unions, waste resulted from skilled laborers doing the work of helpers.[42]

Joint efforts by management and labor might reduce another waste—industrial accidents and deaths. Safer machines, physical examinations, and safety education could significantly lower the industrial death rate, which stood at 23,000 in 1919. The report on waste encouraged cooperation on such issues and so served as a jumping off point for the Conference on Unemployment.[43]

In the summer of 1921, the economic malaise that President Harding had inherited continued to worsen. In August, Hoover wrote to Harding suggesting the President call a conference to find a solution to the crisis, particularly to the problem of unemployment. In the letter, Hoover also indicated his position that the unemployment relief effort should be directed toward establishing community action at the local level and a cooperative effort between economic sectors. Because of the length of the depression, Hoover wanted a conference that could produce concrete solutions and so prevent further deterioration of the situation into the winter.[44]

Nine days after Hoover suggested the conference to the President, a press release formally announced it: a presidential conference specifically designated to address the issue of unemployment would gather in Washington in September, 1921. Hoover, the chairman of the conference, organized it to further his corporatist goals: members would be selected to represent the nation geographically and by industry. He would invite labor leaders and "representatives of the greater groups of industries and thought, and the cooperation of their national organizations will be sought in their selection." "The object of the conference will be to inquire into the volume of needed employment . . . make recommendation[s] . . . that can be properly taken in coordinated speeding up of employment by industries and public bodies . . . and in addition [conduct] a broad study of the economic measures desirable to ameliorate the unemployment situation and give impulse to the recovery of business and commerce." Hoover wished to assemble the key players from the industrial and academic sectors, reach solutions, and implement them while holding to the principle of cooperation and voluntarism.[45]

The Unemployment Conference was the first national meeting of leaders specifically gathered to find solutions to that particular problem. Hoover did not call the conference another "industrial" conference, since he did not see industry per se as the problem. He reasoned that five million people were unemployed in the United States because of a combination of inefficiency, labor strife, soft international markets, concentration of investment capital, and ineffective economic statesmanship. The focus on unemployment reminded the participants of the urgency of the problem and the need for sound, cooperative solutions. Particular industries were suffering from having an unusually high number of unemployed and from government mechanisms, such as construction, transportation, mining, agriculture, and public works projects, and thus required specific attention. Hoover organized committees in these areas, and in statistics, shipping and the business cycle.[46]

Before organizing these committees and calling the conference into session, Hoover formed an economic advisory council and asked it to suggest some initial solutions. This council suggested increased research on such ways of easing seasonal fluctuations in employment as expanded exports to the southern hemisphere and provisions for storing goods manufactured out of season. The government, the committee suggested, could increase expenditures for internal improvements during times of depression and provide information that would allow industry to anticipate fluctuations in the market and act accordingly. The committee did not recommend unemployment insurance. Though Hoover did not commit himself to these solutions before the conference, the report did serve as a basis to begin discussions.[47]

The next task for Hoover was to invite those he thought necessary to the conference's success. As he had indicated in his press release of August 29, 1921, a wide range of leaders was invited to the conference: among others, Clarence Hicks, executive assistant to the Presidents of Colorado Fuel and Iron and Standard Oil, H. H. Raymond, President of the American Steamship Owners Association, C. H. Markham, President of the Chamber of Commerce of the United States, Davis R. Dewey, professor of economics and statistics at M.I.T., Samuel Gompers, President of the AFL, and John L. Lewis, President of the United Mine Workers. In bringing such varied leaders together, Hoover had gone far toward assuring cooperation between corporatist elements, academia, and government. On September 26, 1921, the conference began.

As early as September 29, the conference announced and approved emergency measures unanimously. It suggested that, since unemployment relief was a community problem, the cooperation of mayors would be crucial to the success of its recommendations. It advised repairs of homes, hotels, and other dwellings; municipal construction of roads, schools, and other projects, financed through increased bond sales; plant construction; and reduction in the number of working hours per day. These measures, the emergency-measures committee reported, could put people to work immediately. In the following days, the conference issued reports on longer-term solutions.[48]

As these measures attest, one chronic problem area was the construction industry. The industry usually employed more than one million workers, but the war had produced "artificial restrictions," such as the diversion of capital and labor into other areas, which eventually caused a housing shortage. Additionally, construction was closely related to other industries—for every construction worker, there were 2.5 workers in other industries dependent on construction—and therefore crucial to general prosperity. The construction committee submitted an emergency report on September 29 and a long-term stabilization plan on October 12, 1921.[49]

The committee's plan had seven points. It proposed changes in finance charges levied by banks and a general loosening of credit for new home purchasers. It called for a reduction of freight rates to prewar levels so as to lower shipping costs for construction materials. In the area of labor relations, the committee called for negotiated contracts, but warned that an "employer should not permit the wage his workman to that point at which only provides sufficient earnings to take care of the necessities of life . . . but the workers should be able to educate their children and be able to save [sic]." In return for this, workers should be responsible for delivering "maximum production and abandoning sympathetic strikes and boycotts," as these were "detrimental to the public welfare." Lastly, as part of Hoover's standardization effort, the committee argued that the construction industry would need greater statistical information on trends, practices, of and standardization of materials in order to make itself more rational and more efficient, and to set an example of the benefits of standardization for other sectors of the economy. The Department of Commerce had established a Division of Building and Housing earlier in the year to assist in providing that information.[50]

In its conclusion, the construction committee report placed great emphasis on action. Only by implementing the plan with the cooperation of the various institutions involved in the construction industry, such as banking, manufacturing, labor, and government, could the crisis be relieved in the short term and mechanisms put in place to prevent a recurrence of the depression in the long term. The committee also cautioned manufacturers against raising prices too quickly after the recovery had begun. Prices could be restrained by responsible leaders within the industry and the pressure of public opinion. Neither legislation nor government regulation were mentioned in the report. The conference adopted the resolution on October 12, 1921.[51]

The actions of the construction committee were representative of other conference reports on transportation, public works, and seasonal unemployment. In all of them, viable solutions to the nation's economic ills were drawn from the principle Hoover had been trying to introduce into the public discourse since the Second Industrial Conference of December 1919: addressing problems without further regulation, through cooperation and voluntary agreement to standards and practices from the local to the national level, embracing manufacturing, finance, labor, and government.

The Conference on Unemployment not only helped Hoover promote his economic plan, it also helped him to complete his vision of an associative state based on efficiency, cooperation, and voluntarism. Although much of what historians have written about Hoover concerns these principles, the underlying concepts which determined the language he used and the vision he possessed have gone relatively unnoticed. Cooperation, efficiency and voluntarism had meaning for Hoover in relation to the central concerns and values of his ideology, virtue and liberty.[52]

Underlying the political action of historical actors are concepts that shape the language in and through which that action takes place. James Farr, in his article, "Understanding Conceptual Change Politically," constructs a methodology for analyzing the key concepts of historical actors. Their meaning is affected by context and changes over time, along with conceptual change in the actor involved, and is finally expressed in political activity. Farr also argues that some conceptual conflict may occur and be resolved below the level of language. Hoover defined a concept of liberty and virtue, which he expressed politically in his rhetoric of cooperation. Though Hoover may not have used the specific words *liberty* and *virtue* often, Farr's methodology allows the historian to uncover these important concepts.[53]

The postwar situation created a conflict in Hoover's conceptions of liberty and virtue. In thoughtful, rationally minded people such as he, conceptual conflicts provoke consternation, reflection, and innovation, and are resolved by conceptual change. One can define conceptual change as "one imaginative consequence of political actors criticizing and attempting to resolve contradictions which they discover or generate in the complex web of their beliefs, actions and practices as they try to understand the world around them." For Hoover, the conceptual conflict stemmed not only from the power of the large corporation over society, but also from the wartime response of the command economy. Neither of these positions would allow for the protection of liberty in an individualist sense. To resolve the conflict, Hoover expanded the criteria of liberty to include groups within society and also individuals within the group. Virtue, a necessary condition for liberty to succeed, went through this same conceptual change.[54]

The World War had a profound impact on all its participants, including Herbert Hoover. As an engineer, he had much experience with the science of efficiency and saw the need for rational relationships among groups. The social impact of revolution, starvation, and class-ridged societies disturbed him. Returning from the war, two convictions dominated his thinking. One, derived from the social discontent in Europe, was that the "whole philosophy [of socialism] is bankrupt itself." The second stemmed from his appreciation of the

American experience and his recognition that it "does not allow the use of this community for experiment in social diseases." Confronted by the economic and social problems at home, he constructed a discourse that could solve these problems and simultaneously prevent any desire for "social experiments." Hoover knew the managerial tasks and principles required; more important than these was the underlying reason for a new vision of America—the need to protect liberty and to create a society which would promote virtue in individuals and in government. Liberty was the primary end, for which Hoover had to create a means in the postwar world.[55]

For Hoover, liberty meant "that there should be an equality of opportunity, and equal chance, to every citizen." The "love of liberty" was one of the great ideals of the nation. That ideal was embodied in"that firm and fixed ideal of American Individualism—an equality of opportunity." The theme of providing this equal opportunity recurred in most of Hoover's correspondence, discussions, and articles in this period; usually it appeared first and served as the basis for the ensuing argument. Clearly, Hoover believed fervently in providing people the opportunity to achieve and propel society forward. What exactly did Hoover mean? How did he describe this equality? How could he incorporate his notional concept of equality into a successful, effective framework?[56]

Liberty depended not only upon the actions of the individual, but also upon the attitude and organization of the community. On a personal level, "individual initiative' needed protection. American liberty recognized "that the whole mass can progress in its moral, intellectual and physical standards only through the progress of each individual." The striving of each person toward a particular destiny, in America, prevented what Hoover called "the frozen strata of classes." The protection of liberty through individual initiative could allow an orphan farm boy from Iowa to become Secretary of Commerce.[57]

The protection of liberty demanded that the social structure prevent the domination of one class over another. Hoover recognized that some individuals would succeed and some would not; however, the playing field must be level, the opportunity to succeed must be available to all. This condition would prevent class domination. Socialism, Hoover argued, took away initiative by creating stifling bureaucracies and enforcing an unnatural equality upon the people. To Hoover, the equality of socialism based itself on an ideal of "pure altruism," which perhaps could work, but in the reality of the postwar world resulted in a "bureaucracy of the entire population, in which, having obliterated the economic stimulation of each member . . . character and ability are to be arranged in relative authority by ballot or most likely by . . . some form of tyranny." He saw the failure of this system not only in the chaos in Russia, but also in the failure of attempts to nationalize industry in the United States. For Hoover, individual initiative and equality of opportunity relied on "enlightened self-interest." This was the essence of liberty. The protection of liberty came not from an aggressive Federal Government, in the sense of a large bureaucracy and excessive regulation, but from "education, constitutional free press and free speech."[58]

The growth of capital "into larger units" had threatened this reliance upon individual initiative since the late nineteenth century, and with it came "an inequality of the bargaining power of the individual." If protecting individual initiative was necessary in this new era of mass production and large corporate entities, other groups would need recognition and the playing fields among groups would have to be leveled. This assumption led Hoover to support the right of unions to organize and bargain collectively, the right of farmers to form their own associations, and the right of small business to organize collectives under the Chamber of Commerce and other trade associations. Equality of opportunity for unions, farmers, and small businessmen would prevent the stifling of individual initiative within these groups; "in these groups the individual finds opportunity for self-expression and participation in the molding of ideas." Immediately after the war, these "large industrial units" controlled most of the economic activity in America and through their own readjustment problems threatened "cessation of production and service," which increased the strikes and lockouts that "paralyzed the public."[59]

The solution to the problem, and hence the protection of liberty, rested in cooperation. Common ground had to be found among these different groups. "Unless we can build a bridge of this character we are going to see the community torn to pieces by impossible class conflicts." That common ground lay in the country's economic health. If these different groups could find ways of promoting increased production, higher standards of living, and improved working conditions, all sides would "benefit, not only materially, but spiritually as well."[60]

The Federal Government would play a large role in fostering this cooperation—not through regulation or what Hoover described as "legal repression," but through information that would form public opinion and create an atmosphere in which these groups could cooperate. It was essential that this coming together of different elements of society be voluntary rather than legislated. If not, Hoover feared, government would become the dominant group and move toward authoritarianism, something he feared as much as socialism. In addition, previous attempts at bringing about solutions by government interference had not produced results. This was the problem before the Unemployment Conference. Attempts had been "made at reorganization [and implicitly building cooperation] before, but all of them have gone to the same crematory—the interminable differences in opinion among the executive and legislative officials over details." The Unemployment Conference operated outside judicial and legislative action and provided the forum Hoover sought to build the cooperation needed to solve the country's problems and, thus, protect liberty.[61]

In his opening speech to the conference, Hoover called for cooperation to solve the nation's problems, in terms that bolstered his concept of liberty. First, Hoover made it clear that "the remedies for these matters, must, in the largest degree lie outside the range of legislation." This was necessary not only to prevent statist solutions, but also to ensure that a remedy "could be expected through the mobilization of the fine cooperative action of our manufacturers and employers, of our public bodies and local authorities." If this were done, the country "will have again demonstrated that independence and ability of action amongst our own people . . . saves our government from that ultimate paternalism that will undermine our whole political system." The duty of the Federal Government, Hoover stated, was "not to enforce such programs" by force, but "to mobilize the intelligence of the country, that the entire community may be instructed as to the part they may play in the effecting of such solutions."[62]

Examination of the Report of the Conference shows that each committee's resolutions and methods of attack were grounded in Hoover's concept of liberty. Responsibility rested at the community level, at which success resulted from individual initiative. Different sectors—industry, finance, labor, and agriculture—would have to cooperate to solve large industrial problems such as construction. The government would facilitate this by providing information, not by force. Thus, Hoover's economic plans served as means to an end he felt was crucial to the survival of the democratic system: efficiency, elimination of waste, cooperation, and voluntarism all served to protect and advance liberty.

In his analysis of the depression, Hoover saw not only that a new economic system was necessary to protect liberty, but also that individuals and government should aspire to certain characteristics in order to meet the challenge of the times: the "virtues of hard work, frugal living, more savings, sober conduct and higher honesty." He recognized that if the fundamentals of his conception of liberty were to succeed, virtue, individually and in government, was absolutely necessary. Virtue had not only a moral component, but an economic one as well. The above-mentioned characteristics were to be found in individuals, just as liberty depended on individual initiative. But that initiative needed channeling in positive ways, in harmony with these characteristics of virtue.[63]

Similarly, industry and government had virtuous characteristics necessary to the protection of liberty, to which economic disorder, political radicalism, and statist regimentation were directly opposed. This explains why Hoover stressed the voluntarist nature of his economic policy. A virtuous state that conformed to his vision of liberty could not allow statist solutions of adjudication and coercive legislation. Similarly, such virtuous acts as rationalizing the economy and promoting efficiency and cooperation, corrected economic dislocation and neutralized political radicalism by raising living standards and creating employment. This idea of virtue had to meet one acid test: if virtue could be placed in an economic context how could one reconcile with it the plight of the poor and unemployed?[64]

Throughout American history, the economic component of virtue hinged on a notion that able-bodied people who did not work were somehow morally deficient and, hence, not virtuous. The "Protestant Work Ethic" dictated that those who worked hard, lived soberly, and saved their money were virtuous. The term "unemployed" was linked to the notion of "idleness." Raymond Williams shows in *Keywords: A Vocabulary of Culture and Society* that this connection resulted in the term "unemployed" being taken as a reprehensible personal condition rather than a social and economic situation. This personalization of an economic condition put Hoover and other social reformers into a difficult situation. What role should government take in efforts at relief? Were the poor truly morally deficient, or were they the victims of an economic situation that left them unemployed?[65]

One can see Hoover's answer to this question in his speeches during the Unemployment Conference. One of his justifications for the conference was his belief that "there is no economic failure so terrible in its import as that of a country possessing a surplus of every necessity of life in which members, willing and anxious to work are deprived of these necessities." He clearly viewed unemployment as a result of economic failure, not moral deficiency. However, his belief in cooperation and voluntarism and his distrust of large government interference, led him to reject relief—direct government payouts to the unemployed by the government. "The dole" as he called it, was a "most vicious solution" because it stifled individual initiative by making people dependent on the government, and because it led to large deficit spending.[66] Hoover reasoned that to resort to the "public purse" to solve the unemployment crisis would indeed be "a distinctive step backward in the progress of this country." The eventual recovery of the country in 1922 ended most debate over the dole, but this fundamental position, that the unemployed were victims of an economic situation and yet ought not to receive direct government relief, would haunt him in the Great Depression.[67]

Hoover's concepts of virtue and liberty were the cornerstones of his discourse. The characteristics of virtue for Hoover—economic harmony, political stability and non-statist government policies--shaped his beliefs concerning the protection and advancement of liberty. By promoting cooperation, elimination of waste, and equality of opportunity, Hoover thought his economic strategy would insure liberty. His discourse, introduced during the Industrial Conference of 1919, and renewed in 1920 at the Senate Committee on Reconstruction and Production, finally gained general approval and more importantly generated action at the Unemployment Conference of 1921.[68]

The economic system Hoover envisioned, one based on cooperation and individual initiative with limited government, and the language he used to promote this system, defined New Era discourse. His American Individualism, printed in 1923, and elaborating his beliefs since his return from the war in 1919, served as the political philosophy of the administrations of the 1920s. In his discourse from 1919 to 1921, Hoover expanded the criteria—the definitions of virtue and liberty, and the range these concepts covered. No longer were liberty and virtue concepts that applied only to individuals; Hoover's language and political actions show that the meanings of these concepts were expanded to include the various economic groups within society and that associationalism and cooperation were the proper vehicles to ensure equality among the corporatist economic groups.

Notes

1 James Farr, "Understanding Conceptual Change Politically," in *Political Innovation and Conceptual Change* (Cambridge University Press, 1989) 24-50.

2 Robert K. Murray, The Harding Era: Warren G. Harding and his Administration (Minneapolis: University of Minneapolis Press, 1969) 71-92.

3 The National Civic Federation, "A.Move for Industrial Peace," July 1921, Commerce Papers Box 24, Herbert Hoover Papers, Hoover Presidential Library, West Branch, Iowa. Hereafter referred to as HHP. Murray, *The Harding Era,* 81-83; Ellis Hawley, *The Great War and the Search for Modern Order: A History of the American People and Their Institutions, 1917-1933* (New York: St. Martin's Press, 1979) 44-7; "Wilson's Legacy to Harding," *Nation* February 23, 1921, 282-3.

4 Ellis Hawley, *The Great War and the Search for Modern Order,*81-3; John D. Hicks, *Rehersal for* Disaster (Gainsville: University of Florida Press, 1961) 1-32; Paul H. Douglas, *Real Wages in the United States,* 1820-1926 (Boston: Houghton Mifflin) 55-9. For a detailed account of the causes of the depression see Murray, *The Unemployment Problem* (New York: National Industrial Conference Board, 1921) 1-27

5 Hawley, *The Great War and the Search for Modern Order,* 49-52; Robert K. Murray, *Red Scare: A Study in National Hysteria, 1910-1920* (Minneapolis: University of Minnesota Press, 1955); Ronald Schatz, *The Electrical Workers: A History of Labor at General Electric and Westinghouse, 1923-1960* (Urban: University of Illinois Press, 1983).

6 Hoover to Gompers, May 26, 1917, Pre-Commerce Papers Box 5, HHP.

7 Hoover to Barnes, August 2, 1919, Pre-Commerce Papers Box 1, HHP; Burns to Hoover November 1, 1919, Pre-Commerce Papers, Box 2, HHP

8 "Some Notes on Industrial Readjustment," Public Statement 39, HHP. *Sunday Evening Post,* December 27, 1919, 1-5.

9 Ibid.

10 Ibid.

11 Ibid.; Michael E. Parrish, *Anxious Decades: America in Prosperity and Depression, 1920-1941* (New York: Norton, 1992) 5-47.

12 For an analysis of Hoover's corporatism during his presidency see: Ellis Hawley, "Herbert Hoover and American Corporation, 1929-1933," unpublished draft, Reprint file, HHP. Hawley argues that the goals I have described were Hoover's goals as Secretary of Commerce. Actually, these goals were formed as early as 1919, before the meeting of the Second Industrial Conference. For a discussion of corporate liberalism in general, see Martin J. Sklar, *The Corporate Reconstruction of American Capitalism, 1890-1916:the Market, the Law and Politics* (New York: Cambridge Univeristy Press, 1988); James

Weinstein, *The Corporate Ideal in the Liberal State, 1900-1918* (Boston: Beacon Press, 1968); Jeffrey Lustig, *Corporate Liberalism* (Berkeley: University of California Press, 1982). Implicit in Sklar's argument is the contention that the state served as an instrument of capital. Hoover, through his actions as Secretary of Commerce, sought private regulation of the market by sharing information and limited the power of corporations by advocating the empowerment of trade associations for small business. For an interesting critique of Sklar see, Gerald Berk, "Corporate Liberalism Reconsidered: A Review Essay," *Journal of Police History 3 (1991) 70-84.*

13 Herbert Hoover, *the Memoirs of Herbert Hoover,* vol. 1 (New York: Manmillan Company, 1951) 152-430.

14 Hoover, "Some Thoughts on Readjustment," 4.

15 Robert H. Zieger, "Herbert Hoover, the Wage Earner, and the New Economic System, 1919-1929," in Ellis Hawley, ed. *Herbert Hoover, 1921-1928* (Iowa City: University of Iowa Press, 1981) 82.

16 Hoover, Public Statements 141 and 53 HHP.

17 Hoover Public Statements 141 and 10 HHP.

18 Ibid.

19 Hoover Public Statement 141, HHP.

20 Ibid., 11-13, Hoover Public Statement 53, 6-9, HHP.

21 Hoover, Public Statement 141, 7, HHP.

22 Ibid., 7-8

23 Hoover testimony to the Senate Special Committee on Reconstruction and Production, 66th Congress, September 23, 1920, pp. 609-627.

24 Ibid., 617-8; Hoover, Public Statement 82, HHP.

25 Hoover testimony to the Senate Special Committee on Reconstruction and Production, 617-9, 624.

26 Comments of Senator Eugene Meyer Jr. , Senate Special Committee on Reconstruction and Production, 626-8

27 Ibid., 628.

28 Commerce Papers, Unemployment File, Box 49, HHP, 35-72.

29 Ibid., 36b, 36f. New York Times November 17, 1920.

30 Commerce Papers, Unemployment File, Box 49, HHP, 390.

31 Hoover to Dunlap, Public Statement 106, HHP. Washington Herald, January 24, 1921. Hoover Public Statement 123, HHP.

32 Hoover, Public Statement 128, HHP. Hoover Testimony tot eh Senate Special Committee on Reconstruction and Production, 625.

33 Hoover, Public Statement 128, HHP,2.

34 *New York Post,* February 14, 1921. *Sacramento Union,* February 15, 1921. *New York Times,* February 17, 24, 1921. *Washington Herald,* January 24, February 15,14,1921.

35 Murray, *The Harding Era,* 93-128.

36 Hoover, *Memoirs,* vol. 2, 100-50. Hoover, Pre-Commerce Papers, Correspondence File, Box 75, HHP.

37 Hoover to Harding, Pre-Commerce Papers, Correspondence File, Box 75, HHP.

38 Ibid., 3.

39 Ibid.,3.

40 Edward Eyre Hunt, "Industrial Waste," unpublished draft, November 15, 1921, Hunt File, Box 649, Commerce Papers, HHP.

41 Ibid., 4

42 Ibid.,7-15.

43 Hoover to Harding, August 20, 1921, Commerce Papers, Correspondence File, HHP.

44 Commerce Papers, Unemployment Conference File, Box 644, HHP.

45 Carolyn Grin, "The Unemployment Conference of 1921; An Experiment in National Cooperative Planning," *Mid America* 55 (April, 1973). *Report of the President's Conference on Unemployment* (Washington: Government Printing Office, 1921), 16-19. Hunt to Hoover, Commerce Papers, Unemployment Conference File, Box 652, HHP.

46 Report on Unemployment, 1-3. Hunt to Hoover, Commerce Papers, Unemployment Conference Planning File, Box 652, HHP, 2-4.

47 IBID,. 19.

48 Ibid., 111-18. See also: "Draft Report of the Committee on Emergency Efforts in Construction, August 29, 1921. Commerce Papers, Unemployment Conference Plans File, Box 664, HHP.

49 Ibid., 9-14.

50 Report on Unemployment, 112.

51 Ellis Hawley, "Herbert Hoover, The Commerce Secretariat, and the vision of an Associative State, 1921-1928," *Journal of American History* 61 (June, 1974) 116-40.

52 James Farr, "understanding Conceptual Change Politically," 25. In this article, Farr constructs a methodology for analyzing key concepts of historical actors. Language, its contextuality and changing meaning over time occurs through conceptual change and is finally expressed in political activity. Farr also argues that some conceptual conflict and resolution occurs below the level of language. The implication here, is that Hoover defines a concept of liberty and virtue, which he expressed politically in his rhetoric of cooperation. Even though Hoover may not have used the specific words liberty and virtue often, Farr's methodology allows the historian to uncover these important concepts and analyze them.

53 Herbert Hoover, Public Statement

54 Ibid.,3

55 In the documents used to this print, "especially of opportunity" was used in over 90%. Herbert Hoover, *American Individualism* (Garden City: Doubleday, 1923) 8-9, 16-7. Hoover, Public Statement 76, HHP.9.

56 Hoover makes reference to this is several public statements as well as in *American Individualism*. Hoover, *American Individualism,* 18-9.

57 Hoover, Public Statement 68, HHP. 3; Public Statement 53, HHP; Hoover, *American Individualism*, 52-4.

58 Hoover, Public Statement 53, HHP.3; Public Statement 110-A, HHP; Hoover, *American Individualism*, 42.

59 Hoover, Public Statement 100-A, HHP. 3; Hoover, *American Individualism*, 18-22

60 Hoover, Public Statement 146, HHP; *Report of the President's Conference on Unemployment*, 29.

61 *Report of the President's Unemployment Conference*, 29; Hoover, Public Statement 164, HHP. 2.

62 Hoover, Public Statement 164, HHP. 3; Ellis Hawley, "Herbert Hoover and Economic Stabilization, 1921-1928," in Hawley ed. *Herbert Hoover 1921-1928* (Iowa City: University of Iowa Press, 1981) 43-80.

63 Raymond Williams, *Keywords: A vocabulary of culture and Society* (New York: Oxford University Press, 1976) 273-5.

64 William, *Keywords,* 230-50; see also Michaels B. Katz, *In the Shadow of the*

Poorhouse: A Social History of Welfare in America (New York: Basic Books, 1986); James T. Patterson, *America's Struggle Against Poverty*, 1900-1985 (Cambridge: Harvard University Press, 1986) particularly chapter 1; Walter Trattner, *From Poor Law to Welfare State: A History of Social Welfare in America* (New York: The Free Press, 1986) 231-49; Report on Unemployment, 28.

65 Report on Unemployment, 29.

66 Ibid., 34.

67 Ibid., See report by E.E. Hunt in *Report on Unemployment, 171-8.*

Chapter 2
Herbert Hoover and Political Economy, 1919-1925: An Overview

The United States experienced one of the greatest economic booms in its history during the decade of the twenties. The country dramatically raised its output of goods and services, real wages increased and prices lowered. Gross national product rose at the steady rate of 2 percent annually, and unemployment from 1922-1929 remained below 4 percent. Americans converted these factors into a mass consumption that forced manufacturerers to produce goods at unprecedented rates. In 1922 fewer than 100,000 radios were produced. By the end of the decade over twelve million families owned one. Theaters and the entertainment industry boomed with more people having more disposable income. As a result corporate profits also rose dramatically.1

Helping to propel the economy forward were new technological processes and inventions that created a second industrial revolution in America. New reserves of oil in the Southwest and West gave rise to new powerful corporations such as Texaco and provided cheap power for development in those regions of the country. In addition, petroleum based production rapidly developed in areas such as plastics. Oil provided fuel for large power generators and spread electrification throughout the country. Consequently, production of home appliances rapidly grew. The electric iron, radios, washing machines and toasters became commonplace in American homes. The automobile became affordable for the working class through developments in assembly line production. In short, the decade gave rise to new forms of manufacturing, marketing and consumption habits. Yet there were still important questions that faced national leaders as the decade began. The bright future of the decade was not apparent as the country faced recession in 1921, and Hoover's attempts to address the situation with the unemployment conference revealed his political economy. This chapter will analyze Hoover's political economy, especially the specific relationship between Hoover's economic theories and those of the leaders of the corporatist structure. The economist, corporate and labor leaders Hoover used to form his political economy constitute one aspect of one of the essential publics Hoover relied on to set policy and engage in critical debate over the role of the state in relief as well as the general role of the state.2

One of the most noted economists of the twenties was Wesley Mitchell of Columbia University, whose work exemplified one type of objective, professional approach to the macroeconomic questions relevant to post-war

America. Why Hoover adhered to this particular approach will say much about his own economic philosophy and shed light on how Hoover defined the terms of his political language. Mitchell formed part of the group of economists who understood through their experiences in the war, that the decade presented unique challenges to the profession and opportunity to the nation. The war highlighted the ability of government to cooperate with business and labor to raise production and now the opportunity arose to shape understanding of the economy through methods of economic organization experimented with during the war. One of those methods was understanding and using comprehensive data to analyze various aspects of production. Economists now wished to use industrial data on a wider scale. Mitchell, for example served as the director of the Price Statistics Section of the War Industries Board. He realized that the profession of economists now could become much more scientific through data collection and dissemination and this data also enabled corporate leaders to make more sound decisions. Striving for new theories and applications, Mitchell helped to found the National Bureau of Economic Research to gather and disseminate the statistics and findings of economists to the wider public.

Before the war, Mitchell came to prominence with his publication of *Business Cycles* in 1913. The phenomenon of economic fluctuation had been recognized as early as the mid-nineteenth century, and had begun to receive more detailed analysis in the rapid booms and busts beginning with the crisis of 1873 and lasting into the first decade of the twentieth century. Mitchell studied these fluctuations using voluminous amounts of raw data, and thereby arrived at a theory of what he called the business cycle. Mitchell recognized that business cycles were made up of many separate fluctuations arising from conditions within particular industrial sectors and crossing over into different sectors, ultimately affecting the economy as a whole. The modern business cycle in the industrial economy was thus different from the commercial convulsions of the nineteenth century and seasonal fluctuations in agriculture. The business cycle stretched over time and particular characteristics of the cycle acted somewhat autonomously in industry, finance, and general commerce.

By analyzing its various dimensions, Mitchell found that the cycle was made up not only of "roughly synchronous expansions in many activities" which were "followed by synchronous contractions" but also of many expansions during general contraction and contractions during general expansion. As separate entities in differing sectors expanded or contracted, the aggregate activity of the economy as a whole moved from growth to recession, so that at any one point in the cycle, a particular segment of industry could be going with the aggregate flow or against it, ushering in or phasing out a particular phase of the cycle.

The aggregate movements of Mitchell's business cycle are as follows. During expansion, production rises, as do employment, commodity prices, domestic trade, and most other areas of business. Expansion continues until checked by a reduction in bond trading. This causes a decline in bond prices and sales, which in turn raises long-term interest rates. This leads to general declines in the final stages of expansion: stock prices fall, business failures increase, aggregate business activity stops its expansion and an economic downturn begins. Construction slows, unemployment begins to rise, and soon the economy begins to suffer a rapid decline. Production, personal income, business profits, and all areas of individual statistical measure fall into decline, and economic depression sets in. During the contraction at the bottom of the cycle, bond rates, which arrested the expansion, begin to recover, sales slowly increase, and the interest rate spiral ceases. Rates hold steady and eventually fall. After the liquidation of companies that could not survive the contraction, stock trading begins to rise, construction contracts increase, and aggregate business activity pulls itself out of depression and back to the early stages of expansion.

Employment is affected by several areas of the cycle, among them labor and capital, production and prices. Mitchell found that the level of employment corresponded to the volume of production in the 1919-1938 period; but he understood the relationship was not rigid. Increases in efficiency and the use of more sophisticated machinery increased the output per man-hour, so that employment increased less than output during the upside of the cycle, yet fell more rapidly than output during the downside of the cycle. If efficiency was to increase without reducing employment, consistently expanded production was necessary. Mitchell asserted that "modern plants attain their highest technological efficiency when operated steadily at the capacity for which they're designed." The problem with employment in the cycle arose from irregular flows of work, which caused slowdowns and shutdowns and forced employers to lay off workers. This, in turn, added expenses and thus increased the price of the end product. On the other hand, when the cycle was rising, the volume of work could exceed the optimum capacity of the plant, which also drove up prices and led to layoffs.

One factor determining levels of employment was the wage rate, since it also had a direct impact on the cost of production. Mitchell showed that wage rates had been rising overall since the late nineteenth century as a result of a cycle of wages. When labor was in demand, wages tended to rise. Because of unionization, wages were not cut drastically during the downturns, though labor was no longer in demand. In other words, the overall wage increase was due, primarily, to labor's resistance to wage reduction during downturns, which protected a large percentage of the increases in wages obtained during expansions. At the same time, however, price fluctuations made real wages (the wage one makes when cost of living is factored in) generally lower in the 1919-1938 period than a simple look at the wage rate made them appear. For Mitchell, the key to sustained production, employment, and high real wages was unit cost and the resulting prices for goods. To maintain employment at steady levels, or increase it, plants must operate at capacity, without overproduction, keeping wages at a negotiated level, and maintaining a low unit cost of production.

One obstacle to maintaining this balance was the fluctuating availability of capital during the cycle. One of the primary uses of capital in business is for investment in plant and equipment. Businesses have an incentive to spend on durables during the bottom of the cycle when prices are low. During recovery, however, the need for cash increases as the costs of plant and equipment expansion and maintenance rise, and companies must either spend surpluses or borrow. As this phenomenon spreads throughout the business community, a shortage of cash develops which can end the expansion. As the cycle moves toward depression, the need for cash lessens as sales and demand drop and cash is accumulated through savings from liquidation of goods and reduction in labor.

What is striking about Mitchell's analysis is the impact of capital goods on the overall business cycle. In the years 1921-1938, for example, capital goods formed 18% of the Gross Domestic Product while consumer goods accounted for the rest. Yet capital goods investment accounted for 44% of the total cyclical fluctuations in the period and almost 50% of the cyclical declines. This represented a major obstacle to the proposed plan for maximum efficiency and sustained output at high wages. All equipment and facilities eventually need to be replaced; however, as Mitchell pointed out, since this occurs at random intervals it made for wild fluctuations in the overall business scheme. Any replacement of equipment led to some loss of time, production, and demand for labor. If it happened on a large enough scale the "cash crunch" alluded to above could lead to a downturn in the cycle even if other indicators were strong. Long-term interest rates may not, therefore, have been as useful an indicator of changes in the cycle as orders for durable goods.

Related to this was the effect of capital investment in durable goods on net capital formation. For the 1921-1938 period, gross capital formation averaged $14 billion a year. However, $9 billion was needed to offset capital consumption, leaving only $5 billion per year as net capital savings. Net capital formation was strongly tied to any fluctuation in the cycle, which could have direct effects on the availability of investment capital, interest rate levels, and credit.

In addition to employment, production, and capital, prices might affect the overall business cycle. The layman usually supposes that prices rise when supply is low and vice versa. Yet, as Mitchell knew, R. F. Harrod had shown that "prices rise when goods are turned out in greater abundance and fall in the opposite situation." Mitchell attempted to explain this by examining fluctuations in prices as they related to the manufacturer's ability to control output. He argued that manufacturers in an industry where output could not adjust to demand would alter prices rather than production, while manufacturers in an industry where output could adjust to demand would alter production rather than prices. Thus in the durable goods market, where producers had tight control over output, prices increased as production levels rose because output of goods could be controlled. When demand was high, prices and production climbed. When demand fell, so did production and prices. In contrast, the output of industries such as textiles remained fairly constant over time, so prices rose when demand was low.

Economists, businessmen, and policy-makers in 1921 and into the Depression years sought ways to lessen the severity of the business cycle. Several early suggestions were published by the Business Cycle Committee of the

Unemployment Conference of 1921. Although some committee members differed in their approach, most regarded stabilizing production as central, since employment, prices, and capital investment were all tied to production. N.I. Stone pointed out in his piece "Methods of Stabilizing Production of Textiles, Clothing and Novelties" that stabilizing production would involve several new policies: more marketing and advertising to keep demand from fluctuating too rapidly, lower inventories, and higher quality goods. Sanford E. Thompson argued for many of the same policies in his chapter, "Methods of Stabilizing Production and Distribution." These authors, as well as Mitchell, saw that only stabilizing production and maintaining consistent levels of employment could lessen the severity of the cycle, which would also require, in addition to the measures mentioned above, the lowering of profit margins in order to finance sustained full production.

The state might help to lessen the severity of the cycle. The Business Cycle Committee suggested that the state make counter-cyclical investment in public works, design better uniform statistical methods of measuring employment and production, and establish employment offices and unemployment insurance. In the course of his tenure as Secretary of Commerce and President, Hoover attempted to use such of these solutions as adhered to his own vision of associationalism and the direction of the economy through corporatist structures rather than legislative intervention.

To an extent, Hoover agreed with Mitchell's premise that the business cycle held the key to prosperity or depression: if production could be sustained at high levels with labor peace, the expansion of prosperity could be increased and the effects of the downside of the cycle reduced. He was also influenced by economic theories such as the consumption theory championed in the 1920's by Waddill Catchings and William Foster in their text *Money*, published in 1924. In opposition to other economists, Catchings and Foster argued that money should be central to economic theory, as Wesley Mitchell argued, "money should be the center of economic study . . ." and not viewed as "merely a great convenience in the making of exchanges." In a growing, complex economy, money represented not just paper and coin, but all methods of producing and delivering goods to consumers of all types, including bonds, stocks, credit, etc.

Catchings' theory rested on the assumption that money in its various forms had not just an exchange value, but standards of value in and of itself. Production, profits, labor costs, monetary policy, interest rates, etc., all fell into the category of money. Consumption was one of the key factors affecting production, prices, and profits. As Catchings argued, "Money spent in consumption of commodities is the force that moves all the wheels of industry." Catchings centered the business cycle itself on consumption. When money was spent faster than commodities reached retail outlets, prices climbed and the economy grew. When commodities were more plentiful than consumption, business turned downward. The key to the downturn in 1920-21 was the failure of consumers to "meet the expectation of producers merely by spending as much as in 1919." Thus whatever strategies for growth were proposed, they had to center on raising consumption levels. Catchings and Foster, however were much more aggressive than Hoover in their advocation of public works as a measure to raise consumption. Hoover did understand the importance of such actions, to be sure, but Catchings and Foster placed much more emphasis on such measures. For them, another assumption underlying the economic system was a bias toward under-consumption. Thus, public spending became much more central to keeping consumption levels high. In other words, rather than prudent public works financed primarily at the state level, as Hoover preferred, Catchings and Foster saw large scale public works as a constant in the economy with even larger expenditures during downturns. This stance brought into question Hoover's ideas on wages to sustain consumption.

Hoover's consumption theories rested on the premise that high production levels with sustained high wages resulted in sufficient aggregate demand to absorb the goods produced by manufacturers. Catchings and Foster disagreed. They argued that as long as profits remained high, wages alone would not absorb the output of industry. The solution had to come from increased spending to keep demand high. Otherwise, they argued, in supply side terms, business would be forced to expand indefinitely to create demand and absorb capital. Thus, Hoover and Catchings agreed that consumption was crucial to expanding the economy, and public works played an important role in facilitating that consumption. But Hoover parted company with Catchings when it came to the level of public works and the idea of borrowing to finance these efforts. Consumption continued to play a dominant role in Hoover's thinking as trends in American capitalist development raised the importance of the issue.

As William Leach so eloquently argues in *Land of Desire*, the 1920s was the decade in which "common culture" was born. As overall real wages rose with the income of corporations and banks, the nation entered into a period of mass mergers and consolidation, particularly in retail markets. This combined with what one of the primary critics of consumption, Samuel Strauss, argued was a shift in attitude, wherein consuming goods and raising one's standard of living became a dominant value. To this end, people fed into the chain stores and national department stores to buy not only more goods, but specifically more luxury goods. Standardization, larger units of production, and lower prices ushered in a mass consumer culture, in which consumption appeared the key variable in economic production.

Waddill Catchings was not only an economist writing of the importance of consumption, but, as president of Goldman Sachs, he was intimately involved in its creation. The key to expanded growth was to respond to "underdeveloped desires" and put more money into the hands of consumers, thus generating higher production levels, higher profits, and more jobs. One notable example was Catchings' agreement to finance Warner Brothers in order to create desire for film in large theaters nationwide. Catchings, then, in theoretical and real terms, bolstered Hoover's ideas that the key to solving the Depression of 1921, and later to restimulating growth in 1929-1933, was consumption.

Hoover's philosophy of consumption was based on the premise "that consumption, the satisfaction of wants, would expand with little evidence of satiation if we could so adjust our economic processes as to make dormant demands effective." Government could help raise consumption and production, Hoover thought, by supplying business with detailed statistical analysis that might increase efficiency and help determine consumer tastes. Along with collective bargaining, this would help smooth Mitchell's business cycle.

Hoover saw cooperation, collective bargaining and consumption as the means to attain prolonged prosperity, and therefore found appealing the main tenets of Mitchell's analysis – efficiency and operation at maximum capacity with a well-paid labor force, which uses collective bargaining to establish wage rates. However, Mitchell argued that "only as far as it enhances profit, is technological efficiency valued in the world of business," and that lower profits provided a way to achieve the ends of sustained abundance for all. This Hoover did not accept. Also, though he did see the need for employee representation, Hoover was not, as we shall see below, adamant about union representation per se. Whereas Mitchell doubted businesses' willingness to maintain production, Hoover thought that, with the help of information and the pressure of public opinion, this willingness could be sustained. However, though the two thinkers disagreed on the issue of proper profit levels, other of the ideas of Mitchell and the economists of the NBER generally fit into the range of potential solutions acceptable to both.

In seeking to improve the business cycle, Hoover had to take into account the response of labor, particularly the AFL. Hoover saw that a system of labor representation was necessary to convince workers of the need for high production levels, efficiency, and the elimination of waste. But the AFL might not accept Hoover's voluntarist methods while in the midst of a great battle with employers over the "open shop." And Hoover's support for employee representation and high, sustained wages to increase consumption might not diminish labor's desire for protective labor legislation.

In November of 1920, Hoover spoke to the executive council of the AFL. He argued that mediated collective bargaining would ease labor tensions, and scolded both labor and management for low production levels. He asserted that if labor put its full efforts into production, a large number of men would become employed and the unions would find themselves in "the high esteem of the American people." Clearly, this places Hoover near Mitchell in the acceptance of negotiated labor contracts, and in the emphasis on raising production and consumption levels so as to employ more workers and sustain growth and stability.

For his part, Gompers had been considering the issue of both cooperation and production before Hoover's address. As early as 1919, Gompers had stressed the need for cooperation between employers and workers, which would lead to increased production. That cooperation, however, had to "be earned...by employers who determine with workers the terms and conditions under which production is carried on." Now that government control over industry was loosening, Gompers concentrated on employers' gaining workers' loyalty in areas such as "industrial health and safety" which were "vital" to fostering workers' support. In plants with this type of cooperative bargaining, "workers' production" would "quantitatively and qualitatively exceed" that in plants where workers were constantly pressured to accept falling wages and poor working conditions.

The wave of strikes during 1919 and the movement of employers to the open shop led Gompers to argue consistently over the next 5 years that the problem of rising living standards and the cost of living were due not to labor's demands for higher wages, but to waste and profiteering from management's restrictions on output. "Higher wages in every case have been made necessary by an inflation in prices which has made it impossible for workmen to live without increased income." Lower production outputs and higher prices were conditions brought about by management, not workers. The severe unemployment of 1920, Gompers argued, was "created by the arbitrary closing of industrial establishments" in the midst of what amounted to "propaganda by employers for increased production" which fed the perception that labor was the group responsible for restrictions in output. All this combined, Gompers asserted, to force wages downward. The solution was to grant higher wages and to enhance production through genuine cooperation between employers and employees.

Gompers also addressed the effects of this disastrous industrial situation on the ability to increase consumption. After meeting with President Harding early in 1921, he was distressed at Harding's assertion that labor should accept lower wages in order to put the country on sound economic ground. Gompers pointed out to Harding that "every reduction in wages is a direct blow at the prosperity and well-being of the country." Gompers understood, as did Hoover, that the promotion of consumption would lead to increased demand and sustained production levels. The lowering of wages and laying off of workers had not resulted in a lower cost of living or a return to prosperity, but rather, in the terrible unemployment and inflationary spiral in which the country found itself early in the decade. Thus, Gompers entered the unemployment conference seeking vindication for his own economic theories, which closely paralleled Hoover's in recognizing a need for higher production and consumption. The two also entered the conference committed to eliminating waste in industry, of which unemployment was the greatest of all. Gompers saw the "avoidance of waste in our productive and distributive processes" as one of the keys to solving the economic dislocation following the war. Gompers also recognized that the war had enhanced the authority of a group that could objectively examine the industrial situation and provide recommendations for the elimination of waste in industry: the engineers.

The AFL heartily supported the efforts of the American Engineering Council (AEC), which conducted a study of waste in which it was estimated that idle men and machinery cost $1 billion to the metal trades industry alone. A large part of the waste was due to high labor turnover and accidents, both of which were preventable. The AEC argued that a failure in cooperation between management and labor was the chief cause of these preventable conditions, but that the primary fault lay with management, who fostered conditions antithetical to cooperation. Through employer-controlled employment bureaus and open shops, employers had restricted the movement of workers to new jobs. Consequently, the workers, who could not organize or bargain collectively for wages or job security, were skeptical of any management plans to increase production. Engineers as a body, it was hoped, could encourage employers to change their policies toward labor, which in turn could bring the labor peace and respect for workers necessary for increased production and consumption. If the report of the council did not vindicate Gompers' views, the report of the conference committee on elimination of waste in industry did. One of the most significant points in the report was the observation that 80% of waste in industry was due to management practices, and only the remaining 20% to labor.

Another area of agreement between Gompers and Hoover concerned the role of the courts in labor disputes. Both saw court action as a barrier to cooperation, and as a method of coercion which usually lashed out against employees, thereby weakening collective organization and leading ultimately to the silencing of the union movement. Although Hoover and Gompers agreed on this point, they did so from different perspectives. Gompers was primarily concerned with the impact of court action on collective organization; Hoover with the belief that judicial interference was as an unwarranted use of state power. The two men's positions can be clearly seen in their reaction to the Kansas Court of Industrial Relations.

The Kansas Industrial Relations Act of 1920 provided "for a court of three judges which shall...have the power to adopt rules, hear complaints and judicially determine all disputes and adjust controversies relating to wages and hours of labor." The act allowed for compulsory arbitration of disputes by industrial courts. Championed by Kansas Governor Henry J. Allen, it would ideally create labor peace by having an impartial court decide the merits of complaints brought by either employers or workers. Notably, in establishing a structure for compulsory arbitration, the act required that "all labor unions shall take out charters under state regulations." These did not provide for strikes, which would be considered violations of contract and therefore subject to harsh penalties such as fines or imprisonment.

Gompers argued that this system of compulsory arbitration and mandatory incorporation was nothing less than an open assault on the union movement designed to "legislate men into serfdom." For Gompers, compulsory arbitration was neither warranted nor necessary since experience had shown that "voluntary arbitration has been successful: compulsory arbitration has been the cause of many strikes." The court consistently ruled in favor of employers and served in effect as "an injunction against any cessation of work either before or after the industrial court passes upon wage controversies." This was the road not to labor peace, but to assured unrest. The Kansas law prevented workers from having any impact even on the productive process, let alone the bread and butter issues of wages, hours, and conditions.

Gompers also deplored the impact the Kansas law would have on the entire system of industrial relations. Its obviously biased mechanism for solving disputes would not only subvert future cooperation, it would also open up what Gompers saw as a "menace to every part of [our] social structure," because it placed industrial relations firmly in the realm of politics. Gompers also claimed that the law violated freedom of contract, since compulsory arbitration was often interpreted as compulsory labor.

The Kansas Court of Industrial Relations did find its proponents. Governor Allen traveled to several states in order to promote the Kansas Act, and the New York legislature considered passing a similar act, the Duell-Miller Bill, in 1922. During debate over legislation, Matthew Woll, Vice President of the AFL, was called to testify in hearings and gave one of the more persuasive arguments against the act. First, Woll claimed that not only the unions in Kansas but "about one-third to one-half of private industries in Kansas [fall under] the managerial control of ... the industrial court." Therefore, the courts had the ability to reassert the level of control maintained during the war years, which, even if biased towards labor, would subvert management's attempts since the war to remove government influence from managerial decision-making. An industrial court that had the power to fix wages, etc., also had the power to regulate other areas, including production. Woll argued that this would ultimately lead to falling production levels because of over-regulation, and thus achieve the exact opposite of the intended purpose of the bill, "namely producing will be restricted rather than increased." Second, Woll argued that the Industrial Court system allowed a legislated body executive, judicial, and legislative capacities beyond those of the state legislature itself. This form of "absolute government" was unconstitutional since "the state can not do [something] indirectly that it is not authorized to do directly." State legislators did not have the power to hinder freedom of contract, yet the industrial court undermined that freedom. The court was sanctioned by the state to carry on with no check to its authority. Last, Woll argued that compulsory arbitration by industrial courts served to encourage labor strife rather than labor peace. In Kansas during the four years before the establishment of the court in 1920, there were 705 strikes; in the first year of the court's existence alone, there were 377 strikes, and 228 more in just the first six months of 1921. Such strife resulted in lower wages and productivity, and workers and investors shied away from Kansas because of the hostile labor climate.

Although the AFL strongly opposed the establishment of the industrial courts, it did support state intervention in the area of mediation. Gompers thought very highly of the Mediation and Conciliation Division in the Department of Labor. These bodies were successful because disputes were "adjusted without show of force...but by agreements satisfactory to both sides." As long as the state (represented by the Mediation Division) acted to assist and not force agreement, "both sides are left in a frame of mind that make the relations between them...cordial." Mediation rather than legislation fostered cooperation and voluntarism, two goals Hoover advocated as well as Gompers.

Hoover also opposed the Kansas Court of Industrial Relations precisely because of the coercive power the court possessed. He embraced collective bargaining as a necessary first step towards industrial peace, which might be enhanced only through "effective public investigation with the establishment of public opinion as the only pressure." Using "legal repression" to settle industrial disputes through injunction or compulsory arbitration undermined the employer/employee relationship and led "ultimately to the use of the jail as the solution for disputes." Hoover did not, on this point, clearly call for union organization in particular, but argued that employers accept some form of representation.

Hoover saw a grave danger in the enforcement procedures an industrial court using compulsory arbitration would have to employ. First, the courts could establish minimum wages in particular industries; as a result, Hoover asserted, "wages of all workers, regardless of their ability, fall to the minimum." Second, the courts could determine a fair profit to the employer. Yet, neither "theoretical economists, legislators or courts," had the knowledge to determine what constituted a fair profit. Any court ruling left open a possibility for renewed conflict by both sides. For example, if a plant became unprofitable, instead of shutting down or working to reduce waste, employers could petition the court to reduce wages in order to restore a "fair" profit.

Although Hoover and Gompers both recognized important shortcomings with the industrial court solution to rationalizing production, Hoover was not demonstrably pro labor and the question of industrial peace as well as the rights of labor and those of employers placed Hoover at odds with labor in several instances as well as with other economists. Hoover's stance on public works, particularly accumulating reserves for expenditure during downturns in the economy was an indication of Hoover's understanding that planning with the cooperation of government would be a fixture of his political economy. He resisted calls for more direct intervention, yet his overall philosophy carried with it the institutionalist approach of Mitchell, but did not go as far as endorsing stronger institutionalist ideas such as unemployment insurance advocated by John Commons. Commons argued that unemployment compensation must be an integral part of the industrial system, but not administered through the state. Commons supported the Huber Bill in Wisconsin which advocated employers administrate compensation through their own funds. By 1925, Commons supported stronger action by the state in administering unemployment compensation, arguing that planning on the part of the state would be necessary if unemployment relief were going to be effective. This conflicted with Hoover's ideas on planning that stressed not direct state intervention, but macroeconomic strategies in the monetary field and certainly not direct compensation of any sort.

The political economy of Herbert Hoover indicated aspects of planning through public works administration, yet within the strict bounds of his corporatist vision. His views on consumption and production all formed a general effort in the decade to create new ways to understand economic policy and what the role of the state should bein developing the economy. As the decade unfolded, one of the crucial tests of Hoover's political economy would be his handling of one of the basic industries of the country, coal.

Notes

1George Soule, *Prosperity Decade: From War to Depression, 1917-1929* (New York: Rinehart, 1947) 10-27. Peter d'Alroy Jones, *The Consumer Society: A History of American Capitalism* (Baltimore: Penguin Books, 1967) 36-70.

2 John H. Lorant, "Technological Change in American Manufacturing During the 1920's," *Journal of Economic History* 27 (1967), 240-60; Marquis James, *The Texaco Story: The First Fifty Years, 1902-1952* (New York: Texaco Company, 1952); Peter Fearon, *The U.S. Economy, 1917-1945* (Manhattan: University of Kansas Press, 1987)48-71.

3 In discussing policy formation, it is important to understand the role of economists, politicians and the cultural beliefs and attitudes of the country. These categories of economic knowledge allow the student of policy history to examine the contested views of political economy and obtain an understanding of why certain economic theories are employed and not others. Therefore, a brief review of the categories of economic knowledge is in order. Economists generally fall into the first category of economic knowledge, that of a professional of disciplinary knowledge. The knowledge formed in this category refers to that knowledge which is "based on organized inquiry or research and the systematic collection of relevant emperical data and the formulation of general, middle range and specific theories or models." This knowledge, then, is produced by empirical analysis, which is held to the professional standards of the particular discipline. The result of such research forms the "empirical analytical questions having to do with problems of specific economic states, industries or sectors."
Politicians, as well as journalists, etc. form the second category of economic knowledge, informed opinion. The people classified here are not directly involved in the formal, professional analysis of economics, but rather, "find themselves more or less constantly involved in assessing economic performance and making decisions with economic consequences." The decisions and assumptions of those in this category base themselves on the findings of the professional or academic researcher.
Cultural beliefs and values form the third category of economic knowledge. This includes the expectations, political philosophies, and principles used in assessing economic questions. These overall "guiding principles and assumptions [of what is] beneficial or dangerous to the public good provide a basis for general conceptions of the economic systems an element in the total social order." In analyzing Hoover's unemployment policies, then, we must determine what academic or professional economic knowledge was compatible with his own informed opinion, and his political and moral beliefs. Further, identifying what academic knowledge he *did not* accept gives us further insight

into debates over how the unemployed were to be defined and dealt with in national policy.
For a complete analysis see: Mary O. Furner and Barry Supple, *The State and Economic Knowledge: The American and British Experiences* (Cambridge: Cambridge University press, 1990).

4 William Barber, *From New Era to New Deal: Herbert Hoover, the economists, and American economic policy, 1921-1933* (Cambridge: Cambridge University Press, 1985) 2-5.

5 Wesley C. Mitchell, *What Happens During Business Cycles* (New York: National Bureau of Economic Research, 1951) 3-9. For a concise biography including Mitchell's relationship with other economists in the inter-war period see, David Seckler, *Thorstein Veblen and the Institutionalists: A Study in the Social Philosophy of Economics* (Boulder: University of Colorado Press, 1975) 100-117.

6 Wesley C. Mitchell, *Business Cycles: The Problem and Its Setting* (New York: National Bureau of Economic Research, 1927) 79.

7 Wesley C. Mitchell, *What Happens During Business Cycles,* xvii-xix.

8 Ibid., 130-145.

9 Ibid., 130-9

10 Ibid., 134.

11 Wesley C. Mitchell, Business Cycles: *The Problem and Its Setting:* For a full range of discussion on fixed capital, working capital and securities, see: Mitchell, *What Happens During Business Cycles,* 150-75.

12 Mitchell, *What Happens During Business Cycles,* 153.

13 Ibid., 156.

14 R.F. Harrod, *The Trade Cycle,* (Oxford: Clarendon Press, 1936) 41; Mitchell, *What Happens During Business Cycles,* 176-7.

15 N.I. Stone, "Methods of Stabilizing Production of Textiles, Clothing and Novelties." In Mitchell, *Business Cycles and Unemployment* (New York: The National Bureau of Economic Research, 1923) 116-34; Sanford E. Thompson, "Methods of Stabilizing Production and Distribution." In Mitchell, *Business Cycles and Unemployment,* 135-170.

16 Mitchell, *Business Cycles and Unemployment.*

17 Waddell Catchings and William Foster, *Money* (Boston: Houghton Mifflin, 1924) 3-14. For the position of economists who did not see the study money as central to economic thought see: J. Carver, *Principles of Political Economy* (Boston: Houghton Mifflin, 1919), Emille Lavasseur, *Elements of Political Economy* (New York: Macmillan,

1905); Frank Fetter, *The Principles of Economics,* (New York: Century, 1904).

18 Barber, *From New Era to New Deal*, 54-6.

19 Ibid., 56; Catchings and Foster, *Money,* 277-93.

20 Jim Leach, *Land of Desire: Merchants, Power and the Rise of a New American Culture* (New York: Pantheon Books, 1994) 275-7.

21 Ibid., 353.

22 Mitchell, *What Happens During Business Cycles,* 130.

23 Haggai Hurvitz, *The Meaning of Industrial Conflict in Some Ideologies of the Early 1920s: The AFL, Organized Employers and Herbert Hoover* (Ph.D. Dissertation: Columbia University, 1971) 256-8.

24 Commerce Papers, Unemployment File Box 49 HHP, 35-72.

25 Samuel Gompers, "Address Before the Associated Advertising Clubs of the World." September 1919. Reprinted in *American Federationist,* November 1919, 1026-1047.

26 Samuel Gompers, "Who Limits Outputs?" *American Federationist,* October 1919, 933-56; Gompers to Rukeyser, December 19, 1920 Gompers Papers.

27 Gompers to Harding, August 21, 1921, Gompers Papers.

28 Gompers to McLain, August 14, 1920, Gompers Papers.

29 John P. Frey, "Elimination of Waste in Industry." In *American Federationist*, October 1921. 835-6.

30 *New York Evening Post,* January 7, 1920.

31 Editorial, *American Federationist,* February 1920. 15-6; Gompers to E.F. Ladd, January 6, 1921, Gompers Papers.

32 Gompers to M.S. Rukeyser, December 19, 1920. Gompers Papers.

33 Mathew Woll, "Testimony before the New York Legislature of March 1, 1922." Reprinted in *American Federationist,* May 1922, 318-30.

34 Ibid., 321.

35 Ibid., 322-3.

37 Gompers to Benney, February 7, 1922. Gompers Papers

38 Hoover, testimony to Committee of Education and Labor, United States Senate,

May 31, 1920. 26.

39 Ibid., 29

40 Barber, *From New Era to New Deal,* 52-55; Warren J. Samuels, ed. *The Founding of Institutional Economics: The Leisure Class and Sovereignty* (New York: Rutledge, 1998) xi; Seckler, *Thorstein Veblen and the Institutionalists,*3; John Commons, "Unemployment: Compensation and Prevention(1921)," in Malcom Rutherford and Warren Samuels, eds. *John R. Commons: Selected Essays, Volume 1* (New York: Rutledge, 1996) 288-98.

41 Commons, "Unemployment: Compensation and Prevention," 287-88; John Commons, "The True Scope of UnemploymentInsurance(1925)," in Rutherford, *John R. Commons: Selected Essays,* 360-71. Warren J. Samuels, ed. *The Founding of Institutional Economics: The Leisure Class and Sovereignty* (New York: Rutledge, 1998) xi; Seckler, *Thorstein Veblen and the Institutionalists,*3. Hoover to Hunt, November 13, 1922, Commerce Papers Box 136, HHP.

Chapter 3
A Challenge to Voluntarism: Hoover and Coal, 1921-1927

Hoover tried to bring the post-war economy into a state of rational, profitable, efficient stability by addressing not only the general problem of unemployment, but also problems in particular industries. One industry essential to a strong economy in the 1920s was coal. Although petroleum and other power sources were becoming more widespread, coal remained the major source of industrial power and home heating. However, intermittent employment, overcapacity, excess capitalization, transportation problems, and labor strife continued to plague this "sick" industry as they had for the last 40 years. It therefore provided an ideal laboratory for Hoover's strategies: since the industry failed to operate efficiently even when the general economy was booming, his efforts to "fix" it between 1921 and 1927 reveal the shortcomings of these strategies, which, after the crash of 1929, Hoover nonetheless applied again to the collapsing general economy. This chapter explores the effects of Hoover's policies on the coal industry from 1921-1927 and their implications for Hoover's political economy.

The coal industry, in particular bituminous coal, suffered a critical, ongoing problem of unemployment in the mines, which led to unemployment in urban areas because of intermittent coal shortages. It therefore provides a particularly useful illustration the effects of Hoover's policies, in which employment played a central role. The coal industry's problems grew severe after WWI, when in 1919 it was freed of control by the Fuel Administration. The Fuel Administration itself continued to exist, not to regulate, but to provide a "background for peacetime regulation"; in other words, to provide information to employers and various departments of government, primarily commerce. After the strikes in steel and coal during 1919, President Wilson assembled several bodies to investigate stabilizing these two industries. Herbert Hoover served on the "Committee on the Stabilization of the Coal Industry," which issued its final report in December 1920.

The report suggested that the coal industry by the "nature of its organization, functions economically in a too inefficient manner." The "easy entry, difficult exit and transportation constraints" of the industry led operators to produce as much coal as possible. Yet seasonal fluctuations in demand and high labor costs led to periods of boom and bust in which operators hoped for "cold weather, labor troubles or railroad car troubles," that might drive up prices and so turn depression in the industry into "a comfortable prosperity." Such fluctuations kept employment in the industry to an average of 220 days per year and raised the level of capital investment necessary for operation 30% higher than would have been necessary if operators had distributed employment evenly throughout the year. The organization and administration of individual mines kept miners consistently on the brink of joblessness and consumers often paying inflated prices.

The "cure" for this sick industry, according to Hoover, lay in greater managerial efficiency and cooperation through various means. A central one was cooperation among railroads in the establishment of freight rates to induce summer demand for coal shipments and thereby lessen the severe seasonal fluctuations in the industry. To achieve this Hoover suggested expanded transportation facilities "and a more efficient and equitable distribution of cars" that could end the annual gridlock of coal cars from September through January—often the cause of coal shortages.

Hoover understood that cooperation among the railroads could not alone make the entire industry efficient; yet even this level of cooperation would raise some legislative hurdles. Hoover argued that "no adequate solution can be found except through organized cooperation, of the operators, labor, railroads and large consumers." Such a level of cooperation, however, could be open to charges of violating the Sherman Anti-Trust act. The voluntarist effort Hoover argued for would establish certain price, production, and wage guidelines determined by the parties involved and followed industry-wide, yet this type of cooperation "under the existing laws as to combinations...cannot be carried on." Hoover would have to persuade the leaders of industry to pressure legislators to change the Sherman Act so as to permit such cooperation.

After the great coal strike of 1919, the election of Warren Harding, and the appointment of Herbert Hoover as Secretary of Commerce, the coal situation had not improved. Before the Unemployment Conference, an ICC report warned that the situation regarding coal in 1921 was very similar to that before the coal strike two years earlier. In both situations there was "a period of subnormal production and wide spread unemployment among the coal miners. The discontent caused by that condition of unemployment was the direct cause of the miners' strike."

Production of coal was, in fact, down from the 1913-1920 period. By the end of July 1921, it was down by 52 million tons per month. In an effort to lessen production and price fluctuations in the industry, the Senate introduced bills 1806 and 1807 in June 1921. These bills, called the Frelinghuysen bills after the Republican Senator from New Jersey, attempted to use the state as an information source for consumers, and to give the ICC the power to adjust freight rates when necessary to stimulate the movement of coal. Hoover at this point was firmly entrenched against any legislative measure, arguing that the power of public opinion would prove strong enough to coerce operators and labor into finding a solution through private mechanisms. Even though the bill called for the public release of statistical information, something Hoover supported, its language giving the ICC power to adjust rates "would open the door to unnecessary regulation that would smother the forces of initiative."

Coal operators vigorously lobbied against the measure. Oscar Freemayer, president of the Peterson and Pocher Coal Company, argued that the bill contradicted President Harding's inaugural statement calling for "the omission of unnecessary interference of government with business." Freemayer saw the Frelinghuysen bills as a first step to greater government regulation. Operators saw the measure as "an opening wedge to what is expected to be drastic and sweeping legislation later on for the coal business." For its part, the coal industry worked to forestall any government intrusion by voluntarily providing price information to the government.

In support of his bill, Frelinghuysen argued that "freight rates are sky high, and unless something is done to stimulate buying the panic price of last year in the late spring and summer may be repeated had there been a government agency charged with the responsibility of correctly informing the people I believe the speculators would have been routed and the public saved from extortion." He did not see the bill as regulatory: "to say a branch of government should not study the question and compel information to stabilize the industry . . . is foolish, and to say that this is government interference in business is ridiculous."

The Senate killed the measure in floor debate, affirming Hoover's position. As the depression continued, the coal industry cut wages and provoked further dispute with both union and non-union labor, and consumers faced another coal shortage. Hoover thus appointed a committee on construction, transportation, and mining at the Unemployment Conference. Like the other committees, this had members from academe, labor, and management. John D. Ryan, president of United Metals Company, chaired the committee on mining, which included as well David L. Wing as consulting statistician, John L. Lewis, president of the United Mine Workers; and Mary Van Kleek of the Russell Sage Foundation. The recommendation of this committee centered on the problems of transportation. The committee argued that because "bituminous coal deposits are ample and developed mine capacity is far in excess of the country's requirements safeguarding the nation's coal supply is mainly a question of car supply and transportation." The committee blamed the coal shortage of the previous year on the railroads' system of preferential car usage, which reduced the number of cars available to transport coal and brought "most disastrous results to our people." Preferential car use had been a problem since the war, and was, as the committee report argued, "condemned as an evil by the Fuel Administration in 1918, by the Presidential Coal Commission in 1920 and is prohibited by the Esch-Cummins law." The committee therefore recommended that the Esch-Cummins law be enforced to lower transportation costs and keep coal available. The committee also recommended that railroads stockpile along rail lines "throughout this country a quantity of bituminous coal sufficient to take care of their requirements for a period of at least five months." These additional stores would lessen the use of cars by the largest end users and thus allow more cars for other consumers.

The committee's recommendations concerned only transportation. It made no mention of high spot coal prices nor of general over-expansion, which had led to cut-throat wage/price competition, lower prices at the mine, and correspondingly low wages. In other words, the committee dealt with a major symptom the industry's sickness, but not with its underlying causes—over-capacity and over-capitalization. Unsatisfied with this palliative approach, Hoover attempted to broaden the inquiry. He wished to use the leverage of public opinion on the two key elements in the industry—employers and labor. If he could move the debate about coal into the public arena, the population as a whole, he believed, would help determine rates. The threat of consumer hostility, which might lead to regulation, would bring the industry to self-regulation.

He first attempted to shape public discourse by supporting the government's collection of information concerning the industry, which he regarded as the one means by which it might be stabilized: "The publication of statistics that go to the heart of the matter will be helpful alike to the public and to the coal industry." The publication of information, concerning the price of coal, production practices, and tonnage stored would lead to constructive competition, Hoover argued. Such information would help an already "irritated" citizenry, angered by high prices, find out whether, in fact, these prices were the result of the increasing cost of business, or "whether profiteering is going on." Public opinion would force the industry to charge fair prices. In response to a second flurry of coal bills introduced on Capitol Hill at the end of 1921, Hoover outlined for Congress what he saw as two alternative forms of control. Legislation would either "regulate profits, prices [and ultimately wages] and distribution" or "secure for the public regularly and authoritatively such vital information as will enable it to protect itself from profiteering and danger and at the same time preserve individual initiative and keep the government out of business."

As the New Year of 1922 arrived, all involved in the coal industry agreed that some change was necessary. The agreement between the UMW and bituminous operators would expire April 1, 1922, removing the primary existing price stabilizer; without some change, Hoover thought a strike probable. In February, he took to print to elaborate the factors that might lead to a strike. One was the disequilibrium between union and non-union operators. Non-union operators had adjusted "their wage scale downward thus enabling them to keep down the cost of production at the expense of the unionized mines and miners." Union operators wanted to lower wages to maintain their market share, but John L. Lewis and the UMW refused to accept wage reductions, arguing that the wage agreements of 1920 had already disadvantaged union miners.

Underemployment worsened the union/non-union disequilibrium. While non-union miners averaged 240 days of work per year, union miners averaged only 182, which at the $7.50 average minimum wage per day, gave them but $1,365 a year. Many miners therefore made "a bare living, others less than an existence."

Thus the union's struggle reflected the need for structural change in the industry. Clearly, operators of union fields had to reorganize to close wasteful mines, raise wages, and make employment more steady by lessening surplus labor. Further, the industry had to improve its overall efficiency, introduce more labor-saving equipment, raise exports, and lower transportation costs. Hoover hoped that all sides could work these issues out in some voluntarist fashion, but given operators' desire to lower wages at any cost and the UMW's resistance to any wage reductions, a strike, Hoover lamented, "is inevitable."

The Harding administration did attempt to make an 11th hour proposal to avert the strike by means of a preliminary meeting of coal operators and miners. The operators' refusal left the administration in the awkward position of sanctioning the strike because of the their "breach of faith and a repudiation of signed obligations." On April 1, 1922, approximately 600,000 miners from the bituminous and anthracite fields walked out. The administration, especially Hoover,feared operators might use the strike as an opportunity for profiteering. Both the Commerce and Labor departments asserted that major coal users had bought enough surplus coal to prevent a rise in the price of soft coal and to avert a coal famine for at least sixty days and perhaps ninety. Hoover, then, meant to deal with the strike by maintaining fair prices and promoting voluntarist approaches.

The strike of 1922 crystallized opinions about the troubled coal industry, and brought forth three approaches: regulation, nationalization, and cooperative association. As in 1921, some legislators, including David Walsh, called for more strict government regulation of the industry. To the left, Senator William Borah and some in the United Mine Workers called for the nationalization of coal. Yet Hoover continued to press for a cooperative, voluntarist solution. In so doing, he had to define his assumptions about industrial "order," since he was now engaged in a policy struggle with those who supported nationalization of the coal industry, those who supported strict government regulation, and those who supported the status quo. The strike gave Hoover an opportunity to clarify his position in the ideological debate and to use that position as a practical mechanism for courting others.

The option of nationalizing the coal industry had been raised throughout the progressive period, particularly in connection with the Plumb Plan at the war's end. During the strike of 1922, Senator William Borah warned that if "the coal industry is not reorganized in the interest of the public, then it will be up to the public to try public ownership." "King Coal," as one writer asserted, pitted the miner against the consumer, blaming high prices on the miner, and refusing "to tell his own income, the very suggestion of that is lese-mayeste." And while "all through the world other kings are being deposed king coal laughs."

The National Convention of the United Mine Workers offered three main arguments in support of nationalization. First, the system of production was extremely wasteful: "slack work, accidents, sudden and violent death" were commonplace, and "these ills are incurable while profits rule the lives of men." Second, they argued that coal was a national resource, "the birthright of the

American people for all time to come," and therefore it was the "immediate duty of the American people to prevent profitable waste under private ownership." The answer was "having the government take such steps as may be necessary for the nationalization of the coal industry." Third, nationalization would give labor fair representation in wage questions and bring order and efficiency to an industry that in the UMW's view could not govern itself. Nationalization would not only protect the laborer but the public, who would "receive their coal regularly at a reasonable price, when coal is nationalized. And not before." Not only the "ultimate sufferers from private ownership," but also all other sectors of the economy would benefit from nationalization of coal by raising consumption levels through the higher wages and better health of miners.

John Brophy, chairman of the Nationalization Research Committee of the UMW, published a detailed plan for nationalization in November 1922, which provides an interesting example of a nonacademic using developing methods in research and the social sciences to affect planning and policy. He mounted a serious conceptual challenge to Hoover. In addition to the outlines contained in the resolutions, Brophy also called for a Secretary of Mines and a Federal Commission of Mines to represent consumers and form policy, and for regional and local councils made up of technicians, miners, and the public. He affirmed the right to strike, the process of collective bargaining, and the need for expanding the UMW to all coal fields. He wished to achieve "democratic nationalization" through the ballot box. This would require the formation of a strong labor party, which, Brophy contended, "is the twin brother of a democratic nationalization." The union hoped that the public would support their political agenda once it was educated. Although he did not achieve the ultimate goals of nationalization, his efforts made Hoover's task of solving the crisis that much more difficult; they interrupted any momentum he may have had. Support for nationalization in the coal areas of the country, particularly in the union fields, interfered with Hoover's initial attempt to manipulate the discussion so as to end the strike. Though the UMW did not nationalize the industry, its contribution to the critical debate opened doors to alternatives and contested dominant ideas.

As the strike wore on into May, Hoover and the rest of the Harding administration realized their worst fear; prices for coal began to skyrocket. Even Hoover saw that this would make government action "inevitable if it continues." To prevent the type of solution promoted by the UMW, Hoover decided to step into the crisis by his characteristic method, organizing a conference of operators to stop the "wholly unwarranted" rise of prices.

Hoover saw this sharp rise in prices as an opportunity to push forward with a voluntarist program of stabilization. "There are very large stocks of coal in the country and the problem is one of coordination and cooperation," he counseled. At a preliminary meeting of operators, Hoover first confined discussion to distribution and price, avoiding the wage or strike questions. He reasoned that the first priority was lowering the price of coal to pre-strike levels in order to prevent public hostility and forestall a buying panic. Although the strike obviously upset distribution, he reasoned, "it does seem possible to get voluntary action in the industry to put a stop point on the advance of prices." Such action was crucial; otherwise "the public will govern the industry whether the industry likes it or not."

The evidence suggests that public opinion was fast crystallizing against operators, who were blamed for the rise in prices. One Chicago lawyer, E. E. Donnelley, captured the view of many when he wrote Hoover that "the present coal strike was doubtless arranged by the operators for the double purpose of preventing a reduction of the price of coal and creating undue suffering." Charles Guthrie wrote to the *New York Times* that some type of "collective action" by consumers would force price fairness on the industry, and that "satisfactory legislative enactments," were necessary "to meet such an urgent public need," which clearly "fell within the police powers inherent in the legislative and executive branches." An editorial in the *New York Times* typical of others in several major newspapers pointed out "when the operators refused to keep their agreements for a general conference they clearly placed themselves in the wrong."

The general sentiment against operators certainly influenced Hoover in his actions of May 1922. Understanding that both legislators and the public leaned toward supporting regulation and fearing the UMW's plan for nationalization, he hoped to arouse public opinion to promote his own non-statist solution. Hoover convened a coal price conference on May 31, 1922. This was his first organized attempt to sway operators to rid themselves of the source of most negative opinion, inflated coal prices, a result of their own actions.

As in the case of the Unemployment Conference, a preliminary group prepared recommendations for the body as a whole. Interestingly, the only recommendations outside of committee organization concerned prices. Rather than structural changes that might lower prices, the committee recommended the reinstatement of the price structure for run-of-the-mine coal used during the war by then Federal Fuel Administrator Garfield. In addressing the operators, Hoover stressed that the Garfield structure would offer "an opportunity to the businessmen to demonstrate that moral forces can be established that will prove that the arm of the law is unnecessary in the matter of protection of the public interest." The Garfield scale served to correct unfair prices in some regions and to determine spot coal prices. Hoover argued that operators could form committees to study modifications in the scale, but some structure for uniform reduction and maintenance of prices needed establishment, for which the Garfield scale appeared the most practical. The scale offered the best chance for addressing some of the most vicious evils in the industry, such as runaway prices, profiteering, and speculation.

In a speech to the conference, Hoover addressed his primary points to the public, hoping to sway both public and industry opinion. He placed the onus for changing public perceptions on the operators, arguing that "the operator has, in the public mind, the primary responsibility for the price of coal," even though, "the industry as a whole has operated without profit, and perhaps even a loss" and that fluctuations of 5-15 dollars per ton could make the difference between profit and loss. Hoover asked the public for patience with industry attempts to rectify "a problem of the most stupendous difficulty"; he explained profiteering in coal. Most importantly, Hoover wished to emphasize "that there is not a shred of law or authority to either determine or enforce a fair price" and that "the law itself prohibits coal operators that most operators, "out of their sense of public interest, do not wish agreeing among themselves as to what a fair price would be, even if the operators should place that fair price below cost of production."

An agreement between operators to lower prices would under existing law be open to the charge of violating the Sherman Antitrust Act. Hoover therefore told operators that he would not ask them "to enter into any agreement or combination amongst yourselves to restrain trade or prices whether it is in the public interest or not." Rather, he suggested "inquiring" with operators' cooperation, "as to the situation in the various districts." In acting thus, Hoover would "take the responsibility of saying what is fair, and I am going to ask every individual operator as a public service to adhere to such a basis and that is to be a moral agreement between him and me." Those who broke the agreement would face the pressure of public opinion, but no formal enforcement effort. By framing his solution in this way Hoover hoped not only to avoid the perception of collusion, but also to put himself in a position to organize both the corporatist elements and, through John L. Lewis, labor, while himself representing the government. This unique position left Hoover potentially able to solve the situation systematically; however, unlike at the Unemployment Conference, here a consensus proved difficult.

For example, Hoover sought the participation of the National Retail Coal Merchants' Association, led by the chairman of the board, Roderick Stephens. The steep price increase following the strike led to much public animosity toward retailers. Hoover himself criticized retail price increases in Chicago as profiteering, since by all credible estimates on-hand supply should have been sufficient to prevent such increases at least through May, possibly even June. Stephens responded that the increase was actually due to increased costs passed on to retailers by operators and shippers, and asked Hoover to retract his statements. In his reply, Hoover insisted that retailers should help keep prices in check. Specifically, he advised the association to "handle coal on straight lines from operator to wholesaler without speculative resale" between those points, and he offered other suggestions, including sale of cheaper pre-strike contract coal to homes. Despite the association's agreement to cooperate with Hoover, it did not explicitly accept this proposal.

A continuing problem for Hoover in building acceptance for his proposals was the opposition of congressional supporters of federal regulation of the coal industry. One Senator, David Walsh, was particularly hostile to Hoover's approach. Walsh threatened a senate investigation of Hoover, claiming that the Commerce Secretary was promoting collusion and price-fixing, for the benefit of not of consumers but of operators. Hoover insisted he would welcome any investigation were it not for the fact, as he informed Walsh, that his "interference with the working out of this voluntary arrangement is contributing to make the acceptance of the plan impossible, with the attending result of raising the price of coal." From Hoover's perspective, this opposition by Congress, a part of the corporatist decision-making structure, undermined his efforts by making regulation or other legislative action not a last resort, but an immediate possibility, competing with his own associational method. He challenged Walsh to "take full responsibility of securing from your colleagues in Congress the only other alternative to voluntary action, and that is legislation." Unless Walsh was willing and able to secure this immediately, he claimed, voluntarist methods provided the only real alternative.

Hoover told Walsh that in the short time since the first coal price conference, his methods had achieved some tangible successes. The national average for spot coal had indeed risen from $2.60 to $3.70 per ton before the coal price conference at the end of May. But with the cooperation of some in the industry, spot coal was "averaging $3· 8 on June 5 and $3· 4 on June 12. These averages include districts which are not cooperating and are demanding $5 a ton." By holding to the Garfield scales and bringing more operators into the cooperative fold, Hoover argued, "it is possible that the price of spot coal can be restrained to a range of from $2 to $3 per ton or some $7 to $9 a ton less than it reached in 1920, although I fear you have made such fortunate results less likely." He believed that Walsh's intrusion while negotiations were in progress led some coal operators to refuse to cooperate, and so to more profiteering. Citing the lengthiness of the legislative process, he implored Walsh to "discontinue comfort to those who refuse to cooperate and back his efforts."

Hoover also encountered difficulties in from John L. Lewis and the UMW. For the union, the goals of the strike were twofold: not only better working conditions, more steady employment, and higher wages for its own members, but also organization of the non-union fields of the South, Pennsylvania, and West Virginia. Lewis viewed the coal price conferences and the promotion of the Garfield scale in non-union fields as support for non-union operators. The conference may have addressed prices, but it failed to grapple with the issue of protecting or raising wages. He also objected to the establishment of the Garfield scale because it seemed to provide a way for operators to lower wages still further, by claiming that if prices were to come down, then wages would have to do the same.

Hoover asked Lewis to support his voluntarist effort, which he claimed would allow him to protect the union if Lewis would stop "pounding the non union operators over my back." Hoover also argued that, whatever their differences, only ending the strike would quiet the calls for breaking the union, government ownership, or other harsh solutions. However, the UMW, with the support of the AFL, was clearly dealing from a position of strength, which Hoover could use to his advantage only to force operators to make reforms and end the strike, though he did not want to appear as though he was working expressly on behalf of labor. The strike wore on into the summer of 1922. Hoover persisted in his efforts, however, by slightly shifting focus and lobbying for his voluntarist approach through trade associations. He also became more aggressive in using the government to organize a corporatist solution.

With public pressure rising and winter looming, the Harding administration became more involved in the strike. In late July, President Harding formed a committee, chaired by Hoover with representatives from the Interstate Commerce Commission and the Departments of Justice and Interior, to supervise car distribution, production, and adherence to the Garfield price scales agreed to the month before. The government placed representatives in all coal producing districts to assist operators in conforming to the price/production arrangements. Harding also appointed Henry C. Spencer to the position of Federal Coal Administrator to oversee in particular coal car distribution, which he had done after the dissolution of the old Fuel Administration. In addition, Hoover again asked that state governors use their power and influence to regulate coal prices and allocation within their states, while the presidential committee oversaw the interstate coal trade. Again, Hoover invoked the language of voluntarism, yet the governors and he represented the state. He still wanted a resolution to the coal situation without federal regulation, but his failure to bring about cooperation between the miners and operators forced Hoover to resort increasingly to the powers of the state in order to create conditions sufficient to make voluntarist approaches attractive and viable.

Before his strategy could be fully implemented, the warring parties settled the strike on August 15, 1922, with a new contract signed in Cleveland Ohio. Production in the non-union fields, at 64% of the total by the time of the settlement, helped end the strike. The UMW maintained its $7. 50 per day wage, to which operators agreed through the urging of the U.S. Coal Commission. The agreement set up committees to negotiate a method for further wage agreements and to study the industry. Although the union maintained its wage position, the operators weakened its ability to bargain collectively across states, and gained flexibility in future wage negotiations, a flexibility they would exploit in 1924 at the end of the 1922 contract. Thus the settlement of the 1922 strike was a cease-fire rather than an armistice: further strikes were inevitable, despite another intense round of legislative efforts to stabilize the industry, and new calls to study the industry in an effort to minimize or prevent further hostilities.

On August 16, 1922, President Harding recommended some type of legislation to restrain coal prices. Hoover concurred, arguing that "we must have something more than present authority to control distribution and to stiffen the voluntary agencies engaged in the situation." Hoover's voluntarist strategy had kept most non-union coal mining at a fair price, but he argued that "such a voluntary organization cannot be extended" over all the coal producing regions and, moreover, "the agreements with non-union mines expire with the strike." Thus, despite the partial success of voluntarism, some legislative action became necessary to maintain the price of coal at the Garfield scale: pure voluntarism had proved unworkable. Hoover had to seek authority from the state to force the industry to operate within the distribution and price framework he erected during the strike.

The administration advocated a bill to strengthen the ICC so that, when the president declared a coal emergency, the agency could prevent shortages and profiteering by regulating the supply of coal cars. Coal operators opposed the bill, arguing that any increased regulation would restrain operations and interfere "with legitimate channels of trade." Operators feared that prices would not cover production costs—that "no price can be set for the product of a particular field that is within reason that is not below the cost of production." The legislation advocated by the administration, the Coal Distribution Act, did pass, enabling the ICC to issue priority orders and prevent unreasonably high coal prices. The ICC's increased powers were not permanent, but extended until the president declared the emergency over, or for twelve months.

With the passage of the Coal Distribution Act, Hoover, through the ICC, had greater control over interstate movement of coal. Hoover turned to state governors to insure "proper protection of the public on mine prices for intrastate production." In states such as Ohio, where coal prices remained high, Hoover advocated that fuel committees be established to secure "a voluntary arrangement " to lower prices and prevent priority orders for changes of out of state coal for utilities. With the passage of the Coal Distribution Act, the Federal Fuel Distributor could make "available such pressure as exists under priorities." Hoover could now use the real threat of state power to gain voluntary action. Most operators did voluntarily lower prices, expensive priority orders decreased, as did complaints of profiteering. Apparently the proper combination of federal authority and persuasion made voluntary action in the fields attractive to operators, who, if they resisted the Coal Distribution Act, could expect stricter regulations when it expired.

To take advantage of this window of opportunity Hoover called another conference of coal operators and the US Chamber of Commerce for September 15, 1922. His plan was for the Chamber of Commerce to gain "cooperation on the part of the national business associations, local chambers of commerce and individual corporations to equalize and expedite the distribution of coal and prevent prices from reaching undue limits." He hoped that this would eliminate the need for further regulation, and thereby show the administration that "business itself will solve its problems without injection of the federal government into its affairs." The plan of action endorsed by Julius Barnes, the chamber's president, included confining the purchase of coal to current needs, suspending accumulating advance stocks of coal until the resumption of full production, and turning coal cars around quickly. Local chambers of commerce were to oversee and assist companies in carrying out the plan.

Like the one before the strike, this conference concentrated on transportation, ignoring overproduction and waste. "The problem is one solely of transportation," Barnes argued, and therefore the remedies advocated by the chamber "will have relieved the whole business fabric of a highly disturbing element in coal distribution and prices." Although Hoover welcomed this effort, and it provided for an immediate return to normal conditions, the Chamber of Commerce's plan did not address any of the underlying causes of the coal crisis.

Hoover therefore advocated a second piece of legislation providing for a study of the industry.

This legislation created the fact-finding commission called for in the Cleveland agreement. The United States Coal Commission not only reflected Hoover's belief in the need for detailed scientific study as a basis for policy, but also formed the only area of consensus between operators, miners, and the state regarding coal. Hoover argued that a study of the industry would go far toward solving its two key problems: "the employer-employee relationship [and] economic reorganization of the industry." This would lay the basis for relieving intermittent employment and provide "some return to industrial sanity."

The U.S. Coal Commission, appointed by President Harding, employed at one time some 500 persons under the direction of Edward Eyre Hunt. It published a five-volume report on the coal industry, preceded by a summary volume, *What the Coal Commission Found.* This study marked the first time the government had undertaken "so exhaustive a 'fact finding' concerning any industry." The commission examined both the anthracite and bituminous industries and made several recommendations for legislative and cooperative action.

Hoover had argued as early as 1920 that overdevelopment was a critical problem in the industry, and the coal commission confirmed this: "the two major causes of interference with production and steady running time—no market losses and transportation disabilities—spring from overdevelopment." The overcapacity of mines, intermittent operations, irregular fluctuations in demand, and easy access to new fields during periods of high prices all contributed to the general problem of overdevelopment. Before the publication of the commission report, however, there had never been anything in the history of the bituminous coal industry to discourage overdevelopment. In fact, the rules governing distribution of coal cars exacerbated the problem since "by dividing the cars according to the capacity to produce, these rules have put a premium on overcapacity." Clearly, over the long term, market regulation of the industry had been unable to curtail this destructive practice.

To address overcapacity, the commission recommended federal licensing, like that of the Hepburn Bills of 1908, of those who purchased or shipped coal in interstate commerce. The commission hoped such licensing would provide a way to monitor new mines and prevent their opening if the market was already saturated. In addition, the commission recommended a tax on royalties and differential profits to discourage overcapitalization, a modification of rules for car distribution, and government regulation designed to restrict the opening of new mines when prices spiked. Government policies such as these also would help reorganize the industry by reducing unemployment and help promote collective bargaining.

One of the primary causes of labor unrest in the mines stemmed from the unemployment and underemployment caused by irregularity of operations. The commission's recommendations thus stressed the need for both parties to meet "the fundamental problem of unemployment through stabilization of the industry," and urged the government to take "action against the problem of unemployment as one of its first responsibilities," mainly through the elimination of waste.

The subject of elimination of waste through engineering principles was consistent with Hoover's ideology; this report focused on several issues which paralleled earlier reports on the elimination of waste in industry. One primary means of reducing waste was reducing costs by means of more sophisticated machinery, particularly underground. Although aboveground machinery had become quite sophisticated, few new technological innovations had been introduced for underground operations in the previous fifty years aside from electric motors and undercutting machines. The committee estimated a machine loader could save the industry approximately $200 million per year. Standardization of production and equipment would also bring greater efficiency. To be effective, standardization should include price rates, mine cars, electrical equipment, and car capacity, all of which showed wide variation in 1922. The commission also found a great amount of waste of coal itself because of transportation problems and intermittent operations. The Bureau of Mines concluded that more than 190 million tons of coal lay wasted in the mines in 1921. Most of this coal went unused because of poor management and lack of machinery. However, the Bureau also found that mines with higher quality coal, the fields around Pittsburgh for example, only wasted 10-15% of the coal they mined, while other fields wasted up to 30%. This waste was the result of economic decisions because, as the Bureau found, where coal reserves were large and profits small, wasting coal did not substantially lower profits. The same held true for transportation: because customers, particularly railroads and industrial users, failed to stockpile enough coal, there were car shortages and high prices in peak months. The commission correctly pointed out that the coal industry could solve these problems, and yet, despite efficient production, storage, and transportation, would fail nonetheless if they did not address labor relations.[i]

The relationship between coal operators and unionized miners had always been strained. The commission cited many of the issues discussed above as contributing to the problem of strained labor relations, but another issue, the rise of non-union coal and the growth of its market share, more profoundly shook labor relations. Between 1898 and 1914 a stable system of wage agreements in the Central Competitive Field set the standard for union miners and to a large extent, non-union as well. These agreements limited "the destructiveness of the competition between mines" and prevented "a wage war that led to a wage scale below sustenance" and to bankruptcy for operators. However, operators of non-union fields, free from such agreements, were able to lower wages to adjust to market conditions. This advantage stimulated the growth of non-union fields such as those in West Virginia, which increased their market share from 1% in 1898 to 23% in 1913. The purpose of the strike of 1922, then, was to maintain union control and high wages, and to organize the non-union fields whose continued growth threatened the very existence of the UMW.

The commission reported 37 recommendations for labor relations. None of these advocated further unionization or a standardized wage scale in non-union fields. Instead, the commission recommended greater publicity for facts concerning the industry, better management techniques, and the placement of "umpires" selected by state governors in each district to facilitate bargaining. The commission rejected compulsory arbitration of disputes, and advocated instead compulsory investigation "when the prospect of failure to renew an agreement is imminent, so that the public may have a chance to be heard before conflict arises." The recommendations on labor relations, like other parts of the commission report, fell along Hooverian lines; for example the commission denounced violence and endorsed peaceful union organization, but also suggested that operators engage in collective action to create an "effective district and national organization and a national labor policy among union operators." It hoped operators would organize a labor commission to solve national problems and negotiate contracts.

The report on labor relations, much like the commission's other reports and those of the Unemployment Conference, provided vast amounts of information and stressed cooperation along with efficiency. Yet this report defined a much more clear and active role for the state in licensing as well as a differential profits tax. The commission believed that all of these recommendations, instituted in a comprehensive and systematic way, would create the conditions necessary for structural change in the business of coal mining and eventually lead to more stable employment and wages. Ultimately, as the future of the Jacksonville agreement proved, the goals of cooperation and voluntarism, though noble, were difficult to achieve; the publishing of vast amounts of information was just not enough to bring stability of operation or employment to the coal industry. Without more state oversight, operators and miners continued to make faulty agreements to the eventual detriment to the union effort.

John L. Lewis responded to commission's report in his book, *Miner's Fight for American Standards*, in 1925. For Lewis, unionization could bring stability to the industry by ensuring the maintenance of "such wages and conditions as will force miners unable to produce coal on terms consistent with human welfare and the interest of the consuming public to close." From Lewis' point of view, the union was meeting this challenge put to it by the Coal Commission: when "entering into business agreements with employers the public expects it equally to mention its rights and to discharge its obligation with dignity and good purpose." Attempting to work with dignity, the union had had to strike in 1922 to maintain the wage rate, and it had stood by subsequent contracts, notably the failed Jacksonville agreement. For Lewis, the primary offenders against the wage agreements were operators who sought to break the union and non-union operators who continued to expand profit by lowering wages and opening unnecessary mines. Efficient production, the prevention of strikes, and the maintenance of proper safety and living standards stood in peril "as long as the Union operators permit the non-union interest to occupy the position of spokesman for the industry," Lewis asserted. Although the commission had recommended cooperation and wage stabilization in non-union fields, Lewis found its work disappointing. The recommendations of the commission, according to Lewis, were "superficial" because they did not point to "permanent reform" through restricting overproduction and promoting an appropriate wage scale.

Hoover urged operators to attend the Jacksonville Conference to negotiate a wage scale. In the bituminous fields, Hoover claimed that "continuous operation is the only thing that will stop the economic degeneration in this industry." A period of "continuous operation under free competition and full movement of coal" was necessary to reduce overproduction. The assumption implicit in Hoover's statement was that a comprehensive wage agreement along with continuous operation would force inefficient mines out of the market and raise wages in the non-union fields. The UMW, Hoover, and union operators assumed that the mines that would be affected most by these conditions were non-union mines where surplus mining capacity and supply of workers abounded. This assumption, at least initially, appeared to be correct. Demand for coal in 1923 was very high and transportation was running smoothly.

Thus, the agreements signed in Cleveland in 1922 and Jacksonville in 1924 made it appear that the coal industry was reaching stability. In fact, however, the industry was entering a period of liquidation and new pressures for wage concessions. A reorganization in response to market pressures brought renewed unrest between the signing of the Jacksonville agreement and another mass strike by the UMW at the conclusion of the agreement in 1927.

The demand for coal did not last into the latter part of 1924, and after the Jacksonville agreement, non-union operators responded to lower demand as they did in 1921: they lowered wages. Unionized operators attempted to respond in a similar manner. Some, particularly in West Virginia, closed their operations and then reopened at the 1917 wage level. Most sought to rid themselves of the union and persist in the destructive wage/price game that had plagued the industry for years. They asked the UMW for wage concessions the union was unwilling to give, and another national work stoppage appeared imminent. Lewis and the UMW, under insistent pressure for wage cuts, agreed to district-level negotiations. This brought about the end of collective bargaining and greatly diminished the power of the union, which declined in membership by 420,000 to 80,000 by 1928.

Throughout the decade, Herbert Hoover attempted to bring about stabilization in the bituminous fields. His attempt to build a cooperative framework between miners and management, and to "fix" the problems of inadequate transportation during peak demand and of profiteering were, for the time, novel. They reflect Hoover's voluntarist philosophy at work in one of the primary industries of the nation, one which affected employment not only in the coal fields but also in industrial centers dependent upon coal, and therefore the stability of the economy as a whole.

Hoover responded to the situation in coal as he did to the unemployment situation in 1921. The reports of the Unemployment Conference and the formation and report of the US Coal Commission formed one pillar of Hoover's voluntarist public policy—information, by means of which the industry might be re-engineered so as to become more efficient, safer, and less subject to unemployment. Hoover's policy toward the coal industry, like that at the Unemployment Conference, was greater efficiency and lower unemployment through decreased waste and increased production.

The second pillar of Hoover's public policy, consensus building, never fully materialized in the coal industry except in the establishment of the Coal Commission itself. The coal situation showed the difficulty of achieving a consensus among operators and miners, or even among politicians, given the conflicts in the Congress over regulation. This would also be an obstacle in his unemployment policy, as we shall see.

Hoover's policy depended on a non-statist course of action. In the bituminous industry, this proved to be insufficient for the 1920s, but Hoover's approach occupied the center of debate. He was firm in his reliance on the industry to solve its problems with the cooperationof the state, not its control. The effects of his attempt to enforce his coal policies by manipulating public opinion show us several things. First, this attempt resulted not in labor peace and stability in the industry, but a maintenance of the status quo ante, as reflected in the Jacksonville and Cleveland agreements. Second, Hoover's voluntarist vision was resisted by an industry constitutionally opposed to it. The differences between unionized and non-union fields and the complexities of transportation, over-production, and speculation forced Hoover to promote solutions that pushed the limits of his philosophy. In advocating stability through the Garfield scales, Hoover promoted a form of cartelization, which set prices. That is, he invoked the power of the state, recognizing that there was a limit to the degree he could manipulate the public without state action. He did not support regulation, but clearly he was willing use some state coercion as long as it remained within his conceptual boundaries of liberty and virtue.

The economic boom of the decade may have obscured the problems in coal. Hoover's responses to them provide an important case study of voluntarism on a national scale in a particular industry. We may now turn to the effects of his policy in several cities both in the early part of the decade (1921-1924) and during his presidency (1928-32) to see if information, consensus, and anti-statist philosophy worked as an unemployment strategy in those situations.

Notes

1 Arthur E. Suffen, The Coal Miners' Struggle for Industrial Status: A Study of the Evolution of Organized Relations and Industrial Principles in the Coal Industry (New York: The Mac Millan Co., 1926) 11-74, 94-127. Mary Van Kleek and Ben M. Selekman, Employees' Representation in Coal Mines: A Study of the Industrial Representative Plan of the Colorado Fuel and Iron Company (New York: Russell Sage Foundation, 1924) 3-27, 381-95. Winthrop D. Lane, Civil War in West Virginia (New York: Arno and the NYT, 1969). Michael Nosh, Conflict and Accommodation: Coal

Miners, SteelWorkers, and Socialism, 1890-1920 (Westport: Greenwood Press, 1982) 13-85, 130-56. Perry K. Blatz, Democratic Miners: Work Labor Relations in the Coal Industry 1875-1925 (Albany: State University of New York Press, 1994). Melvin Dubofsky and Warren Van Tine, John L. Lewis: A Biography (Urbana: University of Illinois Press, 1986) 1-113. Price Fishback, Soft Coal, Hard Choices: The Economic Welfare of Bituminus Coal Miners, 1890-1930 (New York: Oxford University Press, 1992). Curtis Seltzer, Fire in the Hole: Miners and Managers in the American Coal Industry (Lexington: University of Kentucky Press, 1985) 8-42. Richard D. Lunt, Law and Order vs. the Miners of West Virginia, 1907-1933 (Hamden:Archer Books, 1979) 11-59.

2 Glen L. Parker, The Coal Industry: A Study in Social Control (Washington, D.C. American Council on Public Affairs, 1940) 86-8; Edward Eyre Hunt to Fisher, Dec. 16, 1920 Commerce Papers, Box 97, HHP.

3 Hunt to Fisher, Dec,16, 1920, p.1-3, Commerce Papers Box 97, HHP; John Bowman, Capitalist Collective Action: Competition, Cooperation and Conflict in the Coal Industry (Cambridge: Cambridge University Press, 1989) 75, Baratz, Morton The Union and the Coal Industry, p.4.

4 Hunt to Fisher December 16, 1920, p.2, Commerce Papers, Box 97, HHP.

5 Ibid., 2

6 ICC report to Harding, August 23, 1921 Commerce Papers box 100 HHP, 4.

7 Ibid.,1-4. Hoover to Freemayer, June 12, 1921, Commerce Papers Box 101, HHP.

8 Oscar Freemayer to Hoover June 6, 1921, Comm Papers box 100, HHP; New York Times, June 25, 1921 Comm papers box 97, HHP.

9 New York Times, June 25, 1921.

10 Report of the President's Conference on Unemployment (Washington, D.C.: GPO, 1920) 13 and 27.

11 Presidents Report on Unemployment, 127-9.

12 Ibid.

13 President's Report on Unemployment, 127.

14 Hoover to Samual Winslow, November 1921, Commerce Papers box 97, HHP.

15 138. New York Times, Jan. 20, 1922, p.17. Hoover to Walter Newton, Dec. 2, 1921, Comm Papers box 97, HHP; "Hoover Explains His Coal Strike Opinion" response of Hoover to Weekly People, Feb. 18, 1922, Comm papers, box 97, HHP.

16 New York Times, Jan. 20, 1922, p.17; "Hoover Explains His Coal Strike Opinion" 2-3.

17 New York Times, Mar. 31, 1922, p.2; "Hoover Explains His Coal Strike Opinion." 3; New York Times, Apr. 1, 1922, p.1.

18 New York Times, Mar. 31, 1922, p.2 Julia E. Johnson ed., Government Ownership of Coal Mines (New York: W.H. Wilson Co., 1923) Anonymous author May, 1922 reprinted in Government Ownership of Coal Mines, p. 191. New York Times, Apr. 2, 1922, p.1.

19 Ibid. UMW Government of Coal (Clearfield PA., 1921) 22. United Mine Workers Journal 32:4 (Oct. 15, 1921).

20 Ibid., 5.; Brophy hinted at the plan just before the strike. See New York Times Mar. 23, 1922 p.18;UMW, "Why the Miner's Program?" in Government Ownership of Coal, 184-5. The plan in its entirety can be found in Labor Age Vol. 11, Nov. 1922, p.4-5.

21 Ibid., 5.

22 Ibid.; Hoover to C. F. Richardson May 13,1922 Comm Papers box 108, HHP; Hoover P.S. 229, May 16, 1922, HHP; Hoover, Remarks at Coal Conference Preliminary Meeting, P.S. 229-A, 18,May, 1922, HHP.

23 E. E. Donnely to Hoover May 24, 1922 Comm papers, box 168, HHP; Charles Guthrie letter to the editor New York Times, Apr. 5, 1922, p.18.; New York Times, Apr. 8, 1922, p.14;. also, see editorials in the Chicago Tribune and Washington Post from April 1 - May 25 which indicate a general opposition to nationalization, but a clear blame for the strike on the operators.

24 Preliminary Recommendations May 31, 1922 Comm papers box 101 HHP. The actual meeting took place May 24, 1922., Hoover address May 31, 1922 Comm papers, box 97, HHP. For information on Harry Garfield see, ibid., Forrest McDonald, Insull (Chicago: University of Chicago Press, 1962) 198-9.

25 Hoover to coal price conference P.S. 234, HHP.

26 Ibid., 6.

27 Hoover to Stephens June 9, 1922 Comm Papers box 97, HHP. Roderick Stephens to Hoover June 9,1922 Comm Papers box 97, HHP.

28 Hoover to Walsh June 13, 1922 Comm Papers box 108, HHP.

29 Ibid., 2.

30 Hoover to Lewis June 14, 1922 Comm Papers, box 97, HHP. NYT May 5, 1922 P.19; NYT Mar. 23, 1922, p.17; strike demands listed in NYT Mar. 31, 1922, p.2.

31 Ibid.

32 Department of Commerce Press Release, July 28, 1922, Comm Papers, box 97,

HHP. Hoover's letter went to 18 coal producing states. Comm Papers, box 97, HHP Ibid., also Coal Strike Distribution Plan, Press Release July 30, 1922. P.S. 250, HHP Parker, The Coal Industry, p.70.

33 Parker, The Coal Industry, 70-5; Bowman Capitalist Collective Action, 153-8.

34 Hoover to Borah, August 18, 1922 Comm Papers box 97, HHP.

35 Coal Age 22 (September 7, 1922) 373; JDA Morrow quoted in Coal Age 22 (August 31, 1922) 335; Coal Age editorial 22 (September 21, 1922) 439; Bowman ,Capitalist Collective Action, 160; Harding to Spens Sept. 22, 1922, Comm papers box 102, HHP.

36 Hoover to Governor Davis of Ohio P.S. 253-A, Aug. 19, 1922, HHP; Bowman, Capitalist Collective Action, 160.

37 Hoover to Alexander Legge, President, International Harvester, September 11, 1922 Comm Papers box 101, HHP; Chamber of Commerce Press Release, Sept. 18, 1922 Comm papers box 97, HHP.

38 Chamber of Commerce Press Release, September 18,1922, p5.

39 Bowman, Capitalist Collective Action 160; Hoover to Frank Kellogg, Aug 31, 1922, Comm papers box 101, HHP. Ibid.

40 Edward Eyre Hunt ed. What the Coal Commission Found (Baltimore: The Williams and Williams Company, 1925) 17, 64.; Report of the United States Coal Commission (Washington, D.C.: Government Printing Office, 1925) 5 vols. Opcit., 17.

41 Hunt, What the Coal Commission Found, 64; .Report of the United States Coal Commission (Part I) (Washington: Government Printing Office, 1925).

42 Hunt, What the Coal Commission Found, 404. Overcapacity also contributed to waste, one area which Hoover had concerned himself in the Unemployment Conference. see Report of the President's Conference on Unemployment (Washington D.C.: Government Printing Office, 1921). For an excellent discussion of the Hepburn Bills see; Martin Sklar, The Corporate Reconstruction of American Capitalism, 1890-1916: The Market, The Law, and Politics (Cambridge: Cambridge University Press, 1988) 228-285.; John M. Cooper, Pivotal Decades: The United States, 1900-1920 (New York: W.W. Norton, 1990) 95-7.; and John W. Walsh, The Hepburn Rate Law (Chicago: La Salle Extension University, 1910).

43 Report of the United States Coal Commission, Vol. III, 1208-10; Vol. I, 155.; Hunt, What the Coal Commission Found, 251-73.

44 Hunt, What the Coal Commission Found, 251-65; Report of Coal Commission Vol. I, 193-255.

45 Bowman, Capitalist Collective Action, 150-52.; see, U.S. Coal Commission, Vol. III 1273-1390, for the complete report on Labor Relations in the Bituminous coal

industry. Hunt, What the Coal Commission Found, 232-263.

46 Report of Coal Commission, Vol. I, 155-60.

47 John L. Lewis, Miners Fight for American Standards (Indianapolis: Bell Publishing, 1925).; for other works on Lewis that are helpful for this period see: Report of Coal Commission, Vol. III, 1275.; John L. Lewis "Report of the President to the and 6th Biennial Convention of the UMW of A," Jan. 22, 1924.

48 Hoover to C.J. Goodyear, Pittsburgh Coal Association Jan. 26, 1924, Comm papers box 101, HHP.; Bowman , Capitalist Collective Action, 163-168; C.H. Krause to Hoover May 7, 1924 Comm papers box 101, HHP.

49 Bowman, Capitalist Collective Action, 167.; Dubafsky and Van Tine John L. Lewis, 143-150.

Chapter 4
Voluntarism and Municipal Government: Chicago, 1921-1927

The success of Hoover's voluntarist approach at the municipal level—the level at which, according to the recommendations of the Unemployment Conference, the primary responsibility for reducing unemployment lay—was necessarily beyond his direct control. Col. Arthur Woods served mayors as a clearing-house for information and ideas, but the federal government provided no aid for unemployed workers; these local leaders had to find their own solutions. In the larger industrial centers, where sectoral and seasonal unemployment was most endemic, the elected mayors were the key public officials, the main source of governmental control. Cities also financed the lion's share of public works. How did mayors respond to the methods proposed by the Unemployment Conference? Was their conception of and response to the unemployed consistent with, or somehow different from, Hoover's view of the virtuous state and citizen? How did the views of the mayors affect their methods of reducing unemployment? And in what ways did they adapt to changing conditions and assert their voices in the larger discussion of the meaning of unemployment? Did they learn new ways of creatively attacking the issue?

Although the scope of this study does not allow us to follow the story throughout the country, much can be learned by careful analysis of developments in three Midwestern cities: Chicago, Milwaukee, and Detroit. These three cities experienced tremendous growth during the war in population and industrial output, and each suffered acutely during the post-war decline, especially from a sharp increase in unemployment. Mayors had to respond to local social and political pressures, as well as to the recommendations of the conference, while they themselves reflected a diversity of views of the role of the local and national state in confronting unemployment. The mayors' response was a critical element, not only in shaping the industrial economy, especially in the areas of industrial relations and growth, but also in forging an urban policy for the 20th century.

Party and ideology were key factors in the mayors' contribution to these processes. Daniel Hoan of Milwaukee, William "Big Bill" Thompson and later William Dever of Chicago, and James Couzens of Detroit spanned the spectrum of available perspectives on contested social issues during the interwar period. Though they differed on the meaning of unemployment and the proper way to address it, these mayors all suggest Hoover's difficulties in promoting through them his voluntarist vision. Hoan, a socialist, worked aggressively to relieve unemployment through municipal institutions while advocating greater national involvement. Thompson, a machine Republican, rejected the Hoover vision in favor of massive public works projects through which he could increase his control of the city through patronage. Dever, a moralist Democrat, was more receptive to the language of antistatism, and Couzens, a progressive Republican, was one of Hoover's strongest supporters. Study of these four mayors will give us a fuller sense of contemporary policy than would be possible through examination either of one city or of national policy.

Early twentieth century Chicago was the industrial heart of the Midwest. Its location at the foot of Lake Michigan and its easy access to the Mississippi and Illinois rivers made it a center for river traffic, and its massive railway hub gave it access to manufactured goods, agricultural products, and people. The city was second only to New York in industrial output, and its population had increased rapidly in the 1900-1920 period. In 1919, after the war, Chicago, like other cities, endured a wave of strikes in the steel, packinghouse, garment, and building trades. The labor movement, in Chicago and generally at this time, was losing its struggle for the closed shop. The city was divided along racial lines, sharper after the disastrous race riot of that year, which was brought on in part by the high incidence of unemployment in the African-American community of the south side and the competition between the expanding population of migrants from the South and immigrants from Eastern and Southern Europe. Of course, war production had employed many blacks, new migrants to Chicago, who after the war were seen as an economic threat by ethnic whites.1 The depression of 1921 exacerbated an already difficult situation, making acute the unemployment, poor housing, and poor sanitation from which the city already suffered. This was the situation in which William Hale Thompson found himself at the beginning of his second term as mayor.2

This chapter explores how Thompson dealt with the question of unemployment; his responses show the intersection of local machine politics and national directives. Chicago, like other cities, had institutional means of formulating policy. The publics Thompson favored included the city council, the Chicago Federation of Labor, headed by John Fitzpatrick, and the Employers Associations. Yet several other publics asserted themselves in discussions of unemployment as the numbers of jobless increased, such as the myriad of charity organizations and settlement house workers who had been dealing directly with unemployment, poor housing, and many of the other social concerns of the growing metropolis. Through this public women gained access to policy discussions, though they were in effect locked out of the patronage system. Blacks, on the other hand, although pandered to for votes, were given no voice in the discussion of unemployment. They were left to rely primarily on their own civic and social institutions to provide relief for the unemployed in their community. Thompson's attempts to address the issue of unemployment in the face of these publics and of federal insistence on voluntarist strategies tells us much about the practical consequences of Hoover's policies.

Again, the economic downturn of 1921 was particularly harsh in Chicago, which was then just two years removed from the great strikes of 1919. Union labor had meanwhile suffered setbacks and remained potentially militant. By September of 1921 the Department of Labor estimated that 134,564 of the city's approximately 1 million workers were unemployed. A survey of several industries showed iron and steel manufacturing, agricultural implements and the Pullman Car Company particularly hard hit, with unemployment rates of 60% 73%, and 49% respectively.[3]

A closer look at some of Chicago's industries shows the severity of unemployment there. In the steel industry, for example, the Illinois Steel Company, which normally employed 31,000 people, employed only 13,900 as of November 1921, 44% of the former total. The Wisconsin Steel Company employed 43%. Unemployment in the farm implement industry was even more dramatic. International Harvester, which normally employed over 34,000 went down to 9,500, only 27% of its normal workforce. The meat-packing and slaughtering industry also showed increases in unemployment, which became particularly acute with a strike in December 1921. However, calculating the number of employed was difficult because of shifts to part-time employment and a lack of uniformity in data collection.[4]

The only areas increasing employment in the November and December 1921 were retail companies, led by Marshall Field's, who added 3,000 employees from November to December. However, this work was seasonal, the consequence of the anticipated Christmas rush. Overall numbers in all sectors showed a slight increase as orders for railroad cars and components began to come in, but these orders only impacted a small number of plants, and real employment gains across the board came only during the general recovery in the spring of 1922.[5]

William Thompson won his first of three terms as mayor of Chicago in 1915. He has been variously portrayed as a demagogue and a buffoon. He clearly strove to build a strong political machine: he changed his policies repeatedly to appeal to whatever constituencies were in the ascendant. He didn't govern by micromanaging, but by the sheer force of his charismatic personality and iron will. He succeeded by the end of his second term in constructing a powerful Republican machine in the city.

How was, however, skeptical, even hostile, to the recommendations of the Unemployment Conference. Thompson particularly opposed the registration of the unemployed through civic committees as a "capitalistic move" designed to establish blacklists, assault union men, and lower wages. In a letter to Hoover, Thompson, using a slightly subtler tone, claimed that municipal improvements were underway, and that these, combined with his Pageant of Progress Exposition held on Navy Pier, would increase business activity and employment.[6]

As an alternative to more direct relief of unemployed workers through soup kitchens or bread lines, Thompson organized and presided over this "The Pageant of Progress" in August 1921. The Pageant of Progress shows a common thread between Hoover's and Thompson's thoughts on relieving the unemployed. Neither supported any form of direct relief, and both sought solutions from private industry without government interference. This position of Thompson's may also account for his stubborn resistance to urging that he appoint a committee for unemployment. His primary approach to unemployment and raising standards of living and wages was through private industry with the assistance of the city administration.[7]

The Pageant of Progress was the largest business exposition to have been held in Chicago since the Colombian Exposition of 1873. It went on for 15 days on the 3,000 foot Navy Pier, where thousands of businesses purchased display booths and 50,000 people a day came to examine the newest appliances and other domestic conveniences for homes, and the newest engineering ideas for construction. The city reported over a million visitors to the Pageant, and a profit of $300,000.00 for the city and of millions for local hotels, restaurants, cabs, and retail merchants, exclusive of the money made at the Pageant booths. Thompson and the administration thought the Pageant as an unqualified success. They had at least implicit support from the Harding administration, as Vice President Calvin Coolidge flipped a switch from Vermont to open the pageant and light the pier, and Secretary of Labor James Davis made one of the opening addresses.[8]

In its second year, 1922, the pageant was not as successful. Local traction disputes and national coal strikes led to fewer visitors. Nonetheless, the mayor and pageant organizers established the Pageant Foundation for Children, a clinic to treat the eye, ear, nose, and throat problems of poor children. As Thompson saw it, an annual pageant would provide facilities to treat an estimated 50,000 poor children per year and save the taxpayers $500,000.00 per year. The foundation would also establish nursing and dental programs. But the pageant and the foundation, irrevocably linked to Thompson, collapsed when he lost to William Dever in 1923. Thompson's most notable achievement in assisting the poor was probably doomed by his close association with it: to continue the pageant would have damaged Dever's political fortunes and his "war with the wets."[9]

Thompson opposed the exclusive emphasis on voluntary measures advocated in Washington; he wanted the Harding administration to correct the primary obstacle to national prosperity in his eye—the railroad industry—by establishing of a popularly elected Railroad Service Commission to regulate and if necessary take over the industry. The railroads, he argued, not only regressively taxed producers and consumers with high freight rates, but also "conspired with the coal interests to withhold cars," thereby restricting transportation generally and raising fuel prices, and ultimately destroying competition and lowering standards of living.[10]

Thompson thought the crisis had international causes as well. Posturing for a move into national politics, Thompson denounced military aid to the co-belligerents and continued financing of reparations. He urged Hoover to intercede in the disarmament conference in Washington and advocate a strict policy of "America first." Americans, Thompson argued, were finding themselves taxed for the expense of "past, present and future wars." Federal dollars should instead finance public works and national unemployment compensation. Thompson actively opposed Hoover's and Woods' attempts from September to November 1921 to make him address unemployment through voluntarist committees. Woods wrote several letters to Thompson arguing that in a city as economically important as Chicago, the immediate establishment of unemployment committees and adoption of other recommendations of the conference were critical. Hoover also beseeched Thompson to "organize committees in your city to address the unemployment situation as quickly as possible." But Thompson remained unwilling, believing such committees useless. "We need more government contracts," he said, "not committees."[11]

Thompson finally did appoint an unemployment committee of 68 members, primarily alderman and business executives, chaired by alderman Robert Mulcahy. The shift appears due, at least in part, to harsh criticism of Thompson's inaction in the press: general accounts and editorials in Chicago dailies had questioned his leadership in addressing the problem. One Chicago Tribune story lashed out at the mayor, quoting letters from James Couzens, the mayor of Detroit, addressed to Thompson and Joseph Neil, president of the Chicago Association of Commerce, that called Thompson irresponsible and claimed that Chicago "should be ashamed of that kind of mayor." Couzens withdrew from several speaking engagements Thompson invited him to "so long as a man so irresponsible was in the mayor's chair."[12]

The mayor's committee on unemployment, established on November 9, primarily devoted itself to passing legislation to speed public works and to lobby corporations to hire additional part-time workers. Long before the mayor appointed his unemployment committee, the city council had already begun attempts to ease the situation. Members of the council saw the unemployed as a potential threat to the city's security. Members feared an increase in crime and fretted about the larger potential for disease. Alderman Clayton Smith of the 28th ward introduced a resolution as early as December 1920 to study unemployment, and suggested more shelter be provided city's homeless population, which was increasing during a harsh Chicago winter. By February, 1921 the situation so alarmed the council that it approved a resolution to "take expedient steps" to increase employment by beginning work early on several projects already approved, including Union Station, the Illinois Central Railroad Passenger Station, and various road and bridge improvements.[13]

The council continued to make what impact it could during the summer, appropriating $5,000 for the lodging and feeding of the indigent unemployed, a figure which would rise to an additional $18,000 by February 1922. But these efforts clearly were not enough to make a serious dent in the situation. Some councilmen openly criticized the efforts of the council itself as ineffective, despite resolutions to hire unemployed men to work in the city sanitation department and several public work projects. One of these projects, construction of a new stadium (Soldiers Field) was approved in November of 1921 but did not begin until well after the unemployment crisis was over.[14]

Spirited motions and public works with limited funding could not put a significant number of the unemployed back to work. Private charitable groups also attempted to address the situation long before Thompson responded to the crisis, led by United Charities of Chicago, which sought to organize labor, business, and themselves to address the situation independently of municipal government. As early as February of 1921, United Charities found itself increasingly regarded as a source of aid by the unemployed, so much so that, recognizing the seriousness of the unemployment crisis, the organization extended its work of providing food and medical aid, interceding on behalf of families to prevent eviction, and where possible finding employment for able-bodied men. As the situation worsened over the summer months, leaders of several agencies, including Hull House, Chicago Commons, Chicago Council of Social Agencies, and United Charities formed their own conference on unemployment in August.[15]

This conference, chaired by Willoughby G. Walling, president of the Chicago Council of Social Agencies, explored present conditions of unemployment, and coordinated the efforts of the city's corporatist elements to meet the crisis. Graham Taylor, head of Chicago Commons, voiced his concern over lack of housing for ex-servicemen, many of whom were also unemployed, and implored the conference to work with several agencies. Reflecting the pressure on many agencies and particularly settlement workers, Taylor exclaimed, "we are all at our wits end, so let us get together and try to get relief."[16]

As part of the conference effort, the Illinois Free Employment Bureau, headed by Charles Boyd, served as a clearing house for employment efforts and data collection. A survey conducted by 30 social agencies under the umbrella of the Chicago Council of Social Agencies sought to pinpoint additional needs facing families. The records of the employment bureau show that jobs in Chicago indeed were scarce. As early as January 1921 the service had three applicants for each position—well over the state average of two. Additional reports summarizing employment in Chicago industries reflected high unemployment in seasonal work such as agriculture, where 150 applicants applied for each 100 openings, and non-seasonal work, where unemployment rates were even higher. In metal trades there were 459 applicants for 100 openings and in factory work, 135.4. All fields had lower rates over the period from July 1921 through October 1921, and this gave some hope that the situation was slowly resolving itself. Boyd agreed that some relief was possible through an expected increase in jobs due to the coming harvest and in the need for coal, assuming that orders soon rose and prices fell. In the meantime, two areas needed addressing by the employment service: transportation and ex-servicemen. Many applicants the service could place had exhausted their savings to the point "they have not even car fare when directed to a job." Boyd lamented that the service did not have the funds to assist potential workers with the meager sum of 5¢ to ride the streetcars.[17]

Another serious problem was a shortage of living space for ex-servicemen, many of whom found it difficult to find employment after returning from active duty and as a result became homeless as the economy worsened. The employment service gave Chicago's 30,000 ex-soldiers particular attention, and joined with the American Legion and Fort Sheridan Association to provide them shelter and employment. As the ranks of the unemployed servicemen and civilians grew, Boyd as well as the groups assisting the servicemen argued that armories and other facilities, such as the municipal lodging house, be opened to accommodate the men.[18]

In addition to the Illinois Free Employment Service, several other local reform agencies conducted surveys in mid September to assess conditions in several areas of the city. One such study, run by the Chicago Council of Social Agencies, examined not only the number of unemployed but also the performance of the various relief agencies in assisting unemployed workers. The results showed that, by a conservative estimate, almost 6,000 families were without any employed workers. In this survey, only those who had once worked full time were counted as unemployed. Of the relief dollars expended up to September, over 25% was aid given to these workers. Furthermore, only 338 of nearly 2,000 people referred to various agencies for work were eventually hired. The statistics of the report indicate just how serious the problem was, considering how many more seasonal and casual workers put pressure for service on the various agencies. Nonetheless, the recommendation for addressing the problem was in accordance with the generally conservative thinking of the time even among local social agencies, who opposed direct government cash assistance. The committee stressed the need for publicly financed work projects, but vehemently opposed cash relief and urged the opening of a central employment and registration bureau.[19]

Another recommendation, not only of the survey subcommittee, but of the conference as a whole, and of John Hartman, Director of the American Legion, was to prevent unemployed workers from outside the city from migrating in to find work. Hartman proposed identification cards verifying that the bearer was a resident and ex-soldier, which a person might present when seeking employment and thereby gain precedence over both migrants and resident civilians. The conference appointed James Houghteling of the Chicago Evening Post to chair a committee specifically charged with making recommendations for "discouraging the influx of non-resident unemployed into the city." As a first step, the committee secured the assistance of Chief of Police Fitzmorris in checking the residency of vagrants, and had several interviews printed nationally to discourage unemployed workers from entering the city. The committee also suggested that railroads recommend that their employees inform potential job seekers not to make matters worse by "flocking in" to the city. Last, the committee suggested the issuance of "blue cards" such as the city had used in the crisis of 1914. The cards, issued to family men with at least six months residency in the city, entitled them to preferences in employment.[20]

The eventual appointment of the mayor's committee created confusion for the city's other committees and for Col. Woods. Clearly, the mayor's committee was formed in response to public pressure rather than the plight of the unemployed, and this raised the issues of control and leadership. Was Thompson really committed to addressing unemployment from the corporatist perspective? His reluctance to act, in which he stood in stark contrast to United Charities, made it clear to Woods at the federal level that leadership came from those charities, not city hall. Within the city, it was assumed that if the mayor's committee was to involve itself actively with the unemployed, it had to fall in line with Walling and his efforts. Politically, this made sense for Thompson and the Chicago Republicans, who could use this as a way to build up their image in the wake of 1919 and Thompson's stance against the war.[21]

One organization involved with both the Walling Conference and the mayor's committee was the Chicago Federation of Labor and its president John Fitzpatrick. Fitzpatrick organized a labor party and ran for mayor in 1919; he was an active member of the national Socialist Farmer Labor Party. As part of that organization, Fitzpatrick encouraged public ownership of utilities such as stockyards, insurance banks, and mines in Illinois. In addition, he championed national health and old-age insurance. Fitzpatrick opposed many of Hoover's proposals, not for Thompson's political reasons, but his own ideological and philosophical ones. Fitzpatrick attacked the monopolies, who in his opinion "manned . . . the government" with dollar-a-year patriots, one of whom was Hoover, and purposely drained the nation's money supply through inflated government contracts. Following the war, workers were "enslaved" by production increases and credit inflation in expectation of continued high prices, and once prices broke depression came. Thus, Fitzpatrick argued that employers, as part of the open shop movement, had artificially created the depression in an effort to lower wages and lengthen hours. He saw the Unemployment Conference as mere farce irrelevant to the goals of organized labor, and on both the local and national stages proposed a socialist, pro-labor solution to the unemployment crisis. In this he shared some common ground with the Walling group and even the city council. At the same time he also advocated a national solution very much at odds with the voluntarist vision and more in line with groups who advocated positions closer to his own—particularly nationalization of industries such as coal and meat-packing.[22]

As president of the CFL, Fitzpatrick sat on the mayor's committee on unemployment and also the Chicago conference on unemployment chaired by Walling. Like other members in both organizations, Fitzpatrick agreed that public works projects were critical, as a temporary measure, to putting unemployed men back to work. He argued that these projects should be developed with shorter hours and increased part-time labor so as to give work to as many as possible. In addition, Fitzpatrick argued that employers support workers by guaranteeing them all a minimum number of hours per week. He also supported the efforts of the Free Employment Bureau, primarily as a reaction against other private employment agencies who charged workers for their service and relied on recruiters operating outside of the city, thus bringing more outsiders in. He also objected to the policies of these agencies, which often required that prospective workers not join the union. Last, Fitzpatrick, like other labor leaders, emphasized the need for more organization of workers both to prevent further layoffs and uphold the morale of union workers, and to gain greater security and higher wages for the other workers who joined. One method of doing this was increasing funding for *The New Majority*, the weekly of the Chicago Federation of Labor (CFL), through increased circulation.[23]

As a member of the Farmer Labor Party, Fitzpatrick also was active in promoting broader solutions on the national stage, such as the "One Big Union" and the progressive ideas associated with it. In this he was at odds with national leaders in the AFL, especially Samuel Gompers, who denounced these ideas and Fitzpatrick specifically as "un-American, Bolshevistic," and a threat to the trade union movement. Nonetheless, Fitzpatrick continued to promote opposition to voluntarism and the conservative approaches of Gompers.

On the national scene Fitzpatrick was outspoken in his support for the Soviet Union. He advocated United States recognition of the newly created nation, which would not only create another foreign market and thereby increase employment at home, but also support what he saw as a government truly representative of the people, the only viable alternative to the "brutal" capitalism of the West in general and the United States in particular. The Bolshevik revolution confirmed in Fitzpatrick's mind that American workers had to organize in greater numbers and become more politically active so that they might "do such a job as Russia has done." In persuading workers to move toward revolution Fitzpatrick not only affirmed his socialist ideology, but as a practical matter sought to prevent what he and the leaders of the Farmer Labor Party saw as the "annihilation" of the labor movement as a whole. As J.B. Brown, National Secretary of the Farm Labor Party lamented, the "situation is so grave" that labor had to "realize the necessity of some common understanding upon which we can unite and stem the tide of reaction." Massive unemployment, together with such actions as the creation of the Kansas Industrial Court and the injunctions against the United Mine Workers, called for radical measures carried out by an activist government on behalf of an empowered labor movement.[24]

As an example of the hostility of the state toward labor and of the need for greater labor action, Fitzpatrick pointed locally to the Landis decision, which he argued "leaves workers worse off and only worsens the question of unemployment and destitution." Judge Kenesaw Mountain Landis's decision, arising from a labor dispute between workers and the Chicago Building Trades, exposed the degree of tension surrounding unionization in the city and also worsened the unemployment situation. In 1919, Chicago carpenters, followed by other tradesmen, found it difficult to find work in the depressed market; those who did were hired at wages below the 1914 levels. So the workers struck for an increase in wages to $1.00 an hour. By November, the strikes in the trades were over, most workers having gained a higher wage. The following year another increase to $1.25 was granted to skilled workers without a strike.[25] However, the increased wage scale came under increased pressure from the Associated Builders, a group of contractors, who argued that a lowering to the $1.00 a day level, demanded by the market, would spark an unprecedented boom in housing construction around the city. As a result of the dispute over the proposed wage reduction, the Building Trade Council and several contractors' associations met in early 1921. Their inability to reach any agreement through May resulted in a lockout in the industry. After consultation between the arbitration boards of the Building Trades Council and the Building Employees' Association, the dispute went to arbitration and Judge Landis of the federal court was selected to settle the matter. Landis' decisions called for a reduction in wages and the assignment of particular work rules, in which many of the unions thought Landis overstepped his authority as arbitrator. It required all workers to register with a central employment office and be issued work cards through a citizen's committee that was clearly hostile to the union. Union men were also required to work with non-union workers, and all jobs had to employ at least half non-union workers. The agreement was contested by unions. Nonetheless, the building trades remained bound by the Landis decision throughout the decade.

The Landis decision did put the industry back to work at a moment coinciding with the 1922 recovery. Given that during 1921 unemployment was at its peak, the trades stagnant, and several work stoppages and lockouts caused more unemployment in a critical industry, the Landis decision may have seemed an effective means of dealing with a difficult situation. However, though it reduced unemployment, it also reduced wages to the 1920 agreement levels. In other words, it put men to work, but not at a living wage, thus creating a large sector of workers living in poverty rather than unemployed and completely destitute.

As an initial step, Fitzpatrick and the CFL supported the measures for relief proposed by the American Association of Labor Legislation. The organization, drawing on members of the labor movement and the academic community, such as John R. Commons, who did not participate in the President's Unemployment Conference, and Edwin Gay and Otto Mallery, who did, advocated several positions in harmony with the Conference and the reformers in Chicago. For example, in the area of emergency relief, the AALL did not support bread lines, soup kitchens, or widespread advertisement of relief funds, and it insisted no provisions be given without work to able-bodied men. It encouraged the opening of municipal lodging houses for those left homeless, but only to city residents, after a work test. The AALL also sought distinctions between the types of unemployed workers. Social workers through "specialized training" would distinguish, among those in the municipal lodging system, for example, between the "unemployable"—the sick, aged, and mentally defective as well as the "shirks and vagrants, the inefficient and sub-standard workers"—and the unemployed. Those designated unemployed would be given industrial training classes and scholarships to assist them in finding work.[26] The AALL also agreed with the other entities and institutions discussed here concerning the need for open, free employment bureaus publicly funded and operated, and expanded public work. Also, the AALL, like the others, advocated a policy of job reference for resident heads of families and part-time work in the form of three to four day of rotations. The AALL also endorsed national legislation providing for unemployment compensation as a way to give the labor force a measure of stability until employment returned.[27]

The efforts of the CFL and John Fitzpatrick reflect struggles within the progressive elements of the labor movement. On the one hand, labor as a whole understood the substantial problems that led to unemployment and vigorously challenged owners of the means of production to reform their practices, while simultaneously attempting to promote a more socially democratic state through political action. On the other hand, alliances between the AALL and the Chicago Conference on Unemployment and the mayor's committee show the limits of reform. Most of the committee settled for practical solutions which at best would do no more than promise work, and which would in no way alter the economic superstructure that produced the unemployed in the first place. Their common solutions resembled, in language and ideology, the solutions of earlier periods: schemes for separating the deserving from the undeserving poor, opening of a municipal lodging house, and expelling vagrants from outside the community had characterized thinking about the poor and unemployed since the Elizabethan period.

Women played a critical role in the disbursement of aid in many charitable societies, and several within the united charities organizations and settlements worked toward expanding the ability of organizations to give relief. To handle the sharp rise in requests for relief, the conference attempted to raise funds through an ad campaign for private contributions. Louise de Koven Bowen, chair of the committee to raise funds, used a two-prong strategy. She spearheaded a group to raise funds from commercial associations such as Association of Commerce, the Commercial Club, and the Industrial Club; and she also insisted that each relief organization attempt to raise additional funds. They agreed to this strategy for several reasons. First, previous attempts to prevent vagrants from coming to Chicago had failed. Chief of Police Fitzmorris reported to Walling that 600-800 unemployed persons entered the city daily, and those who could not find work needed some measure of relief. This influx of unemployed also interfered with the raising of funds. The committee felt that a general campaign advertising for money specifically for relief to the unemployed would violate the dictates of the conference in Washington and increase the number of outsiders coming to the city. So the fundraising was conducted in a "quiet" way to ensure agencies could provide relief through the winter, without giving the impression that money was available for cash grants to the unemployed.[28]

Five thousand dollars were contributed by the Commercial and Industrial Clubs, but Amelia Sears, assistant director of United Charities, pointed out the key problems not only in fundraising, but in relying exclusively on relief agencies with no financial support from any level of government. Sears argued that it "would be absolutely impossible" to meet the needs of the unemployed, homeless, and destitute because the combined efforts of "all the charities combined in Chicago at their highest do not give the public $50,000.00 a month" whereas the amount necessary to provide shelter, clothing, food, secure jobs, and health care to the unemployed in this time of depression would come to four million dollars at least.[29] Several agencies initiated fundraising drives, including United Charities (for $250,000), United Jewish Charities, and Catholic Charities. Yet the amounts raised were not sufficient, and agencies remained under great stress to provide relief through the recovery of spring 1922.

City government, private charity, business, and labor, the corporatist elements of local communities, all certainly mobilized to meet the crisis caused by unemployment, yet the overall effort did not result in either a call for federal involvement, or in much of anything beyond public works to assist the unemployed. Over 25,000 people found employment through the Free Employment Bureau, but the overwhelming majority of unemployed people received meager amounts of relief from an over-stretched private charity system. As the crisis eased, William Dever assumed the mayoralty in April 1923 and appointed Mary McDowell as the commissioner of Public Welfare. Although she was a pioneer in early 20th-century reform and well supported by all constituencies of the city, Dever did not increases her budget, and throughout the decade the city government's only employment strategy remained expanded public work.[30]

Efforts toward relief in Chicago throughout the decade did not stray from the dictates of the Unemployment Conference of 1921. These efforts shows how well conservative 19th-century ideas of reform and charity persisted into the third decade of the 20th century. Social agencies, the city government, the Chicago Federation of Labor, and the various employers associations all agreed to prevent unemployed vagrants from the outside from entering Chicago, to deny direct cash aid to the poor and unemployed, and interestingly, to push for the city to reopen municipal lodging house.

Chicago had established its first municipal lodging house in 1900. As Philpott shows, conditions in many of these facilities were very harsh. Men paid 10 to 40 cents per night for accommodations ranging from a cot and mattress to bare floors and newspaper (provided by the lodger). The lodging house treated its "guests" like inmates. Their clothes were fumigated, their meals consisted of bread and coffee, the following morning they were forced to leave for the day as the institution locked its doors. There were also strict regulations providing that if a man was suspected of weak character, or of not seeking employment, he could be thrown out. The lodging house was in fact similar to the workhouse and asylum of the 18th and 19th centuries. Still unemployment was linked to personal moral failings, though perhaps with slightly less proselytizing.[31]

Although the agencies involved in the Chicago Conference on Unemployment sought information from the growing number of professional social investigators, this was used primarily to justify methods of assistance consistent with the old but still prominent paradigms of relief. Efforts such as those of Amelia Sears to increase money for relief efforts reached to the boundary of the voluntarist model, yet the evidence indicated that neither she, nor the conference as a whole, nor the United Charities specifically, argued that money from some source other than private contributions was necessary to relieve families brought to destitution by unemployment. The primary focus of relief remained on indirect aid, through employment services, exclusion of non-residents from competing for jobs, and the municipal lodging house. Direct aid through cash assistance to the able-bodied continued to be discouraged; public works and aid through the various private organizations remained the only mechanisms to deliver relief. In light of the pleas of Amelia Sears as well as the employment statistics and efforts of relief agencies, this certainly proved inadequate for the relief crisis of 1921 and gave a clear indication of the likely outcome of a future prolonged crisis.

Another important public in Chicago was blacks. As the first "Great Migration" of blacks from the south streamed northward after the turn of the century, the ghettos of Chicago's near south and west sides expanded rapidly. The Black population of the city rose from 6,480 in 1880 to 44,103 in 1910 to 96,642 by 1920. As Blacks continued to arrive in the city, searching for refuge from the social and economic deprivation of the south, they encountered obstacles to employment which their community created institutions to remove. As James Grossman has argued, Blacks faced discrimination from municipal agencies and simple exclusion from voluntary associations, and therefore had to erect their own social welfare agencies to provide relief to their growing and economically oppressed group.[32]

The leading social service institution in black Chicago was the Chicago Urban League, established in 1916. White-controlled agencies such as the YMCA, Salvation Army, and Municipal Lodging House routinely referred blacks to the Urban League, which coordinated services in the Black Belt. It served as employment bureau, housing advocate, and social welfare agency, and was able to function economically on contributions from the local community and white philanthropists. In the immediate post-war years the league assisted over 5,000 people per year. Because of the limited funding of the Urban League and other community institutions—such as Wendell Phillips Settlement House and the Wabash YMCA (the only YMCA in the community)—destitution and poverty remained much worse, despite the black community's struggles to alleviate it, than in the white slums serviced by the larger settlement houses and wealthier charity organizations. However, the Urban League did not pressure the city or national governments for increased state action. It was committed to the self-help doctrine, and this commitment was strengthened by the troubled relationship between poor migrants and the only slightly less poor middle-class. Migrants new to the city were indoctrinated in rules of behavior devised by those who believed that the migrants' poverty was in no small way related to cultural differences between themselves and the older, established black community raised in Chicago. The Chicago Defender, the community's leading newspaper, as well as the Urban League, routinely published rules of behavior for new migrants reinforcing ideas of self-discipline, hard work, and good behavior.[33]

The Urban League placed as many in jobs as possible, primarily as meat-packers and strike-breakers, yet most blacks continued to work as domestics, waiters, and bootblacks. In the downturn of 1921 what was clear since 1900 proved even more obvious: the League did not have a voice in the larger discussions of poverty and relief going on in the city through either United Charities or the city government. In the minutes and reports of United Charities, the Urban League and the black community were mentioned rarely, with the purpose not of aiding them, but of encouraging the Urban League to study their problems and make a future report on south-side unemployment. Throughout the crisis, the conferences in the city addressing the unemployment situation simply did not raise the possibility of increasing aid to the black community. The Urban League, and more generally the black population of Chicago, was left struggling on its own to meet the needs of black Chicagoans. Yet the voice of this public, although unheard, supported voluntarist conceptions of virtue by ideology as well as necessity.

The efforts of Mayor Thompson reflect the general inability to see alternatives to the voluntarist model. The mayor, originally hostile to Hoover's conference as an assault on labor, did finally organize the city council to act on the unemployment issue. However, Thompson and the city council prescribed solutions that fit clearly inside the Hooverian paradigm, such as expanded public works. The Pageant of Progress, although a spectacular success as tourism and marketing, did not produce a significant number of jobs and lay very close conceptually to Hoover's assumption that simply promoting business and consumption could revive the economy. The relief efforts of United Charities promoted reliance on private giving for relief funds. Yet during the short, sharp downturn of the period, the full capabilities of these private agencies, and of philanthropy in general, proved insufficient. Yet despite the obvious failure of relief efforts in the city, no one thought seriously of calling for federal intervention. Apparently, belief in welfare capitalism and the sufficiency of private measures was strong enough to prevent such advocacy. The publics engaged in discussion of the poor were unwilling to seek new methods of relief; they simply reinforced old measures such as excluding transients, increasing public works, and relying on United Charities and Jewish Charities to raise funds and care for the poor. Even the public not given space, the Chicago Urban League, did not call for federal aid. The short duration of the recession masked the problem. Because of the return of prosperity in 1922, companies, the municipal government, and private agencies could continue to approach the unemployed with the same methods. Not until the depression would this change.

Notes

1 Lizabeth Cohen, *Making A New Deal: Industrial Workers in Chicago, 1919-1939* (Cambridge: Cambridge University Press, 1990) 11-53, William Foster, *The Great Steel Strike and Its Lessons* (New York: B.W. Huebsch, 1920). James R. Barrett, *Work and Community in the Jungle: Chicago's Packinghouse Workers, 1894-1922* (Urbana: University of Illinois Press, 1987) 50-120.William M. Tuttle Jr., *Race Riot: Chicago in the Red Summer of 1919* (New York: Atheneum, 1970). For general discussion and background on the relationship of the Federal Government and the cities see: Mark I. Gelfand, *A Nation of Cities: The Federal Government and Urban America, 1933-1965* (New York: Oxford University Press, 1975)

2 Lloyd Wendt and Herman Kogan, *Big Bill of Chicago* (New York: Bobbs-Merrill Company, 1953) 100-206; Harold F. Gosnell, *Machine Politics: Chicago Model* (New York: ANS, 1969); John Bright, *Hizzoner Big Bill Thompson: An Idyll of Chicago* (New York: Jonathan Cape and Harrison Smith, 1930) 68-177; Charles Merriam, *Chicago: A More Intimate View of Urban Politics (* New York: Macmillan, 1929)178-222; Douglas E. Bukowski, *According to Image: William Hale Thompson and the Politics of Chicago, 1915-1931* (Dissertation University of Illinois Chicago, 1989).

3 Report of Lorenzo Plummer, Department of Labor, November 1, 1921 Commerce papers Box 624 HHP.

4 Ibid.

5 Arthur Woods to William Thompson, October 25, 1921, Commerce Papers Box 624, HHP.; Report of Lorenzo Plummer, Department of Labor, November 12, 1921, Commerce Papers Box 624, HHp.

6 Thompson quoted in Chicago Evening American October 28, 1921. Thompson does not have a manuscript collection so the evidence gathered relies on records of Thompson found in other collections, newspapers and secondary sources.

7 Bukowski, *According to Image* 211-16; William Hale Thompson *Eight Years of Progress* (Chicago: City of Chicago, 1923) 144-6.

8 Bukowski, *According to Image* 216.

9 Ibid., Thompson, *Eight Years of Progress* , 148; John R. Schmidt, *The Man Who Cleaned Up Chicago: A Political Biography of William Dever* (DeKalb: Northern Illinois University Press, 1989) 55-75.

10 Thompson to Hoover, October 21, 1921, Commerce Papers Box 24 HHP.: see also Chicago Tribune October 25, 1921.

11 Ibid.; see also Edwin Sherman, Union League of Chicago to Arthur Woods November 2, 1921 Commerce Papers Box 624 HHP; Woods to Thompson, August 23, 1921 Commerce Papers Box 625 HHP; Hoover to Thompson September 27, 1921, Commerce Papers Box 625, HHP; Thompson quote in *Chicago Tribune* October 5, 1921.

12 Hoover to Thompson November 5, 1921 Commerce Papers Box 624 HHP.; Woods to Thompson October 28, 1921 Commerce Papers Box 624 HHP.; for the establishment of the Mayor's committee see Sherman to Woods November 11, 1921 Commerce Papers Box 624 HHP.; For news criticism see Chicago Tribune November 10, 17, 1921 and Report of Lorenzo Plummer Department of Labor November1,1921 Commerce Papers Box 624 HHP.

13 Proceedings of the City Council of Chicago December 29, 1921, p. 1479 Chicago Municipal Library, Here after referred to as CMRL.

14 Proceeding of the City Council of Chicago June 28, 1921, p.580, February 10,1922 p. 1928; Alderman Deveroux's comments of the City Council appear in Proceedings November 23, 1921p.1309 10.r.

15 Charles Frost, president United Charities, fundraising letter March 22, 1921, United Charities Scrapbook, United Charities Papers CHS; Minutes of Conference on Unemployment August 8, 1921 Welfare Council papers Box 75 CHS.

16 Report of Conference on Unemployment, August 8, 1921 Box 75 Welfare Council papers CHS.

17 Ibid., 3; Report of Wilford Reynolds committee on unemployment, Chicago Council of Social Agencies September 29,1921 Box 75 Welfare Council Papers CHS; Report of Conference on Unemployment August 8, 1921 Box 75 Welfare Council Papers, CHS; Statistics of the Illinois Free Employment Bureau for August, September and October 1921 Box 10 John Fitzpatrick Papers CHS; see also Chicago Tribune October 6, 1921 p6.

18 Report of Unemployment Conference Box 75 Welfare Council Papers CHS.

19 Report of sub-committee for surveying unemployment chaired by Edna L. Foley September 24, 1921 Box 75 Welfare Council Papers CHS.

20 Report of conference on unemployment August 8,1921 executive committee minutes Box 75 Welfare Council Papers Box75 CHS; Meeting of Executive Council Chicago Council of Social Agencies October 20 1921 Box 4 Welfare Council Papers CHS; Conference on unemployment October 25, 1921 Box 75 Welfare Council Papers CHS.

21 Edwin Sherman to Woods November 11, 1921 Commerce Papers Box 624 HHP; Woods to Sherman November 16, 1921 Commerce Papers Box624 HHP>; Sherman to Woods November 23, 1921 Commerce Papers Box624 HHP.; W.S. Reynolds to Willoughby Walling November16, 1921 Welfare Council Papers, Chicago Historical Society, referred to hereafter as CHS.jm.

22 C.C. Ousley, Secretary of Employers Association of Louisville, KY. Letter to members April 15, 1922 Box 11 John Fitzpatrick Papers CHS; Draft of speech by John Fitzpatrick September 21,1921 Box 10 Fitzpatrick Papers CHS; see also John Kaiser, John Fitzpatrick and Progressive Unionism, 1915-1925; Fitzpatrick speech to National Conference of Progressive Organizations, February 20, 1922 Box 11 Fitzpatrick Papers CHS; Fitzpatrick notes of CFL meeting January 4, 1922 Box 11 Fitzpatrick Papers CHS.

23 Robert Mulchahy to Fitzpatrick November 14, 1921 Box 11 Fitzpatrick Papers CHS; Chicago Tribune November 10, 1921; Minutes of Chicago conference on unemployment September 16, 1921 Box 75 Welfare Council Papers CHS; Alderman Thomas Byrne to Fitzpatrick February 16, 1921 Box 9 Fitzpatrick Papers CHS; Chicago Conference on unemployment November 16, 1921 Box 75 Welfare Council Papers CHS.

24 William Johnson chairman of trade union committee for recognition of and trade relations with Russia to Fitzpatrick March 15, 1922, Fitzpatrick to Johnson March 20, 1922 Box 10, Fitzpatrick Papers CHS; J.B. Brown, national Secretary Farmer Labor party from Otto Branstetter, Executive Secretary Socialist Party September 29, 1921 Box 11 Fitzpatrick Papers CHS; J.B. Brown to Branstetter September September 29, 1921 Box 10 Fitzpatrick Papers CHS; J.B. Brown to National Executive Committee Farm Labor Party November 1, 1921 Box 11 Fitzpatrick Papers CHS.

25 Royal E. Montgomery, *Industrial Relations in the Chicago Building Trades* (Chicago: University of Chicago Press, 1927) 233-71; An excellent narrative can also be constructed by viewing the *Chicago Tribune* throughout the period.

26 "Standards and Recommendations for the Relief and prevention of Unemployment." American Association of Labor Legislation, New York, September 1921.

27 Udo Sautter, *Three Cheers for the Unemployed* (New York: Cambridge University Press, 1991) 133-40.

28 Louise de Koven Bowen, *Growing Up With a* City (New York: Macmillan, 1926)207-26; Kathleen D. McCarthy, *Noblesse Oblige: Charity and Cultural Philanthropy in Chicago, 1849-1929* (Chicago: University of Chicago Press, 1982) 151-73. Report of Amelia Sears to Conference on Unemployment August 8, 1921 Box 75 Welfare Council Papers CHS.

29 Report of Amelia Sears to Cinference on Unemployment August 8, 1921 Box 75 Welfare Council Papers CHS.

30 Schmidt, *The Mayor Who Cleaned Up Chicago*, 69,76; Dever scrapbook CHS.

31 Thomas L. Philpott, *The Slum and the Ghetto: Immigrants, Blacks and Reformers in Chicago, 1880-1930* (Belmont: Wadsworth, 1991) 100-2; also Harvey W. Zorbaugh, *The Gold Coast and the Slum* (Chicago: University of Chicago Press, 1976) 182-90.

32 James Grossman, *Land of Hope: Chicago, Black Southerners, and the Great*

Migration (Chicago: University of Chicago Press, 1989) 127-8; Allen Spear, *Black Chicago: The Making of a Ghetto, 1890-1920* (Chicago: University of Chicago Press, 1967) 34-50. U.S. Bureau of the Census, Thirteenth Census, 1910, 2:480; Fourteenth Census, 1920, 3:248.

33 Grossman, *Land of Hope,* 140-5; Philpott, *The Slum and the Ghetto,* 310-13; for an example of the Defenders posting of behaviors see *Chicago Defender,* September 18, 1918; Minutes of Conference on Unemployment August 8, September 12, October 7, 1921, Welfare Council papers Box 75, CHS.

Chapter 5
Unemployment Relief Strategies in Milwaukee, 1921-1925

Milwaukee's location, manufacturing sector, and political leadership made it unique among American cities during the early 1920s. Its accessibility by ship and rail made it attractive to European immigrants and to African Americans from the South. Aided by a diversified manufacturing base of breweries, steel foundries, auto makers, shippers, and various smaller employers, the city drew in great numbers before, during, and after the unemployment crisis of 1921. From 1910-1930 its population grew from 373,857 to 578,249. Of that growth, close to 25% were foreign-born whites and over 40% first-generation American-born whites. The black population also increased substantially, from 980 in 1910 to over 7,000 by 1930, but still represented only 1.2% of the population. Politically, Milwaukee was unique in its mayor and at times in its city council. Daniel Hoan, a former city attorney, held the mayoralty from 1916-1940. He was the longest sitting socialist mayor in US history.[1]

This chapter focuses on the Hoan administration's public policy response to the Unemployment Conference of 1921. One would assume Hoan's position on employment would be diametrically opposed to Hoover's, since socialists traditionally embrace government control, and reject corporate leadership with suspicion and hostility. Therefore Hoover's favorable response to Hoan says much about his desire to create a rough consensus in favor of voluntarism in the mind of the public. It also suggests which elements of socialist thought, which had fractured following the war, were admitted to the realm of critical debate concerning relief and the position of the state.

Hoan's response to the growing numbers of unemployed in Milwaukee during the economic downturn of 1921 raises several issues for the historian. First, since the Socialist party was emerging from a split between left and right, socialists and communists, what position did Hoan take in this split—what was his political philosophy as a mayor in a capitalist country? Second, what did his actions during the relief crisis suggest about his conception of the unemployed? Did Hoan organize relief in a manner consistent with Hoover's voluntarism? If so, how, and what does that tell us about voluntarism's range of meaning? What was the relationship of Hoan and Hoover, particularly concerning unemployment? If Hoan was successful in significantly reducing unemployment, did Hoover challenge his methods because of his socialist politics, and if not, what does that tell us about Hoover?

Hoan's innovative municipal initiatives in constructing and financing housing, expanding public works, and organizing services were very effective in addressing unemployment. Though these initiatives reflect his Socialist and progressive philosophy, and though they included municipal ownership programs, of harbors primarily, they nonetheless adhered to essentially voluntarist principles. Hoover's acceptance of Hoan's approach suggests his pragmatism: Hoover welcomed any municipal leader with an effective strategy regardless of politics. Hoan's strategies and Hoover's both fit within the philosophies of both a Socialist and a progressive Republican, even if the Republican rejected Socialism as viable at the national level.

Milwaukee experienced what Hoan called a "golden age" from 1916-1926. The population of the city rose by more than 100,000 during the period, primarily because of Germans and of blacks from the South attracted by the city's bustling, diversified industries. The war had stimulated manufactures in Milwaukee as in other industrial areas; by 1920, the city had established itself as one of the most diversified manufacturing centers in the country. Rail and water transportation made it ideal for iron and steel manufacturing and for engine production, led by the Allis Chalmers Company. It was second only to St. Louis as a producer of beer; it was the home of Harley Davidson motorcycles, of several large shoe producers and auto manufacturers—in all of 1,609 firms employing over 150,000 workers in 1920.[2]

Despite these gains in manufacturing, organized labor did not fare well in Milwaukee from 1919 to 1921. As in the other industrial centers of the country, it attempted to solidify the gains it had made during the war against employers hoping to crush the closed shop. Aided by an anti-injunction law passed by the state legislature, the Federated Trades Council, representing 35,000 union (primarily AFL) men, attempted to organize unskilled laborers in the steel and auto industries. But the intervention in several strikes of the Wisconsin Supreme Court left workers uncovered by the 1919 law. Additionally, labor militancy, the formation of the Communist party, and the "Red scare" began to wear down popular support for labor, and meanwhile disagreements grew among union men themselves, so that by the time of the relief crisis of 1921 they were in a position to succumb to employers' methods.[3]

An examination of the Federated Trades Council in its relationship with the socialists and its actions before and during the relief crisis of 1921 may deepen our understanding of Hoan's approach to corporatist organization and the position of labor—weakened as it was by 1921. Near the close of the war the Federated Trades Council, like labor in general, moved distinctly to the left, influenced by the success of the Bolshevik Revolution in Russia. The Council urged its members to read about the revolution, and to seek recognition and expanded membership. It worked closely with the socialist party, rejecting the conservatism of the AFL. In cooperation with the socialists, it expanded its organizing drives to include unskilled workers, increasing the membership of nine unions including the Teamsters. It also planned strikes for the Illinois Steel and Wisconsin Motor plants. It called for an immediate end to the brutal war following the Bolshevik Revolution and for the withdrawal of American troops.

The Federated Trades Council moved toward the socialists in other ways as well. It had sent delegations to Chicago in an attempt to form a national labor party and, when Samuel Gompers opposed the establishment of such an organization and attempted to remove officials who endorsed it, responded by encouraging members to back the socialist party. This they did in the mayoral election of 1920. The Council overwhelmingly supported Hoan, who won the election by an even larger majority than in the 1916 campaign. The socialist vote citywide came in higher in Milwaukee in 1920 than in 1912, the peak year nationally for socialist party candidates. Clearly, then, Hoan enjoyed the support of organized labor, socialists, and those progressives sympathetic to labor in 1920. Between then and the recession of 1921 however, labor would be severely weakened and this weakness shaped Hoan's response to the unemployment crisis.[4]

From 1918 through mid 1920, the Federated Trades Council grew to its largest numbers since the early part of the century. By 1920, Frank Weber could gleefully report that "28 new unions" had come into existence within one year and that total membership had reached 35,000. In conjunction with the Wisconsin Federation of Labor, the Council exercised this newfound muscle by pushing for protective legislation. The result was the Anti-Injunction Act of 1919, which disallowed injunctions by employers in labor disputes over wage cuts. These gains, however, precipitated an aggressive response by employers, who organized themselves through the Milwaukee Employers Association to establish the open shop and halt the advance made by labor during the war.[5]

The effectiveness of the Federated Trades Council began to decline in 1921, from several causes. First, in June 1920, the Wisconsin Supreme Court struck down the Anti-injunction Act when it was used in a dispute in Milwaukee at the A.J. Monday Plant, which had been planned as the first of several actions throughout the city to protect the closed shop. The court ruled that since the strike did not involve wages directly, the 1919 act did not apply. This, with the growing power of employers to form company unions and with the rise of unemployment in 1921-22, badly weakened the Federated Trades Council. The Milwaukee Employer's Council, representing 28 industrial groups and over 600 employers in the city, promoted contracts designed to prevent workers from organizing through outside unions like the Federated Trades Council. The Employer's Council also retained a small army of lawyers to work aggressively for the establishment of the open shop along the lines of "The American Plan."[6]

Second, the success of the open shop drive in Milwaukee had exposed the inability of Hoan to protect his most vital constituency. The Employer's Council, taking advantage of the court ruling and of the growing recession, successfully organized the large employers of the area so that by the end of the year open shops employed over 60,000 workers. The Federated Trades Council attempted throughout the decade to regain members with various organization drives, but diminishing employment opportunities early in the decade, and the ever-increasing momentum of the Employer's Council throughout the period, drove workers to choose the open shop over unemployment and poverty. The Federated Trades Council fragmented and moved away from the socialist party, which, with third party politics in general, it now regarded as ineffective, particularly after the death of Victor Berger, an important symbol to labor and socialists in Milwaukee. It did not support Robert LaFollette's presidential bid in 1924, choosing a position of "no politics." Yet Hoan, though ineffective against the aggressive tactics of the Employer's Council, still used the rhetoric of a pro-labor mayor and enjoyed the support of labor.

Thus, unlike the Chicago Federation of Labor, which played a crucial role in formulating relief strategies, the Federated Trades Council, without significant support either locally or, after their defection from the AFL, nationally, was almost completely absent from the committees formed by Hoan to combat unemployment. This is not to say that outcomes may have been different if the Council had been included, but issues such as workman's compensation, pensions, and unemployment insurance, all advocated by the Council, may have gained a fuller hearing.[7]

The depression of 1921 hit Milwaukee as hard as it did Chicago and Detroit. Unemployment went from slightly over 2% to over 11% during the year. This represented over 35,000 unemployed workers. The Milwaukee Department of Outdoor Relief reported an increase in families who sought aid from 902 in 1920 to 2,948 in 1921, the largest number in its history. During that year 53,000 men and women applied for work with the Milwaukee Employment Bureau, which placed 24,475, primarily in part-time positions, as manufacturers employed part-timers on shorter shifts. Those who were lucky enough to find jobs did so at much reduced hourly wages, which fell city-wide from 55.5 cents in 1920 to 51.5 cents in 1921 and 48.7 cents in 1922.[8]

Milwaukeeans looked for leadership during the crisis to their mayor, Daniel Hoan. As a Socialist, Hoan had run on a platform of better jobs and a city government dedicated to the working man. Hoan's policies during the crisis were affected by his position within the Socialist party itself, which was going through its own crisis after the war.[9] The war had created both problems and opportunities for some members of the Socialist Party. The Bolshevik Revolution had sent shock waves around the world; in America its significance lay in the socialists' response. Those of Victor Berger and (to a lesser extent) Morris Hillquit were particularly important in their influence in the party generally and on Hoan specifically.[10]

The world war and the Bolshevik Revolution temporarily united the Socialist Party in the United States by providing a model for the end of capitalist exploitation of workers. Berger, Hillquit, and Eugene Debs, all members more of the right than the left wing of the party, came to accept, or at a minimum tolerate the left. All had denounced United States involvement in the war and all praised the revolution in Russia. Berger, for example, though he had criticized the IWW before the war as too disruptive and radical to succeed as a union, was by 1918 arguing that the IWW was the best expression of class consciousness in America, and heartily endorsing the union as the ultimate successor to the American Federation of Labor. But this admiration did not last; after the heat of the post-war red scare and mass labor unrest had abated, Berger actively moved against the IWW within the Socialist Party. He and the other reformist socialist disliked the IWW's calls for the violent overthrow of the capitalist system.

From 1905-1913 the IWW had placed itself at the forefront of labor confrontation through successful actions at McKees Rocks, Pennsylvania in 1909 and the Lawrence strike in 1912. It openly challenged the reformers its leader Bill Haywood described as "step-at-time people whose every step is just a little shorter than the preceding step." Haywood opposed the anti-foreign, craft-based organization of the AFL and reasoned that the only viable future for labor was through industrial unionization and direct action against the capitalist combines: general strikes and sabotage, rather than cooperation and long-term reform. He saw himself and his organization as one that "held the true hope of the working-class." The dominant, reform-minded heads of the socialist party, like Berger and Hoan, saw the ultimate triumph of socialism as one of evolutionary transformation rather than immediate revolutionary change. Though for a short time during the war they underplayed these principles to praise the revolution in Russia and oppose the war, differences as to means and ends eventually tempered Berger's praise of the IWW and exposed the disunity in the party the war managed briefly to cover.[11]

In 1919, when labor protests raged through the country, it appeared likely that a radicalized left of foreigners and revolutionaries might take over the party in the United States. The communist left clashed with the older wing of conservatives, and the party began to fragment. On one side were foreign-language local communists and those who advocated the policy of the Third International; on the other, the older wing of native-born and more conservative socialists not committed to the international or the armed overthrow of the United States government. This faction included Berger, Hillquit, and Debs. Hoan belonged to the same faction as Berger and continued to hold power in Milwaukee through and after the split of the party.[12]

Victor Berger, an Austrian who immigrated to Milwaukee in1881, was important as a Milwaukee socialist because of his experience and knowledge of European socialist movements, his understanding of urban and industrial conditions in the United States, and his closeness to Milwaukee's German population. Berger, like other socialists, defined the solution to capitalist exploitation as the collective ownership of the means of production and distribution. However, as one who did not hold the full revolutionary philosophy of violent overthrow of the system, Berger argued that the achievement of collectivist action would be gradual, yet also inevitable. In the United States, workers needed to exhibit their power through the ballot. Nonetheless, he did support labor confrontation to highlight the deficiencies of capitalism, and therefore the actions of the IWW during the war. Eventually, as the IWW also found itself floundering by 1921, Berger held even tighter to his conservative brand of socialism, in which confrontation over wages and conditions, not revolution, as the only way to move, even if in small increments, toward the future of collectivist control.[13]

Like Gompers since the turn of the century, Berger believed that ultimate social change might come in part not through dismantling monopolies, but welcoming them. Indeed, as Berger stated "the question [over monopoly] is only whether it shall be a private or a public monopoly." For Berger, as monopolies grew in power and control of the market, the only ultimate means of liberation was to nationalize them though the ballot, thereby ushering in a collectivist state. Moreover, the way to get people to participate in this process of dismantling the capitalist state was through policy making toward that end. Berger exemplified this spirit in election to the city council, the Wisconsin legislature, and the United States Congress. He welcomed the cooperation of other progressives so long as it furthered his vision of democratic collectivism.[14]

The labor movement and the heightening of worker class-consciousness was credited, of course, to Berger and all socialists. However, unlike other socialists he saw labor as an autonomous institution not subservient to the party. His belief in the gradual transformation of capitalism drew him closer to conservative unions like the AFL; and they led him, before the war, to denounce more radical labor organizations like the IWW, joining in what Milton Cantor called the AFL's "archaic perspective and the failure of reform socialists to fully appreciate the changing industrial order that the IWW responded to." Berger saw the Wobblies as destructive anarchists. In 1913, at the socialist party convention held in Indianapolis, he initiated constitutional changes that ultimately led to the ouster of the IWW from the Socialist Party. Berger's "constructive socialism," influenced socialists around the country, and particularly in Milwaukee, where he ran the daily newspaper, *The Milwaukee Leader*.

Daniel Hoan identified with Berger, agreeing to a gradualist and democratic approach to social and political transformation, and sided with him when the party split in 1919, supporting his continuing in Congress.[15] Even after the war he did not praise the IWW. He aligned himself with Berger's brand of socialism. As a labor lawyer before becoming city attorney in 1913, he saw the AFL as the most viable form of unionism. He also supported peaceful change through the ballot. He believed that reform socialists might unite with LaFollette progressives in accomplishments like a Widow's Pension Law and Workman's Compensation. He organized a commission of union leaders and businessmen to develop a cooperative home building program that would become a central piece of his economic development plans during 1921. He also stood with the reform socialists in expelling the foreign language locals and Michigan Socialists, who formed the core of the party's left wing.

In the midst of this split in the party, Hoan headed into the election campaign of 1920.[16] As the Socialist Party candidate for mayor, he ran ostensibly on the platform of the state party, which affirmed the legitimacy of representative government and denounced profiteering. The platform blamed the high post-war cost of living on the exploitative practices of corporations during the war and on their drive to cut wages and promote the open shop in the coming decade. The socialists viewed themselves as the ideological front line in assisting working class solidarity and higher wages. Hoan's positions in the campaign on local issues reinforced the state platform, but he also pointed to the growth of the city, its low crime rate, and its relatively high employment rates as firm achievements of the Socialist Party.[17]

As the election drew closer, Hoan's primary opposition came from the Non-Partisan League and its candidate Clifford Williams. The issue at the heart of the campaign was socialism itself, and Hoan's attachment to it. The Non-Partisan League ran as an anti-socialist party, leveling charges that the socialists, particularly in local politics, served not the working class but themselves, for example by raising taxes to supplement wages for conductors and motor-men in the street car system. The Non-Partisans lumped all the socialists under the rubric of the international and tried to tie Hoan to the more radical left wing of the party. The tactic ultimately failed, and Hoan was re-elected, as he would continue to be through 1940. The socialists did lose their majority in the common council, but because of his administrative capability and such ancillary matters as bond issues, this would not prove a major obstacle to Hoan.[18]

The bond issues proposed in the election carried in a largely non-partisan way and proved crucial in the crisis of 1921. The city passed issues for the construction of a new civic center, several streets and bridges, and several new schools. Together the bond issues totaled more than $ 4 million. These projects and the administering of them helped provide continued public work the following year as unemployment increased.[19]

As mentioned earlier, unemployment hit Milwaukee with the same force as other cities like Chicago. Hoan's response reflects his constructive socialist thought. Milwaukee had several social relief institutions in place several years before the crisis, including the Bureau of Poor Relief and the Citizens Committee on Unemployment, formed in 1912. The Citizens Committee, through the Free Employment Bureau of Milwaukee, kept statistics on the poor and unemployed, and encouraged employers to scale back hours so as to employ more of the over 35,000 unemployed in the city. Hoan's various solutions to the crisis provide an interesting perspective on his socialism: public works projects, municipal ownership, and the Garden Homes project, a housing corporation intended to cut out profiteering in construction and real estate: the city built homes in which it retained ownership, renting them to working families.[20]

In August, Hoan also appointed a Committee of Twenty-One, made up of five labor leaders, six businessmen, five social workers, and representatives of the city, to examine ways of cutting through red tape in order to start projects, particularly in construction. The committee began by examining ways to accelerate the granting of building permits, and by administering the permits itself was able to increase construction by 11 million dollars and employ 7,000 idle workers. The committee did not assist unemployed workers in forming unions or seeking higher wages, primarily because it was backed by the Association of Commerce, which had taken the lead in the open shop movement.[21]

The Garden Homes corporation, organized in 1920, allowed the municipal government to construct the first cooperative housing project in the United States. The city annexed 28 acres of land at a cost of $50,000 to themselves and an additional $50,000 to the county. The issuance of preferred stock totaling $500,000 dollars, and of common stock, financed the development. Working men who wished to live in the homes bought common stock in the company instead of paying a realtor. The company owned the homes and the cost to workers was much lower than on the general market: a six-bedroom home and lot cost about $4,600. The Federated Trades Council purchased stock in the company, endorsing what it saw as a commitment to improving conditions of working men. Construction began in 1921, and by 1924 105 units had been completed.[22] The Garden Homes project allowed Hoan to promote the constructive socialist principle that economic development guarded by government minimized the evils of capitalist mechanisms of obtaining profit at the expense of laborer while providing benefits for the whole community. The project employed workers, and provided them with affordable housing.

Hoan's principles appear also in his efforts to use government in municipal construction, especially in his public works projects initiated in 1921, and in the public ownership of the harbors of Milwaukee.[23] As early as 1916, Hoan argued that municipal ownership of harbors and other transportation facilities was necessary to root out exploitative rail rates that hampered business growth, and to provide the wages and security workers needed. Through an inventive financial program that paid bonds quickly and kept the city's budget in the black, Hoan allowed the city to embark on public works projects which he accelerated in economic downturns as a counter-cyclical measure. These both improved the cities infrastructure and reduced unemployment.[24] The bond issues for a new civic center, police station, and court house, which passed during the election of 1920, helped Hoan ease unemployment during the winter of 1921.

The Garden Homes project and expanded public works fit within Hoan's concept of socialism, but what was his position toward the Unemployment Conference and in what ways did he aid the poor directly? Did Hoan's socialism take him outside the paradigm of denying direct aid to the poor and limiting the role of government in areas outside public works—denials and limits that were essential for Hoover and his supporters to protect capitalism and business?[25] Hoan's support for the County Department of Outdoor Relief provides some evidence of his philosophy of the unemployed. During the crisis, this department, founded by the city and county governments, provided various forms of direct aid to its customers. For example, they supplied milk, shoes, clothing, and rent assistance to those families left near destitution by chronic unemployment. The agency's ability to provide aid faced a severe test during the 1921 depression, when the families asking for assistance increased by 2,000 over the previous year. The agency asked the city for more money, and Hoan complied, raising its funding from $100,000 to $200,000. Hoan argued that it was a "proper" function of government to increase funding for agencies directly assisting those impoverished not by their own fault, but by the machinations of a capitalist economy.

There were, however, restrictions on how and to whom aid was given.[26] The Department of Outdoor Relief did not give out any type of direct cash benefit, on the principle that such benefits encouraged dependency. In addition, the agency gave little assistance to transients who could not show proof of residency. As in Chicago, relief workers went out of their way to discourage outsiders from coming to the city and when, unable to find work, looking to the department for assistance. The department preferred purchasing train fare to return transients to their previous place of residency over assisting them in Milwaukee. Of the 2,948 families given assistance during the depression, only 92 were transient, and over 40 of these were provided transportation to their previous place of residence. Hoan raised no opposition to these restrictions; although much less than others, he also believed in limiting the role of the state in relieving unemployment.[27]

When President Harding's Unemployment Conference convened, the city of Milwaukee had already formed the Citizens Committee on Unemployment and the Committee of Fifteen. These committees, established in 1913 and 1921 respectively, both embodied the principles of corporatist voluntary cooperation between city, employers, and labor. In the wake of the Unemployment Conference, Mayor Hoan created the Milwaukee Committee on Unemployment and Relief (MCUR) in October 1921. This new committee, in cooperation with the Milwaukee Free Employment Bureau and the Citizen's Committee on Unemployment, urged employers to employ more men by running 8-hour rather than 12-hour shifts. The MCUR also urged employers to "endeavor to furnish employment" to able-bodied ex- servicemen. In the spirit of voluntarism, the MCUR did not seek any formal mandate from the city council, but relied on the cooperation of employers. And here again, relief efforts were restricted to "able-bodied, deserving" poor. The MCUR also acted as intermediary between Hoover's various committees and the various relief organizations in the city collecting data which might interest Washington.[28]

Hoover and Col. Woods warmly received the MCUR and the relief efforts in Milwaukee, even though they had not invited Hoan to the Unemployment Conference in Washington. If they had any doubts about how this socialist mayor would react to the crisis those doubts were quickly dispelled; and they were particularly impressed by Milwaukee's acceleration of public works and by the Garden Homes project, which they recognized as an innovative step toward relieving housing shortages, and publicized for the benefit of other cities. These accolades arose not from their acceptance of socialism as an ideal, but their pragmatism, and from the efforts of Milwaukee's Chamber of Commerce and Employers' Association. The leadership of these groups, who were fighting simultaneously for the open shop, suggests the limits of Hoover's ability to move city governments to assume any responsibility beyond support to voluntarist organizations through various established committees.

The Milwaukee Leader, the socialist newspaper headed by Victor Berger reflected this tension between voluntarism and socialism.[29] The *Leader* was critical of the Unemployment Conference and of the leadership of employers in the various committees established to relieve unemployment. Berger's criticism of Hoover and the conference focused on their assumptions regarding the unemployed. The federal government's cruel determination to assist the unemployed only by providing information, and otherwise leave such matters to municipalities, was clearly not in the best interest of workers, many of whom had been made destitute by unemployment. Berger argued that within a democratic, capitalist society, socialist reformers should insist on the state's moral obligation to its less fortunate, and therefore on such policies as federally mandated unemployment compensation and direct relief, particularly when many of the unemployed were "veterans of capitalist war."[30]

At the local level, Berger attacked the Committee of Twenty-One and the Milwaukee Committee on Unemployment for their unwillingness to recommend the raising of wages and the hiring of more men. The committee may have urged employers to expand their shifts and lessen hours, but this supported the open shop at the expense of the Federated Trades Council and collective action on the part of workers. Although Daniel Hoan was an ally of Berger and claimed himself a socialist, he was clearly to the right even of Berger by 1921.[31]

Daniel Hoan's actions during the relief crisis of 1921 showed the limits of constructive socialism in relieving the unemployed. Although Hoan ran as a mainstream reform socialist, he nevertheless did not challenge in any significant way the assumptions regarding relief espoused by Hoover and Woods in the President's Unemployment Conference. He did not openly criticize the recommendations of the conference, and he endorsed the efforts of the MCUR, whose leadership embraced voluntarism and avoided state involvement. Interestingly, he was not an obstacle to Hoover's schemes, as one might expect from his party affiliation, but an ally. Hoan showed through the Garden Homes project that the concept of voluntarism allowed for very active municipal leadership. Hoover applauded this municipal ownership of housing, and never challenged Milwaukee's ownership of harbors. Hoan's political association did not prevent Hoover or Woods from praising him in press releases or periodic updates to other mayors. Clearly then, Hoan's socialism, and his advocacy of statist action at the municipal level, did not violate Hoover's ideal of the associative state. Hoover, like Hoan, thought unemployment had economic causes, and Hoan, like Hoover, thought assistance should be conditional on the deserving nature of the recipient. Milwaukee did not offer assistance to transients or the able-bodied. Yet Hoan also realized that in the long term, as populations increased and recessions became deeper, some state action would become necessary; thus his support of unemployment insurance. Whether Hoan's conservative, reform brand of socialism would stand the test of time, or allow Hoan to stay within Hoover's range of acceptability, will be examined in chapter eight.

Hoan stands in some contrast to the other socialist mayor in the country in 1921, C.C. Barewald from Davenport, Iowa. Also part of the right wing of the socialist party, Barewald dramatically increased public works, as did Hoan, and advocated municipal ownership of utilities and other local transportation networks as did Hoan. Unlike Hoan, however, he challenged Hoover and the conference over its assumption that relief was useful only at the local level and over its view of the proper role of the state. Barewald urged, as did Berger, that the federal government shoulder more of the relief burden by providing jobs and indirect relief to the unemployed. Hoan, though he did not join in this, did provide more funding to indirect relief than Thompson in Chicago or Couzens in Detroit. His efforts to provide public works funding to the Free Employment Bureau and the Bureau of Outdoor Relief, although still within the prevailing paradigm of voluntarism, lay close to the boundary of the policy, especially in the latter case.

Notes

1 Joe William Trotter Jr., *Black Milwaukee: The Making of an Industrial Proletariat, 1915-45* (Urbana: University of Illinois Press, 1988) 41; Bayard Still, *Milwaukee: The History of A City* (Madison: State Historical Society, 1965) 476-50.

2 Trotter, *Black Milwaukee*, 45; Daniel W. Hoan, "Milwaukee Registers Progress," *National Municipal Review* (Vol. XII, No.16, October 1923) 576-82. Milwaukee Leader, July 18, 1921. "The City of Milwaukee" Brochure, Hoan Papers, Milwaukee County Historical Society, hereafter referred to as Hoan Papers. Hoan, "Address Before Grand Avenue Business Men," February 24, 1924, Hoan Papers; Paul Glad, *The History of Wisconsin Volume V: War, a New Era and Depression, 1914-1940* (Madison: State Historical Society of Wisconsin, 1990) 129-140.

3 Glad, *History of Wisconsin,* 155; Citizens' Committee on Unemployment and the Public Employment Office of Milwaukee, *Tenth Annual Report* (Milwaukee: Industrial Commission of Wisconsin, 1922).

4 Hoan to Berger, April 30, 1919, Box 18 Hoan Papers; Milwaukee Journal, August 3, 1920, September 22, 1921, November 8, 1913; Glad, *History of Wisconsin,* 130-45. James Weinstein, *The Decline of Socialism in America, 1912-1925* (New York: Monthly Review Press, 1967) 93-106; "Strikes and Labor Disputes, 1917-1938." Box 22, Hoan Papers.

5 Milwaukee Leader, October 13, 1920; Weber to Hoan, December 20, 1920 Box 20, Hoan Papers; Weinstein, *Decline,* 111; Glad, *History of Wisconsin,* 168.

6 Citizens' Committee on Unemployment, Annual Report; Milwaukee Leader, October 21, 1921, Chicago Tribune October 30, 1921; Milwaukee Employers Council, Minutes Box 31, Hoan Papers.

7 Walter Peterson, *An Industrial Heritage: Allis-Chalmers Corporation* (Milwaukee: Milwaukee County Historical Society, 1978) 220; Milwaukee Leader, June 9, 1920.

8 Lewis E. Sawyer, Unemployment Report for Milwukee, December 21, 1921 Commerce Papers box 341, HHP; Unemployment Report, President's Conference on Unemployment (covers the period October 1921 thru Fevruary1922) n.d. Box 26 Hoan Papers. Citizens' Committee on Unemployment, Tenth Annual Reort, and Eleventh Annual Report. Milwaukee Leader, January 3, 1922, March 12, 1921, December 27, 1921; Milwaukee Journal December 18, 1921.

9 Weinstein, *Decline;* Milton Cantor, *The Divided Left: American Radicalism, 1900-1975* (New York: Hill and Wang, 1978) 32-42, 72-80; Sally miller, *Victor Berger and the Promise of Constructive Socialism, 1910-1920* (Westport: Greenwood Press, 1973); James McDonald, *Socialism, Critical and Constructive* (New York: Cassell, 1924)

10 Miller, *Victor Berger*, 10-16, Weinstein, *Decline,* 93-100.

11 Ibid., Bill Haywood, "Socialism, the Hope of the Working Class," International Socialist Review, February 1912; Morris Hillquit, "Socialist Task and Outlook," New York Call, May 21, 1919; Milwaukee Leader February 8, 1920, February 16, 1920, April 7, 1920; for works on the IWW see: Patrick Renshaw, *The Wobblies: The Story of the IWW and Syndicalism in the United States* (Chicago: Ivan D. Dee, 1999) 31-50; Paul Brissenden, *The I.W.W.: A Study of American Syndicalism* (New York: Columbia Univerisity Press, 1919); Frederic Thompson *The I.W.W.: Its First Fifty Years* (Chicago: University of Chicago, 1955) 56-70; Patrick Cannon, *The IWW* (New York: Merit, 1967).

12 Weinstein, *Decline,* 145-9, Cantor, *Divided Left,* 77-84.

13 Miller, *Victor Berger*, 5-18, 44-50; Cantor, *Divided Left, 90-7.*

14 Ibid., Berger to Hoan, October 15, 1921, Box 24 Hoan Papers; Milwaukee Leader August 13, 1921, October 22, 1921, October 25, 1921. Victor Berger, *Berger's Broadsides,* 1912 Milwaukee County Historical Society.

15 Cantor, *Divided Left*, 56; Miller, *Victor Berger*, 81-5.

16 *Milwaukee Leader,* October 18, November 2, 1919; *Milwaukee Journal* October 20, 1919; Beger to Hoan February 15, 1920, Box 20, Berger to Hoan, January 22 1923, Box 25, Hoan Papers; Daniel Hoan "Milwaukee Registers Progress," *National Municipal Review* (Vol. XII. No. 10, October 1923) 574-61; Thomas Duncan to Hoan, August 18, 1921, Box 25, Hoan Papers.

17 *Milwaukee Leader*, February 20, 1920. *Milwaukee Joutnal*, April 3, 1920; Weinstein, *Decline*, 266-8.

18 *Milwaukee Leader*, April 8, 1920.

19 *Milwaukee Journal*, November 9, December 11, December 14, 1921. Charles Bennet, "Fifteen Years of City Planning Accomplishments in Milwaukee," n.d. The item appears as part of an article published in the October 30 issue of "The American City" Box 29, Hoan Papers.

20 Bennet, "Fifteen Years of City Planning. . . " Daniel Hoan, "Cooperative Home Building: The Milwaukee Plan," *Locomotive Engineers Journal*, December 1922, 894-6. "The Milwaukee Plan" Information sheet, n.d. Box 25, Hoan Papers. *Milwaukee Journal* January 15, 19, 22,1922, February 8, 1922 June 17, 19, 20, 1922.

21 Phil Grau to Woods, November 5, 1921 Chalmer Traver to Henry Case, November 4 and 9, 1921, Box 27, Hoan Papers.

22 "The Milwaukee Plan" Thomas Duncan to Hoan, August 1, 1921, Box 27, Hoan Papers; Woods to Hoan, December 11, 1921, Box 35, Comm. Papers HHP.

23 *Milwaukee Journal, March 11, 1923, Twelfth Annual Report, Citizens' Committee on Unemployment, 1924.*

24 "Mayor Hoan Answers Critics," January 10, 1922 Box 25, Hoan Papers. The document is a speech Hoan gave to the common council. Daniel Hoan, *City Government: The Record of the Milwaukee Experiment* (Westport: Greenwood Press, 1974) 63-9.

25 Ibid.

26 Lewis Sawyer, Unemployment Report for City of Milwaukee, November 10, 1921, Box 35, Commerce Papers HHP. Daniel Hoan, Speech at International Harvester Company n.d. Box 27, Hoan Papers.

27 Milwaukee Committee on Outdoor Relief Progress Report, October 30, 1921, Box 28, Hoan Papers. Minutes, City Council November 14, 1921 from *Milwukee Journal* November 15, 1921. Cotizens' Committee on Unemployment, Tenth Annual Report.

28 Chalmer Traver to Woods, December 22, 1921, Box 25 Hoan Papers; Hoan to Woods, December 1, 1921, Woods to Hoan December 15, 1921 Commerce Papers Box 31, HHP. Hoover to Hoan January 8, 1922, Commerce Papers, Box 31, HHP.

29 Woods to Hoan, February 3, 1922, Commerce Papers Box 32, HHP. Woods to Hoover February 8, 1922, Commerce Papers Box 32, HHP; *Milwaukee Leader* December 23, 1921, January 5, 8, February 9, 1922. Miller, *Victor Berger, 76.*

30 *Milwaukee Leader*, January 8, 1922; Berger to Hoan, March 16, 1922, Box 27 Hoan Papers.

31 *Milwaukee Leader,* December 11, 1921; Hoan to Woods, January 26, 1922, Box 26, Hoan Papers; Galbraith Miller to Hoan, Box 26, Hoan Papers.

Chapter 6
Detroit, Automobiles, and the Unemployment Crisis of 1921

Unlike Chicago and Milwaukee, Detroit was dominated by one industry from 1919-1921 and after—the automobile industry. What were the effects of the depression of 1921 on a city dependent on one industry? Was unemployment deeper and more prolonged, or was the industry strong enough to mitigate the crisis? What influence did the auto industry exert on policy makers and their actions to the unemployed? Examination of Detroit's mayor, James Couzens, will tell us much about both the city and the industry: he was the former president of Ford Motor Company, a leader in business and in the progressive reforms of the 1900-1945 period. As such, he viewed municipal leadership as an extension of the business world. He was also the only mayor of our three target cities invited to the Unemployment Conference, of which he was an unabashed supporter. His actions in Detroit provide answers to a number of questions relevant to Hoover's view of relief. Did Detroit rely on private charity to a greater degree than Chicago or Milwaukee? Were employers or organized labor more or less cooperative to the relief strategy proposed by Couzens? More importantly, was the relief policy in Detroit in 1921 an accurate predictor of policy in 1929-1933? Were Couzens' and Hoover's beliefs about the unemployed similar, and what does that tell us about Hoover's vs. Hoan's or Thompson's concept of the role of the state in relieving unemployment?

In this chapter I argue that a particular obstacle to unemployment relief in Detroit was its reliance on one central industry, which gave employers even more influence over relief policy there than in Milwaukee or Chicago. I argue also that Couzens' actions reflect the most thorough attempt by a mayor working with the same underlying concept about relief as Hoover to implement the recommendations of the Unemployment Conference. Finally, I will argue that Couzens, Thompson, and Hoan, despite their widely different political constituencies, all fit within the voluntarist paradigm concerning relief; their cooperation led Hoover to conclude that his methods of organizing the discussion over the state, voluntarism, and relief were valid. This consensus, however, left them and their cities, like Hoover, unprepared to meet the needs of the unemployed early in the depression.

During the war years the population, politics, and economy of Detroit changed considerably. The automobile industry grew tremendously through war orders;

its increased production drew rural whites and southern blacks in search of work, and at first seemed able to absorb them. The city's population grew from 465,766 to 993,678 between 1910 and 1920—the black population from a mere 5,741 to 40,838—making Detroit the fourth largest city in America. In politics, the city experimented throughout the period with municipal reforms, yet its management of relief remained unchanged. The recession of 1921 challenged Couzens' assumption that Detroit's political, economic, and social structure could manage massive unemployment and growing calls for relief.[1]

The development of Detroit's physical, political, and social structure was derived almost entirely in this period from the growth of the automobile industry. In 1914 Ford Motor Company produced 308,000 automobiles, the majority of them the Model T, introduced in 1909. By 1927, when the Model T was discontinued, 15,000,000 had rolled off the assembly lines of Detroit. Correspondingly, Ford's employment went from 450 workers in 1908 to over 36,000 in 1917. Ford led the way, but the city as a whole experienced tremendous growth, particularly just before and after the world war: 200,000 worked there at the peak of employment before the recession of 1921. Between 1900 and 1930, the metropolitan area's population expanded from 305,000 to over 1.8 million. Auto manufacturing accounted for 57% of all manufacturing in the city by 1927. Though production slowed briefly as the city filled war orders, by 1919 it had returned to its peak levels of 1917. This apparently ever-expanding market led Detroit to expect high employment, wages, and growth through the 1920s.

The city entered the decade with one of the premier executives of the auto industry as its mayor, James Couzens, who served as general manager and then the president of Ford from 1903-1915.[2] Couzens entered politics in 1916 as Police Commissioner in order to advocate stricter law-and-order policies and then saw an opportunity to run for mayor as a progressive Republican. He exemplified the party: a Canadian, the son of a small soap manufacturer, he worked as a car-checker in Detroit and saved $2,500 to buy Ford stock in 1903, becoming the primary minority holder of the company by 1917, with 11% of the stock. Couzens quickly rose to join the business elite of Detroit, and although the Detroit Republican Party suffered a severe split between progressives and conservatives, this elite remained overwhelmingly Republican. By 1916, he had become one of the state party's primary contributors. In 1918 he attempted at the municipal level what Henry Ford had failed to do in his bid for the United States Senate, and was able to overcome the polarizing perception of private privilege and status.

Municipal charter reform and municipal ownership of the streetcar system were critical issues in the mayoral elections of 1918.[3] Couzens defeated Democrat William Connolly by less than 10,000 votes. He enjoyed the backing of most employers, led by the example of the Detroit Employers Association's endorsement. He did well with native-born voters with native-born parents, and he was given substantial backing by the *Detroit News*. During the election primary campaign, Couzens had faced the opposition of most of Detroit's upper class, who had supported John Gillespie, the favorite of the wealthy, and the head of the machine system created by John Dodge. Connolly had run the Democratic machine in Detroit and was favored by many to win the general election. David Duffield, the Library Commissioner, was backed by most municipal reformers, having served as the president of the Charter Commission, which had created a new municipal charter replacing the ward system with a smaller, at-large only city council. Couzens ran on a pro-business platform and in a surprise defeated Gillespie in the primary. As the only Republican with any real connection to the business class and aristocracy of Detroit, Couzens won the mayoral election.[4]

He won on a strong municipal ownership platform, which however he failed to fulfill after his election. When most businessmen opposed his proposal to buy the Detroit Urban Rail (DUR) for 31.5 million dollars, which even the Municipal Ownership League believed too high, the common council passed a compromise plan adapted from municipal ownership plans in Cleveland, which businessmen widely supported, since it allowed the city to issue a franchise for the streetcar line on a rider-at-cost basis. Couzens' veto of the plan alienated him even further from the business elite of the city. Throughout his term, he continued to push for greater municipal control of street rails, and for subways to relieve the city of traffic congestion. He was willing to confront the elite so as to expand the influence of municipal government over private enterprise, something he thought "necessary for Detroit's explosive growth." Did he apply the same philosophy of municipal involvement to relief in the recession of 1921?[5]

As Detroit headed into 1921, the auto industry seemed to have weathered the turbulence of the immediate postwar period; its output was increasing, and the coming year was anticipated with hope. However, as in the rest of the country, the recession began in the spring to drive thousands out of work. The press initially reacted with disdain for the unemployed. A *Detroit Free Press* editorial, for example, described a "man on the street" survey in which 50 men were asked if they were willing to work on farms at $40 per month plus board. The editorial argued that all 50 refused because "the city fed and roomed them without working," and claimed that "there is plenty of work available, if the idle were made to take it." The availability of lodging houses and meals, it claimed, fostered an attitude of dependence that the city should work toward ending, rather than promoting. This set the tone for the city's response, at least early in the crisis. By August, over 18,000 men were out of work, and three months later over 50,000 joined them. Still editorials continued to appear preaching optimism about the future, faith in the auto industry, and resistance to large city expenditures on relief.[6] Despite the press's optimism, unemployment continued to worsen. Thomas Dolon, Commissioner of Public Welfare, was forced to ask the common council for $223,000 in late August just to provide relief until the end of the month, since the Welfare Department had already spent over 1 million dollars, most of its budget, in the previous 8 months. Already over 300 men per day were seeking relief in the form of lodging, food, and clothing for themselves and their families.

The council passed Dolon's request, and Couzens argued that the city was performing admirably, "taking care of the unemployed as no other city . . .there have been no bread lines and no soup kitchens." Couzens shared the optimism of John C. Howell, a business economist who predicted the auto industry, and therefore Detroit, would lead the nation out of depression by better marketing and industry consolidation. Apparently the industry shared this optimism as well: Chevrolet lowered the price on its 490 series to $10 below the 1917 price. Ford and General Motors followed Chevy's example. Edsel Ford argued that because of these reduced prices "people are being helped into more progressive times." Ford in fact broke all previous records in August 1921, producing 117,696 cars. National sales faltered however, and inventories increased.[7]

Unemployment continued to worsen in the fall of 1921 and in response Couzens accepted Hoover's invitation to the President's Unemployment Conference, and came to believe strongly in the implementation of its policies. He "felt a keener interest in the success of the movement," he wrote Hoover, "than perhaps some other mayors." Part of that interest stemmed from Couzens' experience while as president of Ford during the recession of 1913-14, when he had showed his corporate liberal philosophy by attacking manufacturers for "allowing their workers to starve while they spend the winter in Florida."[8]

In 1914, taking the lead in dealing with the 82,000 unemployed, Couzens allied himself with Charles Warren, then president of the Board of Commerce, to organize the relief effort. The activities of the board were suspended and its office turned into an employment office. Associated Charities, an umbrella organization of private charities such as United Jewish Charities and Visiting Nurses, sent volunteers, and Ford, Packard and Detroit City Gasses sent employment managers to man the temporary employment office.[9] Doctors and lawyers were asked to provide their services pro-bono to the unemployed through the office. To coordinate the effort, the unemployed were asked to register by describing their family history, financial and medical needs, type of skill, and previous employer. In all 22,000 unemployed registered: 6,000 were directly given full-time jobs, others part-time work, and still others employed by the city on limited public works projects, a total of only 9,000 citizens, then, found assistance of some type through the registration efforts. The remainder, however, had to be given some manner of relief, such as coal or clothing; yet at no time were they given cash assistance or much else in the way of direct relief.[10]

Already in 1914 Couzens' position was close to Hoover's. As a business leader, he had used a voluntarist approach, organizing the business elite to control the unemployment situation through public pressure and refusing to draw upon the city's budget for expanded public works or direct relief. All this closely paralleled the recommendations and methods advocated by Hoover seven years later. One public not involved in Couzens' efforts or in the discussion of unemployment in 1914 was labor: the Detroit Federation of Labor was not even asked to participate in the relief effort. The efforts of these business reformers were thought successful, yet, as mentioned above, only 9,000 unemployed workers of over 80,000 found work or other assistance through Couzens' effort. Yet this method of handling unemployment still dominated local thinking in 1921.

Upon returning from Washington in that year, Couzens began to implement his plans for relief in Detroit. He directed efforts in public works and the Department of Public Welfare, and he organized the business and charity communities in a mayors' conference on unemployment. The city budget already allotted 90 million dollars for public works; this allowed employment in public projects to increase from the usual 10,000 to upwards of 25,000. Couzens felt satisfied that Detroit had already "done everything suggested by the conference except separating those seeking relief from those desiring public work." As in 1914, he urged industry cooperation, arguing that with "greater cooperation from industry we should be able to provide part time work for many of the unemployed." Couzens also planned a conference of his own that would place the corporatist elements—business, charity, municipal government and labor—in a position to attack unemployment.[11] Although he gained the support of the industrial elite, the Detroit Federation of Labor rejected the invitation to join the conference. In an open letter, the DFL argued that the committee "would accomplish nothing"; more importantly in an atmosphere of war over the open shop, the DFL did not want to "create a feeling among the workers of Detroit which would be hard to overcome at a later date." Clearly, the DFL saw the actions of Couzens and the Unemployment Conference as a method of asserting once again the power of the business elite in matters of social policy. Couzens' response to the DFL was low-key: he asserted that although the DFL's support would be helpful, it was not enough .[12]

The mayor's committee on unemployment met in November of 1921, but before then, in October, Couzens began to encourage public works, organize relief measures in the Department of Public Welfare, and call on industry to expand employment opportunities. The earliest report on unemployment came from the Department of Public Welfare, which operated the Employment Bureau. As of October 5, over 37,000 unemployed men had registered with the department for relief. Of that number over 11,000 were placed in jobs supplied by the city and its $90 million-dollar public works projects. The next largest number of jobs, 7,783, came in the form of "non-pay" city jobs: workers exchanged their labor for clothing, coal, and in some cases rent paid to the worker's landlord. Only 3,397 were placed in private jobs, the bulk of these in temporary part-time work.[13]

Couzens, recognizing the low number of placements with private industry, addressed an open letter to the Board of Commerce advising it to ration work, giving part-time work where possible, and preferring married men over single. Although most companies at first ignored Couzens' plea, by mid-October some, such as Ford, began to adopt the plan in various forms. With more inventory building up and fewer orders, most companies initiated mass layoffs, mostly in the form of expanding part-time positions and laying off junior workers. Although the Employment Bureau was expanded and physically moved from the Bureau of Public Welfare, only about half of the laid-off men registered with the bureau.[14]

The Mayor's Conference on Unemployment, dominated by businessmen, met in early November to respond to the worsening conditions. The committee stressed the need for manufacturers to stagger hours and take on workers. Continental Motors pledged to hire 1,500 to 2,000 men in their Muskegon, Michigan plant. Oakland Motor Company and Jackson Motors also made commitments as they attempted to expand their market share by raising production levels and lowering prices. The majority of new positions, however, offered only part-time work, and turnover was extremely high. Couzens pushed for more full-time work, but accepted any commitment. As sales continued to decline through the winter, however, such commitments began to waver.[15]

To expand jobs within the city, Couzens ordered all married women not "dependent on their city jobs for a living to give up their places at once." Couzens' gender-biased position was shrouded in the logic that if a woman's husband was working, then the additional income provided by the wife prevented some other man from earning enough for his family. Couzens also requested assistance from the state: he proposed to send all single unemployed men to the northern part of the state to clear over 300,000 acres of land for farming. The response by the majority of single men was, to say the least, negative. Though Detroit did manage to send several hundred, the project called for 9,000 men from across the state.[16]

Overall, the Mayors' Committee on Unemployment advocated strategies consistent with the voluntarist paradigm, but with little effect. After initial meetings in November, the committee became largely unresponsive to the situation, and Couzens was forced to divert his attention to a re-election campaign, which he won on November 8. As winter approached, Couzens became increasingly disheartened by the lack of enthusiasm, particularly of employers. The number of unemployed continued to rise, and Couzens described the situation as "almost hopeless." His focus in the conference turned to "what we can do to keep up the interest through the winter." Meetings were irregular; the only committee to make an official report was transportation.

The burden of relief therefore fell on the city government and private agencies, particularly on the Department of Public Welfare and the Detroit Community Fund.[17] The Department of Public Welfare provided service to increasing numbers of families over the winter, 828 families at its peak in the first week of January 1922. In administering relief, the Department first "tested the desire of some to work" by asking applicants if they were willing. Those who refused to answer in the affirmative were dropped from the rolls and refused all relief from the city. Those who answered properly were told by the Department that relief "is in the nature of a loan, based on your needs and character." The city meant by these means to avoid giving the impression of making recipients dependent. The bulk of aid came in the form of clothing, coal, and, if the family was facing immediate eviction, rent. And again, this came only to those who showed a willingness to work. Those who, because of pride, discouragement, or alcoholism, stopped looking for work or relief had no recourse but to wait until conditions improved.[18]

By February 1922, the department was assisting approximately 7,000 families per month at a cost of $209,000. Thomas Dolon, as the Department's superintendent, oversaw the Employment Bureau as well as these relief efforts. Since private jobs were nearly unavailable and public jobs already filled, he gave out relief to unemployed workers in exchange for odd jobs such as clearing areas within the city for planting gardens. Many families, of course, appealed directly to the mayor for assistance, but with little success. Such was the case of Ambrose and Amelia Leonard. Ambrose lost his job with Packard in January 1921 and received a pair of shoes, a ton of coal, and 2 months of groceries from the city. He finally went back to work part-time in September, yet he fell ill, missed an appointment with the Department of Relief, and was denied any further assistance, despite a later visit to Visiting Nurses which confirmed that he suffered from tuberculosis. Couzens heard hundreds such stories, yet his methods for distributing relief remained unchanged. Like Dolon he hoped the employment bureau could place more workers and that industry would cooperate in this.[19]

The record of the employment bureau shows that workers were very difficult to place. Applications for work never reached more than 336 in a given week, and placement percentages fluctuated between 10 and 40 percent. Registration of the unemployed was strongly encouraged through the daily newspapers, yet, without the firm commitment of employers, the Employment Bureau quickly became ineffective. Odd jobs or other part-time work became more difficult to provide as the winter progressed, and public works jobs had been filled early in the recession.[20]

The most concentrated effort at relief came through private means. Despite his commitment to public works and the Department of Public Welfare, Couzens, like Hoover, regarded private charitable agencies as the best source of relief. Hoover wrote to Couzens to praise him for not only for his efforts in general, but specifically for promoting "our great private charity institutions who fuel private initiative and provide relief in the right way." In Detroit, this relief came principally from the Detroit Community Fund, which served as an umbrella group for the various private agencies in the city. The city government seeded the fund when it was set up in 1918. When the numbers of those in need increased, the fund sought more money. The target for the 1921 campaign was $3.25 million the bulk of which was designated for distribution through 65 charitable organizations in the city. A mass advertising campaign began in October of 1921: ads and mail-in funds were reported in the major daily papers and fund-raisers were held throughout the city.[21]

Organizers knew early on that the unemployment situation had "thrown the heaviest burden on Detroit's charitable system it has even been called on to assume." As early as February 1921, relief uses were growing rapidly and revenues diminishing just as rapidly. United Jewish Charities, for example, increased relief expenditures from a little more than $3,000 per week in January 1920 to close to $7,000 per week a year later when even more unemployment loomed on the horizon. The Salvation Army increased aid from 95 families to well over 500. In order to meet the growing problem, the Community Union (who administered the funds) agreed to "marshal their forces under the Department of Public Welfare," the common council appropriated $250,000 to the Union; nonetheless organizers knew a massive campaign to raise additional money was necessary.[22]

The campaign got off to a fast start, raising $300,000 in the first three days, most of which came from wealthy elites and area businesses. Hudson Motor Cars Company gave $25,000, the largest early contribution. Campaigning in the downtown district produced almost half of the early total. Other voluntarist strategies included a factory workers campaign, based on the slogan "one days pay for charity." Subscriptions for workers to contribute to the fund were mass-mailed throughout the city and printed in the daily papers. Surprisingly, considering the ever more likely specter of facing relief lines themselves, workers contributed nearly $100,000.[23]

By the end of the fund-raising drive in early November, 3.1 million dollars had been raised, short of the stated goal of $3.25 million, yet clearly the city had responded to their call and organizers were ecstatic. W.J. Norton, secretary of the fund, argued that the campaign gave proof that "philanthropy in Detroit will provide the much needed relief without the burden of the state." Detroit would lean hard on private efforts throughout the crisis and the decade. The Salvation Army, for example, put over 9,000 unemployed back to work at least part-time, fixing up homes and performing other odd jobs; the Catholic Study Club gave milk and crackers twice daily to undernourished parochial school children and medical care both in the home and in hospitals for vaccines and minor illnesses; and organization such as Visiting Nurses were expanded—all with dollars from the Community Fund.[24]

In all, over 190,000 Detroiters received some form of aid from private organizations. Over 38,000 families were assisted during 1921, an increase of over 18,000 from 1920. Interestingly, the reports of the Community Union show that next to care of the sick, the greatest increase in aid went to "character-building, education, and information," mainly through settlement house efforts. Clearly, unemployment was still thought to be linked to moral standing. The work of the Detroit settlement houses like those nationwide focused on temperance and the "Americanization" of immigrants.[25]

In the black community of Detroit as in Chicago, the Urban League, served as the primary institution to coordinate and deliver aid. Also as in Chicago, white-dominated relief agencies, both private and public, discriminated against blacks, leaving them without a voice in wider discussions of unemployment and relief. The Detroit Urban League was established in the city in 1916 and immediately found itself coordinator of housing services, employment bureau, and relief agency. During the recession, blacks lost their jobs first and were rehired last.

The Urban League established an employment office in 1919 under the direction of John Dancy, and attempted to put blacks into jobs that paid a living wage. Unfortunately, most of its placements were in domestic jobs filled primarily by women. Large manufacturers were reluctant to hire blacks, and when they did, only placed them in the lowest paying, most back-breaking jobs available. Some of the black unemployed did receive aid from the Public Welfare Bureau, but the bureau and the major relief agencies in the city routinely pushed many who applied to the overburdened Urban League. In January 1921, the Urban League estimated that "two-thirds of the city's Negro population is out of work." Of the thousands of black unemployed, the Urban League placed less than 200 in that month. In November 1921, while the private charity machinery of the city was raising money and the Bureau of Public Welfare was struggling to find work for the unemployed, the Urban League placed fewer than 300. Mayor Couzens, like other leaders in the city, voiced concern over the situation, but made no effort to assist the Urban League. The Salvation Army refused to give out turkeys to needy black families during the Christmas season and the Employers Association ignored the issue altogether. Though a growing public, blacks were clearly excluded from Couzens' thinking and that of city's relief agencies. The city's failure to respond to the Urban Leagues' call for greater assistance turned them back on themselves, leading them to promote self-help and establish their own training and educational services. Clearly blacks were not going to receive any additional help and their voice was not going to be heard.[26]

As spring of 1922 arrived, Detroit began to pull out of the recession. By April, employment increased from 50,000 to 120,000 as auto manufacturers hired more men following their customary inventory period in December. Couzens was pleased that the situation was quickly returning to normal, and that through the downturn the city had avoided large-scale homelessness and starvation. He gave credit to the Department of Public Welfare and the charity organizations, and congratulated himself for not resorting to the dole. Yet, during the crisis, the city spent 63 million dollars, twice the 1920 budget, on public works, which was the bulwark of employment during the recession. Couzens did not miss this point; in fact he classified public works with relief as part of the city's response. His actions during the crisis clearly mirrored those of 1913-14, and followed the recommendations of the Unemployment Conference. His belief that private charity and the efforts of the Department of Welfare and Public Works could meet the crisis on the surface appeared accurate. Yet labor had resisted his efforts, and private employers had balked at his prodding. Like Daniel Hoan in Milwaukee, he had had to resort to an expansion of the public sector through municipal public works projects to provide enough employment to prevent severe hardship for many of Detroit's working families.[27]

Thus Couzens, Hoan, and Thompson to varying degrees accepted the basic paradigm of the Unemployment Conference. They all relied on private charity first, then public works and organization through voluntarist methods. Even though Thompson sharply disagreed with Hoover's politics regarding the war and thought the Unemployment Conference unnecessary, he nevertheless implemented, weakly, his own conference and relied, perhaps even more than the other two mayors, on private relief. He was clearly the furthest from accepting the Unemployment Conference and Hoover, a position highlighted by Couzens' refusal to come to Chicago because of his disgust at Thompson's unwillingness to act. Hoan, on the other hand, though a socialist, came much closer to the policy recommendations of Hoover. Hoan was not afraid to advocate a strong role for municipal government, and his programs had a much stronger public component than Thompson's. Extensive public works and employment offices, a strong public relief program, and innovative projects like Garden Homes reflected Hoan's socialist ideas, but within a framework that didn't alienate Hoover from his policy. Both Hoover and Couzens advocated voluntarism; but while Hoan used municipal government as the primary relief institution, Couzens relied much more on private charity. He was thus closest of the three to Hoover.

Although the open shop put labor in an overall defensive position during the decade, Thompson advocated labor's cause, and the strength and involvement of Fitzpatrick and the Chicago Federation of Labor reflected that—still, however, it was bound to the predominant theories of relief. The Milwaukee labor movement was mute: the crisis severely limited their voice in policy, and the Detroit Federation, under great pressure, disowned Couzens' initiatives as clearly pro-business and an aid to further gains for the open shop. The DFL's assumptions were correct: organized labor was unable to assert itself during and after the relief crisis of 1921. In all three cities, the business elite largely controlled relief efforts.

The efforts of the municipal and business leadership in Detroit, Chicago, and Milwaukee also reflected Hoover's and most economists' views that however bad the situation, it was part of a business cycle that ultimately would lead to prosperity. This important underlying assumption stifled the voices of those that advocated much stronger federal relief efforts; it kept the focus instead on short-term measures. And the brevity of the crisis tended to support this assumption. Thus, Hoover's conception of the critical debate in the public sphere—or more specifically of the publics he saw as critical—appeared accurate. The mayors viewed here represented three discrete points along a continuum that shows the limits the public sphere and of Hoover's and the mayors' acceptance of the voices of municipal leaders. Blacks, for example, although an emerging, yet still subaltern public, found no voice in the discussion at either the municipal or national level. Women, also of growing importance in labor and the wider social sphere, found a voice only through leadership of the charity and settlement house movements, and not as an autonomous public with specific needs of their own and particular plans to meet those needs. Only during the relief crisis of 1930-33 would municipal and national leaders clearly see the shortcomings of the voluntarist paradigm when the demand for space within the public sphere of formerly excluded voices would shatter the limits Hoover had set on critical debate, and push the discussion of democratic theory, dependence, and the state out of the transitional phase Hoover represented into a new, more statist phase.

Notes

1 U.S. Department of Commerce, Bureau of the Census: *Thirteenth Census of the United States,* 1910: Population, II, 953; Fourteenth Census of the United States, 1920: population III, 496; Richard Thomas, *Life for Us is What We Make It: Building Black Community in Detroit, 1915-1945* (Bloomington: Indiana University Press, 1992) 24-6.

2 Ralph Epstein, *The Automobile Industry, Its Economic and Commercial Development* (New York: A.W. Shaw, 1928); Donald Davis, *Conspicuous Production: Automobiles and Elites in Detroit, 1899-1933* (Philadelphia: Temple University Press, 1988) 57-69; "Mayor Couzens" biographical sketch, n.d. , Mayoral Papers Box 5, Detroit Public Library. Hereafter referred to as Mayoral Papers, DPL.

3 Davis, *Conspicuous Production,* 48-57; Harry Barnard, *Independent Man: The Life of Senator James Couzens* (New York: Scribners, 1958) *Detroit Free Press,* March 6, 15, 23, 1918; Couzens, "Speech Before Area Businessmen," March 14, 1918, Box 3, Mayoral Papers DPL. Raymond Fragnoli, *The Transformation of Reform: The Detroit Citizens League, 1912-1933* (Ph.D. Dissertation: University of Michigan, 1976) 118-42.

4 *Detroit Free Press,* April 8, 1918; Banard, *Independent Man,* 31-50; Davis, *Conspicuous Production,* 47.

5 Davis, *Conspicuous Production,* 53; *Detroit Free Press* October 14, 1920.

6 *Detroit Free Press,* August 15, 1921, September 12, 15, 26, 1921, October 22, 1921; Jewish Charities, Survey of Unemployment, October 30, 1921 , Associated Charities Papers, Box 26 Walter Ruther Library. Hereafter referrerd to as WRL. Russell Sage Foundation, Report of Unemployment, November 30, 1921, Commerce Papers box 25, HHP.

7 Dolan to Couzens August 26, 1921, Box 6 Mayoral Papers DPL; Minutes of City Council, August 28, 1921 Box 6, Mayoral Papers DPL; John C. Howell, "The Present Unemployment Situation" n.d. Associated Charities Papers Box 12, WRL. Davis, *Conspicuous Production,* 57. Couzens to Woods, September 11, 1921, Comm Papers, Box 28, HHP.

8 Hoover to Couzens August 17, 1921, Couzens to Hoover September 7, 1921, Commerce Papers, Box 26, HHP; Couzens to Hoover October 8, 1921, Commerce Papers Box 26, HHP.

9 Couzens to Woods,October 3, 1921, Mayoral Papers Box 7,DPL. The correspondence is adetailed ourline of Couzens' actions in the 1913-14 recession.; Warrem, Memo to Board of Commerce outlining the suspension of activities to assist in employment efforts November 1, 1913, Mayoral Papers Box 7,DPL; Warren to Dixon, October 14, 1913, Associated Charities Papers, Box 11, WRL;

10 Couzens to Woods October 3, 1921, Mayoral Papers Box 7,DPL.

11 *Detroit Free Press,* September 30, October 3, 1921; Couzens to Hoover, October 21, 1921, Commerce Papers, Box 28, HHP. Benard, *Independent Man,* 60-5.

12 *Detroit Free Press,* November 1, 1921.

13 Report of the Detroit Department of Public Welfare, October 5, 1921, Mayoral Papers Box 10, DPL

14 Couzens to Board of Commerce, October 1, 1921, Mayoral Papers Box 7, DPL, *Detroit Free Press,* October 1,2, 1921.

15 Minutes, Mayors Conference on Unemployment, November 10, 1921, Mayoral Papers Box 7,DPL; *Detrioit Free Press,* November 11, 12, 15, 1921.

16 Couzens to Woods November 17, 1921, Mayoral Papers Box 12, DPL. Several responses to Couzens' plan were expressed in letters to the mayor. Of the approximately 30 letters sent to the mayor, all were from workers and all were very negative in tone.

17 Mayors Committee On Unemployment, November 12, 1921, Mayoral Papers Box 13, DPL; *Detroit Free Press* November 1, 8, 12, 1921; Department of Public Welfare, Report, November 15, 1921, Mayoral Papers Box 11, DPL. Detroit Community Fund, Report, November 30, 1921, Box 20, Associated Charities Papers, WRL.

18 Dolon to Couzens January 8, 1922, Mayoral Papers Box 10, DPL; Report of Unemployment Activities in Detroit, December1, 1921, Commerce Papers Box 25, HHP; Russell Sage Foundation, "Unemployment in Cities," December 15, 1921, Commerce Papers, Box 25, HHP; *Detroit Free Press,* December 10, 1921; Couzens to Woods, December 20, 1921, Commerce Papers Box 25, HHP.

19 Ambrose Leonard to Couzens, December 11, 1921, Mayoral Papers Box 9, DPL. This particular box contained over 60 personal letters of Detroit citizens sharing their experience during the crisis.

20 *Detroit News,,* December 15, 1921; *Detroit Free Press,* December 19, 23, 1921; Dolon to Couzens, January 6, 1922, Mayoral Papers Box 7, DPL.

21 Detroit Community Fund, Press release, October 1, 1921, Associated Charities Papers Box 9, WRL. Couzens to Woods, October 5, 1921, Commerce Papers Box 25, HHP. Woods to Couzens, October 18, 1921, Commerce Papers Box 25, HHP; Woods to Hoover, memo on emergency measures in the mid-west, Commerce Papers Box 25, HHP. Hoover to Couzens November 18, 1921, Commerce papers Box 26, HHP.

22 Community Union, "Relief Expenditures for 1921," n.d. Associated Charities papers, Box 11, WRL; Associated Charities press release, October 20, 1921, Associated Charities Papers, Box 11, WRL *Detroit Free Press,* October 2, 1921.

23 *Detroit Free Press,* October 10, 1921; Associated Charities, Fundraising Committee Report, October 15, 1921, Associated Charities Papers, Box 12, WRL. W.J Norton to Dolan, October 30, 1921, Associated Charities Papers Box 11, WRL.

24 Norton to Couzens November 5, 1921, Associated Charities Papers, Box 11, WRL; Associated Charities, Fundraising Committee Report, November 15, 1921, Associated Charities Papers, Box 12, WRL; Couzens to Woods, November 18, 1921 Mayoral Papers Box 10, DPL.

25 Community Union, Report of Relief Expenditures, December 1, 1921, WRL; Norton to Dolan January 8, 1922, Associated Charities Papers, Box 12, WRL. *Detroit Free Press,* December 18, 26, 1921, January 6, 1922.

26 Richard Thomas, *Life for Us Is What We Make It: Building Community in Detroit, 1915-1945* (Bloomington: Indiana University Press, 1992) 63-6, 91-120; Nancy J. Weiss, *The National Urban League: 1910-1940* (New York: Oxford University press, 1974) 36-70; John Chavis and William McNitt, *A Brief History of the Detroit Urban League* (Ann Arbor: Michigan Historical Collection, 1971) 5-27.

27 Russell Sage Foundation, Report on Employment, June 1, 1922, Commerce Papers Box 27, HHP; Davis, *Conspicuous Production,* 63-7; *Detroit Free Press,* May 15, 1922.

Chapter 7
Herbert Hoover, the Great Depression, and the Widening of Voluntarism

At the President's Unemployment Conference of 1921, Herbert Hoover promoted a voluntarist response to unemployment, in which the state served mainly to advise, research, and build consensus, or, at most, institute public works as a counter-cyclical measure. This response appeared successful when prosperity returned in 1922. Unemployment appeared merely an effect of a business cycle, which might be smoothed by strategies arising from study of economic conditions, and specific factors such as seasonal fluctuation, banking reform, and consumption economics. Most mayors' acceptance of Hoover's approach increased its apparent validity, as did his own handling of the coal situation, although it never fully stabilized the industry.

When he was elected president in 1928, he expected to end the decade presiding over a prosperity that, as he joyously stated, "would end poverty." It was not to be. Black Tuesday and the ensuing depression challenged all Hoover's assumptions about economics and the role of the state, about state virtue and individual liberty.[1]

The depression forced on Hoover a change not only in policy, but in the assumptions and language underlying that policy. This chapter explores Hoover's struggle to retain his voluntarist assumptions in the face of a crisis much deeper than that of 1921. Mass unemployment and growing opposition forced Hoover to expand the meaning of voluntarism, but he tried to avoid sacrificing his most deeply held philosophy. The publics he had manipulated now rose against him. In response he sought to rework his idea of voluntarism so as to appease opponents in Congress while continuing to advocate his earlier positions. He did this mainly through the President's Emergency Committee on Employment and its successor, the President's Organization on Unemployment Relief. How did these committees organize? What did they recommend, and what was the response of labor, businesses, and local governments? What challenges did they face? How successful were they and what did this indicate to policymakers opposed to Hoover's philosophy? Discussion of these issues will illustrate the transition from voluntarism to the New Deal. The most important challenges to Hoover's policies came from Robert Wagner. His initiatives and Hoover's response to them show the emerging consensus in favor of a more activist government morally obliged to do more to assist the poor. Finally, a discussion of the 1932 presidential campaign highlights the transition from Hoover's position to a new one, which, though clearly more statist, had a significant base in associationalism.

Following his nomination as the Republican standard-bearer for the 1928 campaign, Hoover ran on a platform that proudly proclaimed the economic health of the nation and claimed that if the policies of the last eight years continued, then "soon with the help of God poverty would be banished from this nation." Hoover pointed to rising wages and lower prices, to standardization, cooperative effects in industry, and the rise of industrial associations as proof that his initiatives laid down in the Unemployment Conference of 1921 were successful. On the surface it appeared that Hoover's associative vision and his economic and moral philosophy were indeed about to take America into an age of ever-rising prosperity.[1] [2]

However, not long after taking office, Hoover saw trouble brewing. Within days of the stock market crash, he worried that the high cost of money and rampant speculation in the stock market might disturb the prosperity of the country. The former was already being felt in some industries; Hoover feared it would lead to inflation which, if sustained long enough, might trigger a downward spiral in the business cycle. The latter brought a risk of devastating economic collapse. He was relieved at the decline in stocks the week of the 16th of October, and hoped that the market might settle down. He said he had "given more thought to both these situations" than any other in the administration up to that time. His fears were realized—on the 29th the market collapsed; and the greatest trial of Hoover's abilities began. He declined to intervene in the market for fear that more harm than good would result.[3]

The crash affected employment almost immediately. Hoover's Secretary of Labor, James Davis, a fixture in the cabinet of the presidents of the decade, warned that if some type of immediate action was not taken the administration "will find ourselves in the midst of an unemployment situation such as we have not experienced since 1921." By December, Hoover confided to Julius Barnes that 3 million people were already unemployed. Yet, remembering the 1921 conference, he recommended asking leaders of industry to begin repairs, deferred maintenance, and clean-up projects to keep as many men employed as possible. At this early stage, he believed if the country made it through the winter, the economy would recover from a correction in the market, and avoid a more severe recession.[4]

Hoover therefore called business leaders to a conference in Washington. Above all he wished to ward off "undue pessimism, fear, uncertainty and hesitation in business." Hoover outlined several steps to head off further economic decline: in addition to the maintenance efforts he had recommended to Barnes, he urged employers to maintain wage rates and labor to keep peace in the workplace. He also called for counter-cyclical investment in public works at higher levels than in 1929. He believed that the agreement of those present in Washington with these plans, clearly based on the Unemployment Conference of 1921, showed that the decade's work of voluntarism had changed the corporate conception "of the relationship of business to public welfare." Continued lower interest rates, the voluntary action of business, and prudent public works would revive the economy and prove conclusively the value of voluntarism and the associative state. Hoover's actions were praised not only by businessmen, but also by economists such as Waddill Catchings, who argued early in 1930 that Hoover's plan was "the finest piece of constructive leadership in our generation." The fact that employers agreed to hold the line on wages indicated "that for the first time in history, the heads of our largest businesses are ready to follow [Hoover's] leadership." But as economic conditions worsened, this first triumph turned to defeat as employers ultimately chose their profit margins over the public welfare.[5]

In the spring of 1930, Hoover believed the worst was over. He held another gathering to promote the important findings of the committee on Recent Economic Changes, which had issued its final reports the previous year. The primary focus of the committee's report was the establishment of "economic balance," sustained growth based on consumerism and cooperation informed by "research and study, the orderly classification of knowledge" which ultimately "may make complete control of the economic system a possibility" without statist measures. He had in mind such instruments as the Business Survey, the various reports on unemployment and the business cycle, and the more complete census for 1930.[6]

Meanwhile, the relief situation had already reached near crisis proportions. The Russell Sage Foundation reported that requests for relief among 149 agencies nationwide were significantly higher for the last quarter of 1930 compared to the same period in 1929. Requests for April 1930, for example, were 57% higher than for April 1929. To respond to the rise in pressure for relief efforts Hoover called on "especially [men and women of wealth] to give generously of their substance and if necessary from their surplus." To relieve the "especially heavy burden" placed on private charitable institutions, Hoover called for the raising of $75 million to meet the needs of the unemployed. For Hoover, it was a matter of national moral obligation for all who earned more money than they needed to make donations. Even though charities were stretched to their limit, the proper response was not legislation, in his view, but private action. To help make municipal relief organizations and private charities more effective, Hoover sought to organize national relief organizations along the same voluntarist lines as industry, outlining particular objectives for various organizations. His relied on the Association of Community Chests and Councils to survey the relief needs and available funds for cities over 25,000 and organize the overall fundraising campaigns. He expected the association to organize in locales that did not have a community chest and to develop "through national channels [understanding of the necessity] for using all available resources, public and private, for absolutely essential relief."

This last clause, although not specifically defined, implies Hoover's still stern opposition to giving any sort of aid that might foster dependence. All assistance, whether through municipal or private agencies, should be restricted to emergency shelter, clothing and, in extreme cases, rent or food. The crisis was not yet over, but believing the country was in position to recover, Hoover's goal was to get through the winter only; he made no long-term plans. He felt more information was needed. The National Business Survey Conference had shown that unemployment was still the bedeviling problem it had always been and, he felt, some independent committee to gather information and make recommendations was necessary if the pressure on relief agencies was to ease in 1931.[7]

On October 21, 1930, Hoover announced the creation of the President's Emergency Committee on Employment (PECE). To head the organization, Hoover called on Colonel Arthur Woods, the former chair of the Emergency Measures Committee of the Unemployment Conference of 1921. The committee was to serve as a "special action group" to coordinate and "accelerate efforts to provide employment." It was merely a "booster": Woods and Hoover made great efforts to reiterate that there was nothing wrong with the existing structures for information or relief. PECE was organized only to "supplement, in a brief emergency period, the efforts of existing agencies which had functioned or are now functioning in a normally satisfactory manner." The committee centered on proposals for public works and on coordination between local public and private agencies to offer not relief but employment. Hoover was eager to assure employers and mayors that the committee was temporary and that the crisis would soon end.[8]

To reassure the public and control discussion, Hoover and PECE mounted a vigorous campaign to publicize the level of cooperation of business. Several corporate executives gave public radio addresses outlining what industry was doing about employment. These bear close scrutiny as they show the reliance on company welfare to stem the tide – a strategy that rested on the assumption that the crisis could not strain the companies enough to impede such welfare. These addresses also illustrate just how advanced company welfare had become. Policies instituted by some of the largest corporations provided more relief than most private or public agencies, but in several ways also made the worker indebted to the company, e.g., by loaning money to laid-off workers. Farm implement maker International Harvester, for example, made no-interest loans to laid-off workers as advances against future wages. Loans were made available only to those Harvester intended to hire back; and to receive the loan, workers had to lay open their finances to a company group that determined eligibility. A worker with savings was ineligible. Further, the loans only carried a four-week guarantee. A worker, then, had to be destitute to receive assistance, and then only for 4 weeks, after which there was no guarantee of continued help. General Electric, which already provided a pension, life insurance, and mortgage assistance, did not provide an unemployment program until 1930. Although its unemployment assistance program was sound in principle, based on equal contributions by employees and the company, GE was not at all prepared to assist the numbers of workers laid off as the depression worsened in 1931.[9] Similar problems plagued other employers. Eastman Kodak, for example, strongly supported the construction and maintenance programs advocated by PECE, but again as the depression lengthened, these methods of employment stabilization were not sufficient to absorb the numbers of workers affected by ever-lower sales.[10]

The inability of employers to provide adequate relief put more pressure on the administration to act. PECE, recognizing the severe relief needs anticipated for the winter of 1931, continued recommending limited relief and limited public works. The crisis, and Hoover's response to it, eventually brought discord into PECE, as Col. Woods' resigned when Hoover rebuffed his ideas of expanded relief. The efforts of PECE from August 1931 through the winter of 1932 showed the first cracks in the utility of voluntarist action. I will discuss these efforts, and then the national legislature's attempts to subvert Hoover's plans.

Hoover looked to the winters of '31/'32 with a certain degree of optimism, based in part on a statistical report from the census bureau which showed "less sickness, less general mortality, less infant mortality" than in 1928, a year of full employment. Hoover decried the calls for increased public money for relief as exaggeration. The answer for the coming winter, Hoover argued, was continued public works within budget, construction work, and increased activity by local municipalities and private charities for any additional relief needs. Hoover vehemently opposed any widespread government relief as "misguided" and insisted that the adoption of "doles" in Europe had brought these countries "close to demoralization." In addition, Hoover argued, consumption as well as savings deposits were up and the harvest of 1931 "indicated recovery from the drought." From Hoover's point of view, "the underlying forces of recovery are asserting themselves." To stem calls for the dole, Hoover pointed to the efforts of the public works activities of PECE as an example of properly limited government action.[11]

The views of Woods and Hoover came to differ markedly over time, particularly over the extent of public works. In Woods' view, public works and construction were an integral part of the plan for addressing unemployment. Woods hoped that emergency appropriations for 1931 and 1932 would allow states to give work immediately to the unemployed. The appropriation for 1931 for roads, public buildings, rivers and harbors, ship and aircraft production was doubled over the 1928 figure of $276,567,000 to $530,455,000. In addition, Congress passed additional appropriations of $90,500,000 for highways and $30,000,000 for public buildings. Even with the additional appropriations, however, only 50,000 more workers found employment than in 1929.[12]

As unemployment rose, Woods argued that current public works projects did not increase consumption or employment sufficiently to stimulate recovery. He believed the state should make a more concerted effort to this end, and in this he diverged from Hoover's determined reliance on the private sector. Woods, testifying at a senate committee on relief efforts, recommended at least one and perhaps two or more billion dollars in government spending for public works. He was joined in this by powerful senators such as Robert La Follette, Jr., of Wisconsin and Edward Costigan of Colorado, and by other public figures such as William Randolph Hearst. They regarded public works as a productive relief measure, superior to the dole, and no threat to the economy of government. However, since such works went beyond simple counter-cyclical investment, Hoover disapproved of them. Along with Leo Wolman and Otto Mallery, he argued that the unemployed in 1929-31, as in 1922, would return to work "because business has revived and not through their employment on public works." Projects beyond budget would, for Hoover, move the area of public works into the realm of relief and—as Theodore Joslin, Hoover's press secretary argued—into a "demoralizing dole." This disagreement, and legislative actions in 1930-31, would end the relationship between Woods and Hoover. In the meantime, outside of public works, PECE attempted to assist in the realm of private charity.[13]

PECE approached the area of public and private relief in much the same way the Emergency Committee had in 1921. It brought the major national relief organizations together, and provided them an academic foundation to report on levels of relief in particular cities and general trends in unemployment, in the hope that, over time, these organizations would be able to keep up with demand while the crisis worked itself out. This would prevent any increased calls for federal aid and thereby prove again the power of voluntarism. For Hoover, this was essential: "personal responsibility of men to their neighbors is the soul of genuine good will; it is the essential foundation of modern society."[14]

Significantly, before his split with Hoover, Woods arranged cooperation between the Association of Community Chests and Charities, the Family Welfare Association, the American Association of Public Welfare Officials, the National Association of Travelers Aid Societies, and the Russell Sage Foundation. Each organization was to perform specific tasks. The Association of Community Chests was to lead the organizing effort along four lines: collecting data on relief needs and funds, organizing charitable fund-raising campaigns, organizing in cities under 25,000, and nationally promoting the "widespread understanding of the necessity for using all available local resources, public and private, for absolutely essential relief." The Family Welfare Association compiled a field staff to consult on administering relief in small communities and provided information on trends in the relief field. The American Association of Public Welfare Officials concentrated its efforts in managing "local social and economic resources" and refining methods of delivering relief. Traveler's Aid dealt with the increasing problems of transient families. And the Russell Sage Foundation provided current statistical information on all aspects of relief. With this team, Hoover confidently assured those in the relief field, private charity, now as in 1921, "can relieve the situation" and "will work in the present crisis."[15]

During the summer and fall of 1930, relief levels had risen sharply, by as much as 57% from April to June over the same period in 1929. The largest percentage of aid came from public agencies such as Mother's Aid and from non-sectarian agencies. This aid generated mainly seasonal work that lowered relief for summer, but could be expected to fall off during winter. Woods found that the administration's direct relief went mainly to transients who flooded larger cities in search for opportunities. He therefore urged as the relief demand grew in the fall and winter that the unemployed remain in their home communities. Following older poor law precedents, Woods recommended and public officials announced that "they are providing jobs or national relief for local residents first, they are giving second thought to strangers." To drive the point home, Woods advocated use of registration bureaus to screen potential recipients for legal residence. He argued that provisions should be made for temporary lodging and food for only those transients who showed credentials from the bureau, and that those transients should if possible be returned to their home communities at the expense of those communities. He argued, quite correctly, that if transients flooded into the larger cities, a potentially disastrous winter would only get worse.

In the meantime, Woods and Hoover worked to raise funds, a critical voluntaristic activity.[16] Payments for outdoor relief had doubled from 1929 to 1930 and the winter of 1931 threatened to strain all channels for aid. Hoover repeatedly begged those who had money to give it to charity. He asked people to buy as in normal times, to provide work for the unemployed, such as painting or gardening, and most importantly to support relief organizations. Hoover saw the problem of skyrocketing unemployment as economic, and therefore claimed that all who were needy deserved help. He urged people to help one another as the only way through the crisis. He understood direct relief was now necessary, primarily in matters of health and "character building," but felt it must come from private and local sources because "no government action, no economic doctrine, no economic plan or project can replace that God-inspired responsibility of the individual man to his neighbor." For Hoover, this moment was a spiritual test of the very virtue of the American people and the state.[17]

Hoover, Woods, and later Fred Croxton, used a nationwide advertising campaign to raise awareness and funds. They organized the mailing of pamphlets to thousands of companies and associations; they placed newspaper articles and advertisements; they set up radio addresses. They distributed over 300,000 pamphlets between February and April 1931 alone. Dozens of local radio campaigns and fundraising efforts combined to raise even more private funds. States were asked to provide more money for public welfare boards and municipal relief agencies. However, this public money barely kept up with demand, and as the depression worsened, fell short. Private campaigns raised fairly large amounts from philanthropists and those still working, but these too were finally overwhelmed.

A review of the statistical data indicates that voluntarist organizations, to which municipal and private contribution is critical, could not stand in the face of an acute or prolonged crisis. Relief expenditures by November of 1930 rose dramatically with unemployment throughout the country. The Russell Sage Foundation report on 86 public relief departments in cities showed an increase of over 100% in families seeking aid and of almost 200% in expenditures over 1929. More than 100,000 new cases of aid were reported for the month of

October, which cost over $3 million. In the same period, 129 private relief agencies, including Jewish and Catholic relief, showed a similar increase, 100% increase in families aided and 100% in funds spent. Over 46,000 families requested aid for the month at a cost of over $800,000. These statistics showed relief at the highest level to date, and nonetheless in 1931 relief agencies would find themselves stretched even more.[18]

Even in months when relief was usually low, such as September, a "marked upturn in relief occurred." One significant trend throughout 1930 and 1931 was the increasing pressure on public relief agencies. By September 1931, over three-quarters of all relief came from such agencies. Private funds were completely inadequate and, as the financial crisis worsened, municipal bodies asked for more money from state governments that themselves teetered on bankruptcy. For the first 3 months of 1931, 81 cities spent over $30 million in relief, mostly from tax revenue, but that revenue was quickly evaporating. For September 1931, from 449 agencies reporting, over $10 million of relief went to families, of which 73% was administered by public bodies for outright relief—rents, food, clothing—and 27% for wage relief. Clearly, the promise of corporations to provide loans and relief to laid-off employees had long since been broken. In many cities, such as Detroit, Milwaukee, and Chicago, expenditures rose over 400% from September 1929 to September 1931. The tremendous increase in relief, and widespread publicity of Hoovervilles and bread lines, led Hoover to press for even more private charity, but it was not enough.[19]

An alternate vision of expanded government aid was rising in Congress to challenge Hoover's voluntarism. The transition to democratic statism began with debate over the Wagner Bill, which crystallized two, now clearly competing, views on relief and the role of the state. PECE under Wood's leadership had organized relief efforts with municipalities and the larger private agencies, but eventually Woods would abandon PECE as voluntarism appeared ever more inadequate, leaving Hoover an embattled president unable to lead the country from 1931 until his landslide defeat in 1932.

In early 1930, Robert Wagner, the reformist senator from New York, sent three bills to the floor. The first, S3059 would provide for expanded public works approved by the president and administered by a federal board. The second, S3060, would abolish USES in favor of state-led employment exchanges coordinated by the federal government. The third, S3061 would coordinate statistical information gathering under the direction of the Secretary of Labor. Wagner argued that levels of unemployment and destitution in the country had reached a point where positive action by the federal government was critical. His three bills would provide the first effective movement towards alleviating unemployment and "practically eliminate [cyclical] unemployment." Wagner, as a reformer, was committed to the idea of the welfare state and saw eradication of unemployment as the most pressing and necessary step toward providing "better organization to the existing system." He wanted an economic system that preserved private institutions yet was simultaneously able to distribute more effectively the benefits of production to all citizens.

A careful reading of the bills indicates that Wagner was a democratic statist, one of a group of reformers who, as Mary Furner has defined them, believed in a "more positive conception of what the state could accomplish without itself becoming a threat to liberty." Nonetheless, Wagner was unwilling in 1930 to propose legislation that clearly and significantly moved in that direction; these bills were merely preliminary steps to a more activist state. In the debates surrounding the bills, however, a strong voice clearly emerged for collectivist planning, as well as the reactionary voice of conservatives, including Hoover, who saw even these incremental steps as clear harbingers of drastic statist involvement in the economy.[20]

The Statistics Bill, S3061, passed easily in both houses and Hoover signed it into law July 7, 1931. The passage of S3059 and S3060 would not be so smooth. Wagner argued that the employment stabilization bill was consistent with Hoover's ideas of public works and would finally "arrange [public works] in a manner to stabilize industry [through proper timing of construction]" achieved through advanced planning. The emphasis on planning was certainly consistent with thinking on the business cycle during the 1920s, when there was consensus that public works served best as counter-cycled investment. Yet Hoover did not support the bill specifically, and in his address to the nation in January 1931 he implied a need for only $100-150 million in additional appropriations for public works. This number was "absurd," according to Wagner, who originally requested in his bill appropriations of over $1 billion. Therein lay one level of Hoover's opposition to the Wagner proposals, as well as other, similar legislation. He saw these amounts as nothing less "than a raid on the public treasury," which clearly put the balanced budget in jeopardy and moved the state closer to the center of the economic machine. In response to Hoover's inaction, Wagner pushed S3059 and S3060, and Hoover signed S3059 with significant modifications in February 1931. However, the most contested of the three bills, S3060, remained unsigned, as a result of which Woods left PECE and debate was more clearly defined over what "doles" were and more generally over the value of voluntarism itself.[21] This bill fundamentally violated Hoover's principles by giving the federal government the role of managing state and local employment bureaus. Since it called for the abolition of USES, it raised the fundamental issue of the financial relationship between the states and the federal government in an employment service. In his veto message, Hoover argued that USES "is today finding employment for over 130,000 men and women" per year. He insisted that abolition of the Farm Labor Division of the Department of Labor and of the veterans' employment service, both operated by USES, was inadvisable, since they and state employment agencies were flexible enough to go where the most need appeared, and the USES could facilitate interstate job opportunities. In other words, he claimed, the current apparatus functioned properly and better service required keeping control at the local level. Moreover, if the services did need strengthening, that would come not by abolishing the bureau, but by "statistical data gathering" through the Commerce Department, and Hoover proposed that Secretaries Lamont and Davis institute such gathering. In addition, S3060 called for the federal government to bear what usually was a state responsibility, the setting up of agencies, and this in Hoover's mind overstepped the boundary between facilitation and undue control. Hoover and his supporters viewed S3060 as one step toward the dole, and he vehemently opposed on those grounds. Along with other pieces of legislation, such as that proposed by Senator Caraway for cash payments to veterans of $3 billion and Senator Brookhart for $37.5 million in additional federal subsidiaries for roads, this bill was simply an attempt to "legislate the depression away" that would in fact "indefinitely prolong it."[22]

Hoover believed his first duty to both the employed and the unemployed was "insistence upon a stable financial position of the government as the first requisite for recovery." Again, national relief, Hoover argued, came through "cooperation" of largely private interests, and the "ill-timed, rash" legislation proposed in the Congress would "create more unemployment and more distress." Hoover insisted that the Wagner bill, if signed, would not create one new job because it would take several years to organize. Ultimately he feared the Wagner Bill's effects after the depression ended. If the agency led people to expect a dole from a federal employment service, they would insist on the same dole in prosperous times. Hoover feared the federal government would find itself obliged to give wages regardless of the status of the economy.[23]

From the private sector, manufacturers gave Hoover most of his support. Opposed to the Wagner bill were the Metal Traders Illinois Manufacturers Association and, most importantly, the National Association of Manufacturers, whose counsel, James Emery, wrote a brief calling S3060 unconstitutional. The crux of the argument concerned the appropriations for the bill, which gave the federal government the ability to coerce a state to create employment agencies even if it opposed such action. The bill redirected authority from local leaders to an enlarged federal power. This, as Hoover warned, must be avoided at all costs, lest the dole come to the United States.

The supporters of the bill saw the measure in a very different light. They came from various corners of the corporatist structure. From labor, community organizations, municipal leaders, and academia, vocal support for S3060 was immediate and clear. It came, for example, from Paul Kellog, editor of the *Survey*, from United Jewish Aid Societies, from the Central Traders and Labor Assembly of New York, from the Central Employment Bureau of the YWCA, and from such reformers as Jane Addams.

More significantly, academics involved in the reports of the Unemployment Conference of 1921 also supported the Wagner Bill. Bryce Stewart, a participant in the 1921 conference, argued that the Unemployment Conference itself was recognition of the problem as Manufacturers of California, Chicago Manufacturers Association, a national, rather than a local or state matter, and that legislation creating a national agency with the ability to coordinate all employment operations was clearly necessary at the time. Louise and Colum Gilfillon, caseworkers and researchers from the President's Research Committee on Social Trends also supported the bill. Gilfillon equated the goal of "getting the idle man [quickly and cheaply] to the best vacant job" to sending a letter. A national monopoly was crucial because of just how "numerous, small local and unreliable private employment exchanges" had become.[24]

Mary Van Kleek of the Russell Sage Foundation, who early in the twenties supported Hoover's efforts, broke with Hoover in an article in the *Survey*.

Van Kleek offered several arguments for the passage of the Wagner Bill. First, the achievements Hoover attributed to USES and the Veterans' Service and Farm Labor Board were really the work of state employment agencies which the Wagner Bill was designed not to kill, but to enhance. And yet only twenty-four states already had such employment agencies. Van Kleek also disputed Hoover's argument that the measure would take several months to become operational. Section 10 of the Bill provided for a seamless transition to the new format. The heart of Van Kleek's argument was that the very structure of the Wagner bill had been advocated for years in several different arenas. As early as 1914, the American Association for Labor Legislation offered the idea and, more significantly, the recommendation of the Unemployment Conference of 1921 was consistent with it. The Public Works Committee of the President's Unemployment Conference had argued that states should operate employment agencies with the support of the federal government, though not that the national government should operate the agencies. Later, the Committee on Business Cycles gave "hearty approval" to a national system of employment bureaus. In Senate hearings in 1929, several recommended that "USES should be reorganized." It had only twenty-four state agencies; and none of the agencies coordinated with each other because no definite procedures for doing so were ever established. Rising unemployment had created "an unprecedented need for the most effective possible machinery for dealing with the task of finding employment." Hoover's veto was a serious blow to recovery and a clear signal that his idea of cooperative government action had grown more conservative over the decade. It led to the defection of many of his supporters, who favored a more active federal role than Hoover could allow.[25]

The most drastic sign of this split was Woods' abandonment of PECE. Woods strongly supported strict local autonomy in 1921 and organized the Emergency Measures Committee of the conference. However, during his years with PECE, he shifted to a much more statist position, as several of the measures he advocated clearly show. Woods recommended over $3 billion in new appropriations for highway construction, reforestation, and other projects. The administration rejected the highway appropriations, which Woods thought might employ approximately 340,000, as too expensive. The administration also rejected the reforestation because it feared the political risks of acknowledging how far the Department of Agriculture had fallen behind in conservation. The last straw for Woods was the Wagner Bill, which he saw as essential for coordinating unemployment relief. At loggerheads with Hoover, Woods quietly stepped down from the chairmanship, departing for Europe to study conditions and leaving Fred Croxton to take over. He reported to Hoover from Europe that he still opposed the dole, but did approve of loans to the states for employment agencies the activities of which might be coordinated by a non-political commission, and so, by implication, of the Wagner Bill. With Woods gone and Croxton in charge, PECE lost steam; it was replaced in 1931 by the President's Organization on Unemployment Relief, another attempt by Hoover to reassert his voluntarist vision.[26]

In an attempt to derail the Wagner Bill, Hoover's new Secretary of Labor, William Doak, who succeeded the newly elected senator, James Davis, offered a substitute. Interestingly, Doak, a former vice president of the American Association of Labor Legislation, had supported S3060 before his appointment. The House of Representatives overwhelmingly voted to block the substitute and the Wagner measure passed on to face Hoover's pocket veto.

In the spring after the veto of the Wagner Bill, the administration unilaterally reformed USES. The service would now open "at least one employment bureau in each of the states [to cooperate with State and local authorities]." The Farm/Labor Service and the Veterans' Placement Service would both be expanded and the "industrial activities of the Untied States Employment Service will be reorganized." Superintendents coordinated the efforts of several divisions, including the building and needle trades, mining, and transportation, all of which fell under the leadership of John Alpine as supervising director. Wagner claimed the reorganization was the theft of his ideas and in fact it mimicked his Bill. It appears, then, that Hoover had vetoed the bill, even at the cost of Woods, rather from budgetary and political motives than anything else. The Hoover-reformed USES operated on a budget less than half that Wagner proposed and, importantly, Hoover was limiting subsidies to the states while appearing to strengthen local control and coordination.[27]

In August of 1931, Hoover made his last determined effort to defeat continued calls for direct federal relief to the unemployed—the dole. "Proper assistance to the deserving" had to be maintained, and therefore a new association more attuned to Hoover's vision—more loyal, and better able to assist Hoover in regaining the upper hand in the public discussion of relief—needed to assert again the moral as well as fiscal legitimacy of voluntarist action. This new organization, the President's Organization for Unemployment Relief, was dominated by business leaders who realized that if such relief measures as increased unemployment compensation were instituted, the increased taxation would fall to them. The head of the organization was one of the most aggressive business leaders of the time, Walter Gifford, President of American Telephone & Telegraph. Supporting Gifford was a who's who of American business: among them Owen D. Young of General Electric, Walter Teage of Standard Oil and Pierre DuPont.[28]

Gifford, who clearly believed in Hoover's voluntarist vision, appointed Owen Young to coordinate yet another national relief campaign to raise money for local organizations. Such leaders as these, it was hoped, could sway more of the wealthy to give and more business owners to reintensify efforts at keeping as many men employed as possible. To preserve continuity, Gifford continued to use the agencies and foundations cooperating with PECE, but his clear focus was fundraising. He reorganized the committees according to their importance: fundraising, employment plans, and administration of relief (all headed by Fred Croxton), cooperation with national groups, and public works. Backed by organizations such as the National Association of Manufacturers, who had consistently fought against any increased federal spending for relief, Gifford attempted to use POUR to promote voluntarism and resist growing favor of increased government intervention. Soon after forming the new organization, Gifford appeared before the Senate Committee on Manufacturers, who were investigating unemployment. Strong advocates of increased intervention, such as La Follette, grilled Gifford on the administration's preparations for relief in the coming winter. Gifford assured the committee that voluntarist efforts, especially private groups, were on the rise, and that the nation could survive the winter without "government excess." Along with Silas Strong of the U.S. Chamber of Commerce, Gifford objected to federal relief for the jobless, but the burden of proof appeared to have shifted away from the statists and toward Gifford. The situation continued to shift as the winter of 1931 approached and more municipal agencies and even state governments were finding it difficult to fund relief. POUR therefore needed to provide more than optimistic rhetoric; it needed sufficient data to prevent the Congress from going even further than the Wagner Bill in the area of relief. For Hoover and the voluntarist vision, POUR stood as the last defense against the shift in the national conversation over the responsibility of the state toward the poor and the unemployed.[29]

Hoover's supporters, however, continued to rely on the argument that unemployment was not as serious as most critics had asserted and that relief should be "dealt with locally through some local agency," as Eliot Wadsworth claimed in October 1931. Because unemployment remained essentially a local matter, POUR did not embark on a national drive for relief with a central clearing agency to distribute funds to areas in need, but rather continued to rely on local drives for specific communities. And much of the earlier voluntarist rhetoric remained unchanged. Spreading work or making work remained central, as well as the assertion, over a year into the depression, that the situation was "a temporary emergency which is testing the fundamental American policy of freedom of action and self-reliance." One of the early reports of POUR simply restated the solutions offered at the Unemployment Conference of 1921: resumption of normal buying, expansion of credit, special work, increased public works, and focused community surveys.[30]

POUR's report on public works and care of the homeless reflects the now stale philosophy of voluntarism and Hoover's and POUR's lack of initiative. The report makes much of the fact that the 10-year project of public works begun in 1926 was cut by three years because of increased appropriations in 1929 and 1930. However, it does not support recommendations for increased appropriations for projects other than those scheduled in 1926, because such appropriations could have no effect on unemployment for the winter of 1931 or the spring of 1932. The committee also discouraged appropriations for projects that were recommended but not authorized, since such appropriations could "not meet in any appreciable degree present unemployment conditions." Long-range planning for public works through the Federal Employment Stabilization Board was clearly necessary, but there was still no a formal strategy for such planning. Apparently, as far as POUR was concerned, the over $300 million in appropriations through 1930 was all that should be spent on public works.[31]

The committee clearly opposed federal money for municipal and/or state projects. Despite diminishing state revenues and increasing demand on states to care for the poor, the committee concluded that "such appropriations would mark a departure from the policy that such works are the obligation of the localities." The committee, like Hoover, feared that federal assumption of state or local works projects would lead directly to boundless spending and more importantly "would weaken the sense of responsibility of the municipalities and states to provide for their local needs and welfare."[32]

Much the same tone characterized POUR's report on the homeless. Lenton Swift, Executive Secretary of the Family Welfare Association of America, reported that the numbers of homeless in American cities now represented "an army of thousands [new recruits] to poverty." But under the voluntarist scheme, dollars to assist the homeless were scarcer than ever, and, more importantly from a conceptual point of view, the idea of total reliance on self-help and local resources placed those administering to the population in what Swift called the difficult position of having to find a middle ground between "harshness and sentimentality; between niggardliness and over-generosity; between exploiting the homeless or being exploited by them." Above all, the committee felt that any measure dealing with the homeless must not destroy their self-respect as did those scourges of degradation Hoover abhorred so much, the bread line, the soup kitchen, and public handouts, all of which were exploding in numbers in the winter of 1931. Instead it preached self-reliance and local, centralized administration, measures that had not worked for two years. The report called for increased local funds to care for the homeless and also more scrutiny in differentiating the able-bodied poor from the "chronically homeless [flophouse] type." Once again, the emphasis was on efficiency rather than relief. Centralized agencies would refer different "classes" of homeless men to different agencies. Thus newly homeless "white collar man" would be sent to agencies where work was given in exchange for services, while the chronically impoverished man would be sent to professionally trained social workers. The report urged that the police be encouraged to crack down on begging and panhandling, and to establish procedures to handle the transient. Meanwhile, in cities like Milwaukee and Chicago, efforts to ship transients back to their home communities resulted in mass confusion as ever greater numbers of migrants looking for work flooded the cities. The situation was only worsening, yet in both public works and in policy regarding the homeless the administration refused to abandon its moralistic assumptions about personal responsibility and the proper role of government. In consequence, the public began to see Hoover as paralyzed by the crisis, and the forces contesting Hoover's vision pushed even harder for increased relief. These efforts were centered in the Congress, where more relief bills came to the floor. It was clear by February 1931 that Hoover and his vision were facing failure. In August, Congress refused to continue funding POUR, signaling the end of the voluntarist version of relief. Hastening this development was the battle for unemployment compensation and the continued legislative efforts in Congress that opened the presidential election cycle for 1932.[33]

The tide in Congress shifted permanently toward the advocates of federal relief during debates on the Emergency Construction Bill of 1932. Although the measure itself did not stray far from accepted notions of public works, these debates helped define the meaning of relief and the role of the state in providing it. The bill, a compromise offered by Wagner, dealt a final blow to Hoover's original ideas of voluntarism, but the debate which led to the act was most vociferous in reaction to the bill it replaced, the LaFollette-Costigan Bill. This bill called for public works paid for by the federal government and made available to the states through grants, and for additional monies for unemployment relief. Discussion of it revolved around the word "dole" and the proper role of the government in relief. Opponents charged that outright government relief constituted a social evil which, as James Emery of the National Association of Manufacturers argued, impaired states rights and individual initiative. William Green of the AFL, however, strongly urged Hoover not only to pass this measure, but also to institute a mandatory 5-day week. For Green and several social activists and relief workers as well as a growing number of state officials, the time for more direct intervention had come. Hoover refused to back the proposal, however, because he would not support any measure in which the federal government gave grants to the states. He did suggest he might support a modified bill which allowed money to the states in the form of loans, on condition that the states requesting the money could show that there was no other way they could raise the money they needed. The two sides reached a compromise and the bill passed. Even though the final bill called for loans, it clearly marked the "entrance of the federal government into the field of relief." Meanwhile others called for expanded welfare-state initiatives in other areas. While these struggles for relief took place, Hoover's efforts shifted from POUR to the Reconstruction Finance Corporation organized in 1932. This corporation clearly suited Hoover's voluntarist ideas: it injected the state into the position, not of regulator, but financier for business. As William Bock commented, "it is relief but for the wealthy and the bankers." The RFC attempted to stimulate businesses through a variety of measures designed to evade the swirling rhetoric of the dole and maintain the private sector as the prime mover toward recovery. A short discussion of its organization will show how different was Hoover's philosophy from those who advocated the Emergency Construction and Relief Act, and other more statist measures now arising in the states, most importantly unemployment compensation.[34]

Hoover first unveiled his program for a financial mechanism in October 1931. While still clinging to the notion that the depression had European causes and that Americans regarded it with "foolish alarm," he urged a cooperative effort between banking and the government to restore confidence to depositors and ease the credit crunch. He called for bankers to form a voluntary consortium with $500 million "to assure our banks may attain liquidity in case of necessity and thereby enable them to continue their business without the restriction of credit." In addition, he asked the Federal Reserve to make advances on the securities of banks already closed to eliminate the deflation that kept the business cycle from moving toward recovery. Last, he proposed the RFC operate "with available funds sufficient for any legitimate call in support of credit." The key to the effort, Hoover argued, was to create financial stability while "stimulating private initiatives and local and community responsibility." In other words, Hoover's philosophy led him to create relief for large institutions that might stimulate recovery from the top down: the RFC inserted the state in the economy not as regulator, but bail bondsman. Nevertheless, with proper funding, Hoover saw the RFC as "the final campaign against the depression."[35]

The RFC was officially approved in January 1932 with Eugene Meyer, Governor of the Federal Reserve Board who earlier headed the War Finance Corporation, as Chairman and Charles Davies, former Vice President under Coolidge and a prominent Chicago banker, as President. The banking community applauded the action and Hoover confidently asserted that the loans made by the RFC would cushion any further shocks to the system, thus enhancing "credit, banking and railway structure, in order to permit business and industry to carry on normal activities." By March, the RFC had made $183 million in loans, the majority to banks and trust companies, and lesser amounts to railroads and agriculture. Hoover assumed that he had sufficiently dealt with the financial crisis and that the continuing authorization of the RFC would allow bankers to remain solvent. The reality was that the loans by the RFC were not enough to rescue the banking system. Hoover quickly moved to expand the work of the RFC in areas of relief and public works.[36]

For Hoover, the RFC was preferable to "massive" public works projects. He cited as an example loans to the Pennsylvania Railroad of $27 million as part of an arrangement to assist the railroad in electrifying several of its lines. Reports to Hoover stated that the railroad would employ 28,000 men. Some of the money was a loan in exchange for securities; the loans cost the government nothing. By contrast, Hoover opposed public works projects based on grants for highway construction, since they added to the nation's debt, imposed "a tax on the people" and employed only 55,000. For Hoover, the former method was clearly more prudent. In addition, the RFC would finance public works that produced more in tolls, etc. In other words, works subsidized by the working poor in regressive taxes should be used to employ the jobless—in direct contrast to proposals such as the Garner Bill, which called for millions in public works through government bonds which would make "balancing the budget responsible." The RFC also made loans in the area of relief: Hoover proposed the RFC to underwrite state bonds or make direct loans to states to a total amount of no more than $300 million for the entire nation.

The RFC was more than an extension of voluntarism, however. As an officially appropriated lender to the private sector, it had much broader powers than the War Finance Corporation, and because of its specific mission the RFC moved the state much closer to the center of the economy. This raised concerns from the left and right. For those on the right, the broad powers of the RFC looked like centralized banking or "state capitalism." The RFC was not an anti-statist enterprise; on the contrary, it was more statist than any other measure instituted before the New Deal programs. For Hoover it provided the last hope of preventing the state from entering into full relief. Hoover saw the RFC as an extension of voluntarism, which increased its range of meaning in relation to the state and unemployment specifically, and the market more generally. The RFC also faced a strong critique from the left because of the way it operated. Its loans seemed to many a "top down" solution to the depression. Hoover may not have cared, so long as the loans eventually put people to work, but to people like Norman Thomas of the League for Industrial Democracy, such loans were reprehensible. Thomas scolded Hoover for not giving any reassurance or real relief to the unemployed or enough money to the states. In the area of public works, Thomas observed that money loaned by the RFC, in essence, "has not employed anybody."

Against both sides, Hoover defended the RFC as an institution that in fact would employ many over time without destructive state interference: "We must avoid burdens upon the government which will create more unemployment in the private industry than can be gained by further expansion of employment by the Federal Government." Hoover clearly implies that there is a limit to how far he will go in public works, and steadfastly clings to his "no dole" position. The real solution is the RFC, even if it involves the government in private affairs.

State governments began to fill the gap in aid left by the administration's stubborn adherence to voluntarism. Their efforts took the form of another initiative Hoover had rejected at the federal level, unemployment insurance.[37] Two days after Hoover signed the RFC into law, Franklin Roosevelt, Governor of New York, called the Albany conference to discuss state action to mitigate the depression. Representatives from seven states attended, and one of the centerpieces of the conference was unemployment insurance. The majority of states politicians and academicians at the conference favored the idea, including representatives from New York, Ohio, Connecticut, Pennsylvania, Massachusetts, Rhode Island and New Jersey. Though these did not represent the majority of states, they did represent 32% of the nation's population and 49% of all wage earners.[38]

William Levinson of the Ohio State Unemployment Commission was one of the leading advocates of insurance. He argued that it was "nothing more than an extension of workman's compensation systems in effect in most states." Unemployment could not be completely eradicated, but the risk and lost buying power of unemployment could be diminished. If labor was as important to industry as capital, "there is no reason why the public should not support industrial workers in times of unemployment. This should justly be a charge on industry." The real "dole" for Levinson was the lack of accountability in industry for layoffs, since these workers became the responsibility of the Red Cross or other private or public relief agencies. This, in essence, amounted to "subsidizing industries."[39]

Paul Douglas agreed with Levinson's analysis and added that any unemployment insurance plan must be national and enforced through mandatory legislation. Managers, he argued, would not voluntarily support such measures: "after a decade of experimentation less than 1 percent of the nation's workers" were covered by voluntary unemployment insurance. A reserve fund on which workers could draw for a limited period of time, made up of contributions from workers, employers, and perhaps state or federal government, was in the best interest of all, because private charity could not meet workers' needs, and the continued purchasing power provided by the insurance could "check the downhill sweep of business during periods of depression."[40]

John Commons preferred over unemployment insurance a system of compensation. Commons argued that the first, best measure against unemployment crises in the future was prevention, but in the event of unemployment, some corrective measure was clearly needed. He reasoned that compensation would prove more economical and efficient than insurance, because employers, compelled to create a reserve fund for unemployment, would clearly be motivated to create "the employment spirit" just as they had created the "safe spirit." in promoting workplace safety. Insurance, on the other hand, was inefficient. Drawing a contrast with British law, Commons claimed that "it penalizes the efficient employer for the benefit of his competitor." In contrast, in his plan, "the efficient employer who gives steady employment is rewarded." The passage of such a plan appeared doubtful, but in some respects it came as close to Hoover's ideas of individual initiative as any of the unemployment insurance plans. Some states, however, including Wisconsin, already were on the way to passing these plans into law.[41]

Opposition to unemployment insurance came from various quarters, including the AFL, manufacturers, and Hoover himself. William Green, president of the AFL, argued that compulsory unemployment insurance "would fasten the dole system on American labor and industry." It added another level of paternalism above labor and, to make matters worse, the benefits received by workers "would supply them with only a minimum of sustenance." Green offered the alternative of voluntary insurance funds, but only in seasonal industries, and advocated division of work rather than the spread of part time work, and a guaranteed yearly wage. Unemployment insurance, argued Green, was just another form of charity, and the idea that workers should contribute to any reserve fund when they were at the mercy of employers was outrageous. Workers should be allowed to contribute or not as they chose. As in 1921, labor, still fighting for bread and butter issues through arbitration, did not advocate any statist solutions. This would drastically change by 1935 with the advent of the New Deal. Hoover, like Green, resisted the idea of federally legislated or funded unemployment insurance. He emphasized the potential impact of such measures on individual initiative and questioned the role of the state and the financing. In relieving individuals and private institutions of their responsibility to the public, mandatory insurance ran counter to the major premise of Hoover's thinking. It encouraged idleness rather than mitigated it and placed the federal government in the position of underwriting cash payments to the unemployed, the "dole." Of all the proposals he had heard that for the most part "amount[ed] to the dole," "the largest is unemployment insurance." The only reserve Hoover would support would be made up of voluntary contributions paid by a cooperative effort of industry and labor only.

By summer 1931, voluntarism was clearly in eclipse, but Hoover continued to stand behind it. The RFC might make loans, public works might be increased, but the strategy of federal assistance violated all the principles that formed the foundation of voluntarism.

Nonetheless, at the state level, the discussion continued.[42] The tremendous financial pressure states found themselves in led some to initiate policies that directly undermined voluntarism in favor of increased governmental action. A growing number of states instituted unemployment insurance. This led in late 1932 and early 1933 to a violent turn in public opinion and policy that ended the Hover era and ushered in the more mature welfare state of late 20th century America.

The election of 1932, then, was as much about voluntarism as any other issue. The campaign pitted the clearly more statist FDR against a more broad-minded, but still voluntarist, Hoover. Hoover clearly saw the election as a referendum on his depression policies and his vision of an anti-statist, corporatist associationalism that could lead the country into recovery. He was aware he faced an uphill battle against the charismatic FDR, but his faith in his actions and the office he held, he hoped, would help him win. He drew a sharp line during the election between his views and policies and his opponent's, in a final effort to sway public opinion back to his side. The election, as Hoover saw it, was a "contest between two philosophies" in which the very essence of virtue, individualism and associationalism was under attack by the dangerous forces who wanted statist, regulatory, interventionist government.[43]

Beneath the extreme rhetoric and demonization typical of any campaign, Hoover was clearly concerned with the philosophical issues. From 1921 forward, Hoover remained true to his anti-statist vision of self-government and the virtuous state as "the fundamental principles of an economic and social system." Those principles created "ordered freedom," the test of which was the maintenance of equality ofopportunity through a cooperative effort of private institutions and individuals, in which the state played the role or coordinator, or instituted mild counter-cyclical corrections. Most importantly, the state "must secure cooperative action which guilds initiative and strength outside of government." This ideal shaped the policies of the Hoover administration.[44]

The efforts of PECE and POUR, according to Hoover, showed the effectiveness of cooperative efforts by "carrying a victorious battle" through the winters of 1930 and 1931. Although in fact these efforts fell short, Hoover's vision permitted no other action. His own recognition of the RFC's role in relief reflects his thinking. Hoover was not al all happy with the RFC's loans to state governments, which he feared could "be made a pork barrel operation rather than [relief] based on need." But the policies advocated by Roosevelt stood dangerously on the brink of "European socialism." This, clearly, was too vitriolic, but Hoover saw in Roosevelt a threat to "ordered freedom."

In defending his vision, Hoover moved in several directions. He repeatedly claimed that the depression originated not in America but in Europe, and that therefore, though it was something America had to see its way through, it did not suggest any fundamental flaw in the American capitalist system. Such arguments, however, had finally lost their impact with both the right and the left. On the left, democratic statists had finally taken the initiative with the Emergency Construction and Relief Act, which proved that legislatively Hoover's conception of virtue and liberty as formulated in 1921 was dead. On the right, large businessmen and even the NCF abandoned Hoover. Gerard Swope, President of General Electric, advocated compulsory economic planning through trade associations, but with federal supervision, a form of cartelism which left labor and capital free to control production and agree to price controls. This plan also placed the state more centrally in the market, as a regulator of a cartel economy that also stifled Hooverian individualism. Thus, with no constituency, facing a groundswell of hostility from veterans, and the desertion of municipal leaders from the left and right, Hoover and his vision suffered the crushing defeat of November 1932.[45]

The Hoover presidency, and his years as Secretary of Commerce, stood then as the beginning of a transition to a mature welfare state and a statist liberalism that continues into the late twentieth century. Moreover, study of the decade reveals not only a transition from an anti-statist to a democratic-statist policy, but Hoover's particular philosophy of the public sphere and critical debate. It is to this area we turn next.

Notes

1 Hoover Public Statement 127, HHP.

2 Wilson, *Forgotten Progressive*, 128.

3artin Egan to Lamont, Oct 23, 1929 PPF Box 168, HHP.

4 Davis to Hoover November 12, 1929 Presidential Papers Box 337, HHP. Hoover to Barnes December 7, 1929 Presidential Papers Box 337, HHP.

5 Schwarz, *The New Dealers*, 32-59. Hoover address to business leaders at U.S. Camber of Commerce, December 5, 1929, P.S. 1178, HHP. William Trufant Foster and Waddell Catchings, "Hoover Verses the Economics of Despair," in Review of Reviews, January 1930.

6 Preliminary Report of the Committee on Economic Stabilization, President's Committee on Recent Economic Changes, Presidential Papers Box 327, HHP. Memorandum of Committee Assignments in the Field of Community Organization and Relief, n.d.Presidential Papers Box 330, HHP.

7 Hoover to J.H. Case, October 18, 1930 PPF Box 18, HHP. Report of Russell Sage Foundation, June 1930, Presidential Papers Box 348, HHP. "What President Hoover Has Done in Relief of Unemployment During the Depression from November 1930 to September, 1931." n.d. Presidential Papers, Box 336.

8 "Preliminary Report of President's Emergency Committee for Employment" n.d. PECE Papers, RG 73, National Archives, Washington, D.C.

9 The transcripts of several of the radio addresses are included in, "Unemployment: Industry Seeks a Solution." PECE (UGPO: 1931) address by Cyrus McCormick December 20, 1930; Cohen, *Making A New Deal,* 175. Shatz

10 Ibid. 32-41.

11 Hoover speech September 8, 1931. Presidential Papers box 345, HHP. *Public Papers of the Presidents* 1931, 298.

12 "Government Expenditures on Public Works." December 23, 1930, Box 335 HHP. Hoover, PS 1447, HHP. Arthur Woods, Press Release December 13, 1930, Presidential Papers Box 343, HHP.

13 Ibid.

14 Hoover to H.D. Gibson, Chairman Emergency Unemployment Relief Committee of New York, October 6, 1932, Box 1130, HHP.

15 Memorandum, "Cooperative Arrangements in the General Field of Community Relief." n.d. Presidential Papers Box 336, HHP. Allen Burns, Executive Director Association of Community Chests and Councils to Hoover October 27, 1930, Presidential Papers Box 337, HHP. Hoover to Perry Davidson, President Mutual Employment Agencies, September 1, 1931, Presidential Papers Box 335, HHP.

16 Report of Russell Sage Foundation, June 1930, Presidential Papers Box 348, HHP. Woods radio address December 9, 1930, Presidential Papers Box 346, HHP.

17 Press release November 7, 1930, Presidential Papers Box 342, HHP. Community Chest fundraising efforts were up 6.2% for 1930 over the 1929 level. Census reports indicated outdoor relief payments for 1929 at $9.9 Million up to $18.1million for 1930. Census Report August 8, 1931, Croxton Papers, RG 73 series 7 Box 1100 National Archives. Hoover radio address PS 1684 October 18, 1931, HHP.

18 Report of Russell Sage Foundation, Relief Bulletin for November 1930, Presidential Papers Box 348, HHP.

19 Report of Russell Sage Foundation, Relief Bulletin, September 1930, Presidential Papers Box 348, HHP. Fred Croxton address to Association of Community Chests, June 13, 1931, Presidential Papers Box 345 HHP.

20 New York Times April 7, 1930; H.L. Lurie, "The Place of Federal Aid in Unemployment Relief," Social Science Review (Vol. V; Dec 1931) 523-38. S3060 71st Congress 2nd Session; Rexford Tugwell, *Mr. Hoover's Economic Policy* (New York: John Day Co., 1932) 15-30. Mary Van Kleek, "Toward a National Employment Service" *Survey* April 15, 1931. Schwarz, *Interregnum of Despair,* 23-45. See also, Otto Mallory to Croxton, March 24, 1931, RG 73 Series 7 National Archives for analysis of state appropriations for planning. Furner quote from Mary O. Furner "The republican Tradition and the New Liberalism" in Furner and Michael J. Lacy, *The State and Social Investigation in Britain and the United States* (New York: Cambridge University Press, 1993) 176

21 Schwarz, *New Dealers*, 33-5. New York Times, Dec. 10, 1930. *Commercial and Financial Chronicle,* February 21, 1931. Hoover Radio address, Box 345 HHP. Wagner to Hoover March 7, 1931, Presidential Papers Box 348 HHP. Hoover veto message Box 348 HHP.

22 Hoover PS 1507, March 7, 1931. Van Kleek "*Toward a National Employment Service*" E.E. Hunt to Thomas Taylor, February 13, 1930, RG 73 series 1 National Archives.

23 Hoover address Dec. 12, 1930, Presidential Papers Box 348, HHP. Ibid. Washington Star October 25, 1931. Chicago Journal of Commerce, February 24, 1931. Shelby Harrison, Russell Sage Foundation to Hoover, Feb. 24, 1931 Presidential Papers Box348, HHP. Schwarz, *Interregnum of Despair*, 27.

24 Harrison to Hoover, Feb. 24, 1931, Presidential Papers Box 348, HHP. Gilfillan to Hoover, Feb. 27, 1931, Presidential Papers Box 348, HHP. Van Kleek "*Toward a National . . .*"

25 Van Kleek, "*Toward a National . . .*"; Recommendations of the President's Conference on Unemployment, 42.

26 New York Times, Jan. 16, 1931; Washington Daily News Jan. 15, 1931; Woods to Hoover August 7, 1931, Presidential Papers Box 338, HHP; Hoover to Woods, August 11, 1931, Presidential Papers Box 338, HHP.

27 Schwarz, *Interregnum of Despair*, 38-40. "Hoover's Job Plan Under Fire." *Literary Digest*, May 9,1931.

28 Report of the Activities of the President's Organization on Unemployment Relief, Presidential Papers Box 341, HHP. New York Times August 20, September3, 1931. Washington Star October 25, 1931. Hoover announcement of Gifford as head of POUR, Presidential Papers Box 341, HHP. Hoover PS 1643, August 19, 1931, HHP.

29 Report of Activities of POUR, Radio address by Elliot Wadsworth, Chair of Committee on Cooperation with National Groups, October 11, 1931, Presidential Papers

Box 341, HHP. New York Times Nov. 13, 1931, U.S. Senate hearings, subcommittee of the Committee on Manufacturing. Hearings on S. 174 and S262, 72nd Congress 1st. Session, 308-58.

30 Walter Gifford Statement POUR, Sep. 25, 1931, Presidential Papers Box 341, HHP. Transcript of radio address by Elliot Wadsworth, Oct 11, 1931, Presidential Papers Box 342, HHP.

31 POR, Report on Public Works, Dec. 16, 1931, Croxton Papers, RG 73 Series 7, National Archives.

32 Ibid.

33 POUR, Report on Homelessness, Dec 19,1931, Croxton Papers, RG73 Series 7, National Archives.

34 New York Times, July 9, 1932. Hoover, *Memoirs,* 136-40. Edward Williams *Federal Aid for Relief, 40-50.*

35 *Public Papers of the President of the United States, Herbert Hoover, 1931* (Washington: USGPO, 1976) 433-36, 583-87. Hoover remarks to delegates of Pa. Unemployed, Jan. 7, 1932, PS1753, HHP.

36 *Public Papers of the President, Herbert Hoover, 1931-1932* (Washington: USGPO, 1977) 101-2. Jordan Schwarz, *The New Dealers: Power Politics in the Age of Roosevelt* (New York: Vintage Books, 1993) 50-1.

37 *Public Papers, 1932,33,* 211-12, 227-8, 244-6. Hoover, State of the Union Address, December 1931, PS1729, HHP. Norman Thomas to Hoover, April 23, 1932, Presidential Papers Box 340, HHP; James Olson, *Saving Capitalism: The RFC and the New Deal, 1933-1940* (Princeton: Princeton University Press, 1988) 15-20; M.C. Rorty, "How May Business Revival Be Forced?" Harvard Business Review, April 1932, 385-98.

38 New York Times, Jan. 24,1931.

39 Ibid.

40 Ibid.

41 Chicago Tribune, October 5, 1931.

42 New York Times, September 8, 1931. Irving Weinzweig, "The Unemployment Insurance Plan of the Amalgamated Clothing Workers of America" The Unemployment Review, June 25, 1931, 13-15. Michael Parrish, *Anxious Decades: America in Prosperity and Depression, 1920-1941* (New York: Norton, 1992) 281, 351-2. Hoover address to Indiana Republican Editorial Association, June 15, 1931, PS 1587, HHP. Hoover, PS 1939,HHP.

43 Parrish, *Anxious Decades,* 354-61. Hoover, PS 2031, October 31, 1932,HHP.

44 Hoover, PS 1939,HHP. See also Wilson, *Forgotten Progressive.*

45 Wilson, Forgotten *Progressive,* 151-5. Barry Karl, *The Uneasy State,* 105. Schwarz, *New Dealers*, 38-50. Hoover PS 1939, HHP. PS 1999 October 15, 1932,HHP. PS 2031, October 31,1932,HHP.

Chapter 8
Municipal Government and Voluntarism: Chicago, Milwaukee, and Detroit— The Great Depression

The Great Depression was felt most deeply at the local level, and municipal government consequently bore the brunt of providing relief during the crisis. Unemployed, homeless, and destitute people in unprecedented numbers presented a critical challenge to the mayors of Chicago, Detroit and Milwaukee. Under pressure from a national policy of voluntarism that relied primarily on municipalities for relief, would these mayors, like the national legislature, push Hoover towards greater federal aid? While a cursory glance at the Depression as a whole would suggest that they did, during the period 1929-1933, the issue was not so clear. At the national level, as we have seen, Hoover was reluctant to cross the boundary of voluntarism into the realm of direct aid. The same reluctance also occurred at the municipal level. This chapter chronicles the impact of the early Depression in these three cities, and municipal leaders' response to it and to Hoover's policies.

The first city examined here is Chicago. As the Roaring Twenties came to a close, William "Big Bill" Thompson was again mayor, reclaiming his post in 1927 by defeating William Dever, the man who had displaced him in 1924. Thompson's goal was to resurrect a political machine through which he could assert complete political authority and to re-establish the corporatist structure Dever had established, but with the addition of an ascendant labor element. Thompson placed key labor leaders in positions of authority in his administration to strengthen his political labor machine. Michael J. Kelly, president of the Wage Earners League, was made Director of Labor for the Board of Education. Edward Moore, president of the Heating Engineers, became a Deputy Commissioner of Public Works. Thompson also strove to reinforce his own authority over employers. Having put together a solid political machine, he assumed that with increasing prosperity his mayoralty would take him into national politics. The crash of '29 and the Depression, however, ultimately left him defeated.[1]

In the immediate aftermath of the crash, Mayor Thompson, like other business and civic leaders locally and nationally, still clung to the ideal of perpetual prosperity and, reflecting back on 1921, saw this depression as if anything briefer than the last. Thompson fully expected the year 1930 to "be one of prosperity," and agreed with Secretary Mellon that the crash did not pose a severe threat. He encouraged the City Planning Commission to accelerate projects for physical expansion of the city and he expected that since population and manufacturing had not slowed, any downturn would be brief.[2] As fall of 1930 approached, however, it appeared that, in fact, conditions were getting worse and that action had become necessary.

The impact of the crash was felt rather swiftly in the city government. Because of several years of deficit spending and a voucher program to float salaries, the city treasury was empty as early as 1930. When City Treasurer Charles Peterson disclosed that the city could not pay its employees, proposals were made to slash police and firemen from the city budget. According to Peterson, for the city to have any money, 1,000 employees needed to be removed from its payroll. Thompson warned, however, that he would veto any such proposals. Meanwhile unemployment, though not acute in January 1930, threatened to devastate a city already $11 million in debt. Ultimately a budget was passed preventing cuts to police and fire, but it plunged the city even deeper into debt. Lacking the resources to take on a growing number of unemployed, the city eagerly welcomed the formation of a state committee to handle the situation.[3]

Governor Emmerson appointed an unemployment commission in October 1930 with Benjamin Squires from the University of Chicago as its temporary chair. Officers appointed to the commission included Clifford Barnes, Vice Chairman of the Chicago Association of Commerce, Brittain Budd, President of Chicago Rapid Transit, John Fitzpatrick, President of the Chicago Federation of Labor, and Joel Hunter, President of United Charities of Chicago. The group's strategies for providing relief were solidly based on the assumptions and activities of 1921. All saw the Depression as very brief, and all agreed that unemployment was best handled by private organizations and limited public action. This was readily apparent in its first two measures. First, Budd organized a contingent to go to Washington and urge Hoover to speed up government contracts for public works. Such projects for Chicago, Budd argued, "would greatly relieve the pressures of unemployment" in the city. Second, the commission initiated a private donation drive to raise $5 million in contributions for distribution through already established charity organizations such as United Charities of Chicago.[4]

Meanwhile unemployment, particularly in the winter of 1930 through 1931, grew worse each month; a fact which ultimately led Thompson and his successor Anton Cermak to bolder measure than those proposed in 1921. In September 1930 the Census Bureau estimated unemployment in Chicago at 4.3% or approximately 145,352. The amount of relief reported by United Charities, Salvation Army and the County Bureau of Welfare was $234,334. In a year, these numbers rose dramatically. In September 1931, an estimated

$859,264 in relief was spent on an estimated 250,000 unemployed in Chicago, a number which rose to 350,000 by the end of 1931. Soup kitchens and bread lines expanded all over the city and "Hoovervilles" became commonplace sights as families lost their homes.[5]

Private employers expanded their own relief efforts throughout the year. As in 1921, they sought "to keep men off charity," and they used many of the strategies they had used then. U.S. Steel, for example, refused to allow its employees to seek aid from private or public agencies. While it had to limit its employees' hours, U.S. Steel provided them food and rent assistance and, in limited cases, cash loans. Other employers set up in-house employment bureaus for laid-off employees. Throughout 1930, corporate welfare plans remained the dominant source of relief. County and city agencies targeted their relatively small efforts at the most destitute families. In the fall of 1930, and the laying off of more and more men brought on more aggressive tactics, such as the Governor's Commission. Yet public and private efforts were related. The Governor's Commission, for example, was run by the employers as a way to distribute relief through mechanisms they might control.[6]

The first and primary goal of the Governor's Commission was raising private funds to be distributed through local relief agencies. The Commission hoped to raise $5 million to "feed, clothe, and shelter the victims of unemployment." In addition, it tried to "pressure government agencies and private capitalists to stimulate construction [set a policy of shorter hours] and raise community chests." To get an accurate picture of the unemployment situation, the Commission asked the Chicago Association of Commerce to take a census of the unemployed in the Cook County area. Various corporate leaders, such as Samuel Insull, strongly encouraged employees to make voluntary contributions to the Commission; in fact, he required his employees to donate one day's pay per month toward relief. Insull's vast utility companies with their several thousand employees contributed over $100,000 to the fund-raising effort. Other large employers, such as U.S. Steel, Northern Trust Bank, and Armor Swift, also set up employee-contribution plans. The $5 million goal was reached by February 1931, but by that time it was clear that this could not meet the needs of the city.[7]

As fund-raising continued, the number of unemployed, as we noted above, grew rapidly. Two measures were undertaken by the Commission to bring immediate employment to some and aid to others. To increase the effectiveness of the Illinois Free Employment Bureau, the Commission undertook a massive drive to register the unemployed. It opened several registration sites, and employers with openings, or private citizens with odd jobs around their homes, were encouraged to bring them in. Over 1,000 applied per day, for an average of only 50 to 100 jobs, most day labor. The program, as in 1921, was supposed to allow large numbers of people to find some earning method, but unemployment was much worse, and many homeowners, mostly white collar employees, did not respond as they did in 1921 because the Depression threatened them as well: they hoarded their cash instead of spending it on home improvement projects.[8]

Those who did find employment were chosen by a ranking system devised by the Illinois Manufacturing Association. Married men with families were given highest priority, single men or women lowest. As in 1921, one qualifying attribute was the residence of the job seeker. Residents of Chicago were given a higher priority than residents of the surrounding suburbs, and those coming from out of state were routinely turned away.[9]

The second strategy, one absolutely opposed by both Thompson and Hoover in 1921, was to increase food kitchens and emergency shelters. Hoover routinely discouraged soup kitchens as unnecessary and morally appalling. Yet in Chicago, as elsewhere, they became necessary when voluntarist approaches failed to work. The tremendous pressure of unemployment led the Secretary of War, Hurley, to allow the city to use Army equipment to care for the jobless. Army posts released to the Commission blankets, cots, and mobile kitchens for the feeding and shelter of the destitute in converted Army barracks. By the end of the 1931, it was clear that the Commission's voluntarist reliance on private funds and the Free Employment Bureau was ill judged. Nonetheless, adhering to its belief in "noblesse oblige," the Commission still hesitated to advocate direct aid from the state or the federal government, which it still identified with the socialist "dole." At no time did the Governor's Commission advocate the passage of the Wagner Bill or endorse the statist solutions offered in Congress during the Hoover presidency.

A Committee on Unemployment, initiated by Mayor Thompson, in some ways paralleled the Governor's Commission, but in other very marked ways, the mayor and his committee deviated from the voluntarist model.[10] At first the efforts of the city council were very limited. Following a special session of the council in October 1930, a five-member committee formed to address the situation. The primary focus of this committee, led by Alderman Albert Horan (29th), was public works and pressuring companies, primarily railroads, to provide work through upgrading facilities. Horan threatened the Pennsylvania Railroad with sanctions, for example, if it did not begin a $14 million project to upgrade elevated tracks. Horan estimated that this alone would provide 2,500 jobs. Other projects included a bond sale for various work around the city. The South Park District planned an $800,000 upgrade to Soldiers Field. The City Council approved a $28 million bond issue for the November 7th election. This passed, but even planned projects did not have start dates earlier than January.

In the meantime, the city sought also to expedite the issuing of building permits. In the first 11 months of 1930, 2,343 permits representing $87 million of construction contracts were approved by the city, sharply down from the 5,946 representing $195 million in the first 11 months of 1929. The Council was influenced by the argument of E.M. Craig, President of the Building Construction Employers Association, that employers in the industry were reluctant to lower wages any further and "because of the current low prices of this time of materials, an increased letting of permits would be a shot in the arm for the local economy." Permits rebounded through 1931, but only by 200, because of a lack of private capital for new projects.

In addition to these measures, Mayor Thompson, in his usual flamboyant way, launched several others, and various attacks against some of the private methods of providing relief. As in 1921, Thompson, always looking to improve his political position locally and nationally, advocated Federal relief and municipally-controlled corporatist activity. One of his favorite targets was the *Chicago Tribune* and its "Good Fellows" program. The paper, in cooperation with the Governor's Commission and the Free Employment Bureau, took in applications from the unemployed and attempted to match them with jobs provided by the Bureau, and also encouraged private giving funneled to United Charities. Thompson viewed this as an effort to get "public spirited citizens to send cash to the *Tribune* so that they might create soup houses for those for whom they are making it impossible to find jobs." The Good Fellows program, argued Thompson, promoted the "aggrandizement of the *Tribune*" rather than the welfare of the poor. In fact, the daily feel-good stories gave the impression that anyone could find work through Good Fellows; and though the program did raise several hundred thousand dollars, it averaged a placement rate of only 10 jobs per week.

Though hostile to this approach, Thompson did support other voluntarist efforts.[11] His first proposal was creating a "municipal wood pile," a surplus of wood for heating. This and other small projects, such as park cleaning, were developed so that "in exchange for a day's labor, homeless men are given food and a night's lodging." Thompson's most substantive and heavily promoted plan, and also his most controversial, was intended to stimulate buying in the city. He argued that though the crisis was worsening, there was still a substantial number of employed people, most of whom, having lost in the stock market, or fearing a lay-off, consumed less. Thompson wanted to stimulate consumption to create jobs, in accordance with the classical models espoused by Hoover and others during the entire decade of the 1920s. His plan was quite novel. He advocated that patrons at stores be given coupons awarding daily/weekly cash prizes. This idea, although commonplace in the 1990s, was then attacked on all sides at the time. The Chicago Association denounced it as "irresponsible and reckless given most people's situation." The Chicago Federation of Labor claimed it encouraged people to spend money they may not have and to buy on installment; this did not "help workers, but this plan hurts workers and will not help the economy." In fact, Thompson's idea may have had an impact in the Chicago of the late 19th century, but in the much more integrated economy of the1930s, such a local promotion was powerless given the scope of the crisis: it required infusions of capital and spending at rates the average consumers of one city could not possibly effect. Thompson relied almost entirely on public works from bonds and on the United Charities for care of the poor. Parades, woodpiles and ill-conceived strategies for consumption did nothing either to consolidate and invigorate corporatist strategies or to lead toward non-statist solutions. Thompson was impeded in part by illness, but more importantly by corruption and the powerful influence of organized crime in city politics. Thus, as the mayoral elections approached, private agencies stood almost alone against unemployment.[12]

The leading relief agency in the city, the Chicago Council of Social Agencies, steadfastly held to the idea of private relief for the poor. The member agencies employed several strategies, all of which ultimately showed that private charity alone simply did not meet the needs of an overwhelming number of the unemployed and destitute victims of a capitalist system in crisis. By January 1931, the Council had opened over 90 relief stations in the city to feed and clothe the poor. Yet even this early in the crisis, agencies were simply overwhelmed. United Charities, providing shelter and food to roughly 200 destitute families per day, began simply to send families away, recommending they seek assistance from the Good Fellows program and leaving hundreds with no aid at all. The Council, however, measured their success not by numbers assisted, but by private funds raised in comparison with earlier years. W.B. Reynolds, Director of the Council, argued in February 1931 that the raising of $10 million proved that private charity could shoulder the burden. Reynolds argued that "no one is starving in Chicago and we feel the public will continue to respond to the appeals for aid to the destitute, Chicago will take care of its own emergency." Reynolds was in complete agreement with Hoover that federal aid through direct appropriations was an "unwarranted invasion" of the field of relief. Further, Reynolds thought unwise any relief beyond already planned public works. The thought "smacked of the failed policies of Europe and will crush the initiative of our citizens." Reynolds applauded Hoover's stand against the Wagner Bill and other calls in the Congress for expanded federal action.

By 1932, however, the situation had forced Reynolds to modify his views. By fall of that year, the numbers of the homeless and destitute, of the unemployed and underfed, had so increased in Chicago as to prove beyond all doubt that the city's and even the state's corporatist voluntarist strategies just were not working. There was no recovery, and the levels of giving fell so far below what was necessary that the private charities themselves called for a new, statist approach. Insisting still on their own ability to administer relief, they suggested that they distribute direct government aid to the poor. Reynolds himself commented in November 1932 that Roosevelt's relief plans in New York were clearly a better alternative, if executed on a national scale, than to continue "to try to give relief when the city and the state are near bankruptcy and unemployment continues to worsen." Reynold's shifting views reflected the changes in conceptions of relief that led to the elections of both Anton Cermak and FDR. Allegiance to voluntarism in Chicago to the exclusion of increased federal involvement was near an end.[13]

Anton Cermak's election as mayor meant not only the end of Thompsonism, but also the beginning in Chicago of statist economic solutions, particularly in relief. As President of the County Board, Cermak had argued for a tax of $1 a day or 1% of county employees salaries to be used specifically for relief distributed by the county. In this mayoral election race, Cermak urged on several occasions not only further study and surveys of the unemployed, but also new approaches beyond reliance on municipal funds and private charity: "the situation requires not only a city government free of corruption, the state and federal governments must also assist" Cermak won convincingly, and he made managing the Depression his top priority.[14]

Upon taking office, Cermak attempted to mobilize the corporate public, primarily the banking and business communities, to help the city, then teetering on bankruptcy, pay employees and continue municipal relief. He also tried to organize two other essential publics in the city, labor and relief agencies, which he needed to help him mount a public relations campaign to ease tensions as demonstrations increased in response to the worsening Depression. Realizing that the city's voluntarist structure was in complete disarray, Cermak shifted gears early in 1932 and led demands, not only from Chicago but also from the state, for direct federal relief aid. This was a significant shift away from voluntarism toward statism. The weight of the Depression left no alternatives and, as we shall see, even those most hostile to "the dole" and statism were silenced.[15]

Several factors influenced Cermak's decision to call for direct federal aid. First was the ever-worsening condition of the city's finances. The primary problem facing Cermak was over $600,000,000 in unpaid taxes. Only 60% of taxes levied in 1929 were paid and only 50% in 1930. In addition to Depression conditions, which forced some to choose between paying taxes and buying necessities, real estate owners, arguing that property taxes were unfairly high, refused to pay.[16]

The Thompson administration had responded by paying banks and corporations with a type of scrip, similar to a bond, to be repaid by collection of taxes. By the time Cermak took office, these bonds had lost most of their value. The city had fallen behind on payment on this scrip of over $10 million in interest. The city services the scrip had financed were in danger of ceasing altogether. Thus one of Cermak's first public announcements was that the city of Chicago "cannot meet obligations [we have no cash] the city is broke."[17]

Cermak made appeals to the state legislature as well as the financial community to which he was so well connected for funds to keep Chicago functioning. He knew that the city's financial straits made organizing and influencing the banking and financial community his most urgent priority. He approached this part of the corporatist structure through direct personal negotiation and through the Citizens' Committee on Public Expenditures. This group, perhaps the most powerful association of financiers in Chicago, was led by William Sargent, Chairman of Northwestern Railroad and included the presidents of several large banks in the city, including LaSalle and National, as well as railroad and manufacturing executives. Since the city was at their mercy, however, they demanded tax reforms, few of which the mayor could pass, and anyway the money available from these financiers was not nearly enough to run a city. Cermak tried to appease them, but soon shifted his efforts to Springfield, the state capital, where he would have to come with proposals to save the city before a Republican legislature that thrived on Chicago/downstate rivalry.[18]

Cermak's initial efforts to appeal directly to Governor Emmerson were not completely futile. The Governor offered little emergency aid, since he was also under increasing financial pressure for relief funds from every community in the state. But he saw that the Chicago's tax policy required review, and that the state needed new approaches to raising revenue as well. He appointed a panel to recommend strategies for tax policy that he might take to the legislature. Cermak initially suggested expanding the powers of the city in licensing and enforcement of the existing tax structure in Cook County. The Governor's Tax Conference, however, rejected this suggestion, arguing that Chicago tax policy required revision, not enforcement. The proposal accepted by the Committee and taken to the legislature called for a state income tax to assist the state in providing relief, public works, and education. In addition, the Tax Conference recommended taxes on tobacco and, for Cook County, a new tax administration. Although Cermak opposed the income tax, the plan enjoyed the support of the leaders on both sides in the legislature, of the governor, and of the major Chicago dailies. The tax passed with ease and was then challenged in the courts. Though it made a provision for the future, it didn't provide immediate relief, for which Cermak continued to press the legislature. Unfortunately for Cermak and the distressed in Chicago, no significant relief funds were passed; the legislature ended its session and Cermak was left with no source of relief funds except Washington.[19]

Cermak turned to the federal government not from any carefully formed political economic philosophy, but from fiscal desperation. The city's first foreign-born mayor, he was not one to seek assistance. He believed in self-reliance and the primacy of municipal control, and he was wary of dependence in any form, particularly on an institution as removed as the federal government. He was a firm believer in the primacy of market control and a minimum of government interference. As County Board President he had practiced the same corporatist, voluntarist, anti-statist rhetorical game as most of the politicians of his generation. He believed in individualism, self- help, and hard work. Only an economic catastrophe as profound as the Depression could move him to abandon voluntarism for statism. Only after all other avenues were exhausted did Cermak turn to Washington.[20]

In his first foray to the nation's capitol in May 1932, he met with several congressmen, whom he urged to agree to what he called a "prosperity loan" to the city. The purpose of this loan was to provide money for public works and construction projects which would "reestablish public confidence." As the projects progressed, people would have employment and return to depositing money in banks and, more importantly, spending money in the city, thus returning production to normal. Clearly this approach was advocated by LaFollette and others in the Congress who, by that time, were forming significant opposition to Hoover's policies, but the proposals Congress was formulating provided funds to the states, while Cermak was arguing for direct loans to municipal governments.

When no serious attention was given to Cermak's initial proposals, he asked the Reconstruction Finance Corporation for direct loans; again he was turned down. The RFC made loans to financial institutions, not municipal governments, and local bank leaders did not want such loans. Many of the banks in Chicago were so unstable they were unable to borrow, and others were not willing to accept RFC money merely so that they might lend it to a city government already badly indebted to them. Eventually, through political pressure on the Illinois delegation and persistent lobbying, Cermak did secure two loans from the RFC, but these, totaling only $6 million, were not enough to correct the city's financial position or provide significant relief through public works.[21]

Although Cermak did not come home with the money he had hoped for, he was the first big city mayor to clearly enunciate statist solutions for relief. In addition to loans, he also argued for direct federal aid in relief. After all private and municipal avenues for relief had failed, he argued there was no other solution, that "the Federal Government must provide relief to Chicago, we can't do it and our people are starving." He lobbied for direct food aid for the city in grain, for example, which might be baked by relief agencies and distributed through their swamped relief stations. As the election of 1932 grew closer, Cermak continued to push for federal aid and enthusiastically supported Roosevelt's New Deal proposals and his efforts in New York as governor. From purely pragmatic motives, Cermak was driven to seek aid from sources outside the voluntarist framework. However, his aggressive battle for federal support also indicates the completeness of the shift in his views toward statist methods. This shift in outlook was also reflected in the actions of the mayors of Detroit and Milwaukee.[22]

Shortly before and after the stock market crash of October 1929, the situation in Milwaukee resembled that in Chicago. Milwaukee like our other cities was in relatively prosperous condition in 1929. Just before the crash, Merle Thorpe, editor of *Nations Business,* addressing an audience of the Milwaukee Association of Industrial Advertisers, argued that the nation was past the time of the business cycle. Industry was so capable of meeting shifts in the market that there was "simply no time for depression." Thorpe confidently predicted the decade would not only end stronger than it began, but continue in ever-growing prosperity for another decade at least.[23]

After October 29, Milwaukee, as all of America, came face to face with a severe and prolonged depression. By spring of 1930, over 15,000 Milwaukeeans found themselves out of work and the numbers rapidly climbed to over 35,000 by November. J. Handly of the Wisconsin Federation of Labor conservatively estimated 20,000 unemployed in Milwaukee as early as March, and agencies such as the Milwaukee Family Welfare Association were already dangerously close to expending their entire budget for the year by the end of April. Hoan's early response to the crisis was to petition the President to expand public works immediately. Expecting like others that the crisis would be brief, Hoan adhered to the already established paradigms of public works and increased fund-raising by private agencies. In the area of public works, Hoan supported the Wagner Act and the National Unemployment League's proposals for a stronger commitment by the federal government not only to public works, but also to unemployment insurance.[24]

These proposals, however, came under attack by communists and by more radical socialists than Hoan. One such group, The Unemployed Council, led by the growing Communist Party in Milwaukee, attacked Hoan's slow and moderate response as of the summer of 1930. Hoan's claim that the depression was a short-term issue showed him to be "a lackey of the capitalist class." Workers facing lay-offs and wage reductions argued that the socialist mayor should be their champion, rather than a complier with the status quo, indistinguishable from a Republican or Democrat. To advance this view, the unemployed held marches through the city protesting the lack of jobs and adequate relief.[25]

The first of these took place on February 5, 1930, when a group of over 400 unemployed men marched to city hall to petition Mayor Hoan. They demanded public funds for direct cash relief to the jobless, and free food, clothing, shelter, and medical care for the poor. Hoan responded that the city lacked the funds to provide all this. Police disbursed the demonstrators, claiming that in blocking traffic they presented a safety hazard; several were arrested and jailed. The Unemployed Council organized another protest on March 6. Again, several hundred protesters marched through the city to City Hall. Unlike the first, however, this demonstration grew violent. Protesters and police clashed in front of city hall; as a result eight protesters were injured and over 30 arrested. Though Hoan had all the arrested protesters released, in the eyes of many, particularly the left, he had "sold out the workers to the greed of . . . capitalists."[26]

The Unemployed Council announced a 17-point plan to the city council in June to "expose the true nature of the capitalist government and their socialist lackeys to the working class." Among the demands of the council were guarantees of work at the 1929 wage rates for those already employed, unemployment insurance compensation equal to full wages for the unemployed, and a combination of both for those in part-time positions. Funds for the plan were to come from federal, state, and local treasuries, and from a tax on corporate profits. In addition, the council called for full housing subsidies for the unemployed and an immediate halt to all evictions in the city that resulted from unemployment. The Unemployed Council used the platform to set a standard which, if not met, gave them leverage against Hoan, with which they hoped to push him toward some type of aggressive action.[27]

Hoan's response to the council and to the crisis as it worsened into the fall of 1930 adhered to the methods used throughout the decade. In fact, during the winter of 1929 he responded mainly with patient optimism that the economy would soon turn around, and only under some pressure did he convert an unused building into a dining hall to feed the jobless. From December 1929 through

February 1930, volunteers served over 59,000 meals. Hoan consented only after ensuring that the funds for this did not compromise the budget of the Bureau of Public Welfare. Financing for the dining hall came from contributions of city employees and other private citizens.[28]

In the fall of 1930, Hoan's response began to change. In October, the city council called for an additional $200,000 for public works. Although the funds were scheduled for 1931, the council was prepared to move projects ahead if necessary. The limits of the council proposal help make clear the gradualness of Hoan's shift. One of the criteria for receiving employment on any city sponsored work project was residency. Anyone seeking employment on public works "must have resided in the city for a period of one year." Another criterion was "urgency of need" based on present income and family size. Workers registered for work through the City Services Commission, and the work was rotated among those who qualified; 500 at a time were to make $.60 per hour for three-day periods. By December, 1,500 men were registered; work had begun at the end of November. This was obviously not enough; at the end of November Hoan finally proposed a more comprehensive solution.[29]

He was motivated to act by several factors: the demonstrations of the jobless, the inadequacy of the public works efforts of both the federal and local governments, and the strapped financial condition of the city. More importantly, he with other mainstream socialists saw the deepening crisis as an opportunity to reassert the socialist agenda and thereby provide powerful support to statist solutions that ultimately would usher in a socialist state. Hoan therefore advocated unemployment insurance as a first step in this evolutionary process. He realized that "all local efforts are wholly inadequate" and that any permanent solution to relief "can be accomplished only by the . . . the Federal Government." Unlike Thompson in Chicago, Hoan very early abandoned the voluntarist ideology of the 1920s and shifted wholeheartedly towards a strong statist position. He vigorously supported a Wisconsin bill to create unemployment insurance and urged that the president introduce such legislation nationally. Both Hoover and Woods responded by encouraging municipal action and strong private charity efforts. Hoover specifically argued that the bill proposed in Madison was "a dangerous step toward the dole and which cripples individualism and equal opportunity [sic]." Hoan responded that Hoover's reluctance to confront unemployment more aggressively showed that "the policies of the present administration are clearly bankrupt and a new leadership willing to put the full resources of this nation to relief is needed now."

However, Hoan himself, though not bound to the voluntarist efforts of 1921, was slow to engage the public with a new discourse of statist action. To be sure, he now supported various statist positions besides unemployment insurance, such as reducing the retirement age from 70 to 65 locally and nationally; and reducing hours in industry nationwide. But because of the climate in Washington, Hoan found it pragmatic also to advocate more corporatist and voluntarist measures.[30] For example, He accepted the voluntarist measures recommended by the Wisconsin Citizens Committee on Unemployment, meeting in Madison. This conference, chaired by Governor Kohler and including the mayors of the state as well as industrial leaders and relief workers, recommended the establishment of local committees on unemployment organized along voluntarist lines. Its recommendations for relief closely paralleled those of the Unemployment Conference of 1921: expansion of part-time work, odd jobs in the community, public works, and registration of the unemployed and coordination through private charity organizations.

Realizing that this was not enough to provide a permanent solution, Hoan pushed for discussion of permanent reduction of hours and elimination of child labor. The conference did consider Hoan's recommendations, but Governor Kohler and the Citizens Committee refused to stipulate any definite plan of action concerning them. Hoan was furious. Writing to Don Lescohier, Executive Secretary of the committee, Hoan urged the governor to call a special session of the legislature to mandate an eight-hour day. In Milwaukee, the largest employers, such as the Allis-Chalmers Corporation, Nordberg and A.O. Smith Company, were still operating twelve-hour shifts, and showed no sign of willingness to change their policy. Hoan threatened that if Wisconsin companies did not go to the three shifts "I may have to speak in louder tones. I am told the trades union movement here is contemplating a public demand of this nature in the near future."[31]

Governor Kohler and the rest of the leadership of the committee fundamentally disagreed with Hoan's positions. Kohler, like Hoover, saw cooperative efforts through voluntarist structures as the virtuous way to solve employment and while avoiding state "authoritarianism." Although the committee worked vigorously to formulate a detailed plan, by the summer of 1931, it had produced nothing but that plan. For example, it was considering means of making public employment offices run more efficiently, while those offices, largely neglected by the jobless, were placing fewer than 15% of those who did try them. The Governor did not move on unemployment insurance, and by the time he lost the gubernatorial election to Phil LaFollette in 1930, the citizens' committee and voluntarist efforts throughout the state had largely failed. During the campaign, the views of Hoan and other progressives, who saw state-centered policies as the only solution, had clearly prevailed. As it had been by Cermak in Chicago a year earlier, the corporatist philosophy in Wisconsin was not only challenged, but defeated. Hoan supported LaFollette's bid for governor and a flurry of legislative bills passed in special session immediately after the election: an unemployment compensation bill in December 1931, the first in American history, and an Emergency Relief Act, pooling over $17 million for direct relief to the employed and public works.

In Wisconsin, as in New York, a clear change in thought was manifesting itself in policy. Hoan saw the bills passed in Wisconsin as a first step in an inevitable evolution toward socialism. The Depression magnified the "artificial prosperity which followed the war," and the numbers of destitute on the streets of Milwaukee and other cities now made it obvious that "legislation not only in

Wisconsin, but in Washington, will be the only way for relieving their burden."[32] Meanwhile, Hoan acted to put in place "whatever temporary measures are necessary." Milwaukee County tripled its relief budget and the city diverted funds into the County Bureau of Public Welfare. At the municipal level, however, Hoan continued to stress that no city government could raise enough money, or coordinate agencies to the degree necessary to combat the problem effectively.

Likewise, in Detroit, Mayor Frank Murphy ultimately abandoned the voluntarism of Couzens and Hoover in favor of statism. Detroit, a city that relied heavily on one industry, felt the pain of the stock market crash and ensuing depression more quickly and intensely than most other cities. Over 5 million vehicles rolled off assembly lines in 1929. By the end of 1931, that number was down to 1 million. Consequently, unemployment and poverty rose rapidly, and the overburdened municipal government began to look for federal aid. Mayor Charles Bowles and his successor, Frank Murphy, faced unprecedented levels of hunger, poverty, and fear. They responded quite differently, and as a result one destroyed his political career while the other established his.[33]

After the crash, levels of unemployment skyrocketed. In 1929, the automakers employed half a million men. By mid-1930 over 125,000 had lost their jobs, and over the next year they were joined by 100,000 more. Most of those who kept their jobs moved from full to part time. In addition, small businesses failed by the score as money dried up and extending credit became foolish. In 1929, only 3,500 families sought relief from the city. In January 1930, 12,500 received assistance. By 1931, over 200,000 people were completely dependent on city relief. And blue-collar workers did not suffer alone. Many of the new middle-class of supervisors and low-level managers found themselves among the ranks of the unemployed.[34]

Mayor Charles Bowles took the reigns of the city in January 1930. His first task in office concerned the city's finances. Detroit already bore a heavy debt load from bonds issued in the later 1920s for infrastructure improvements. It was difficult to meet the city payroll with what the rising welfare rolls left in the budget. Bowles argued that the city "can hold on through the present downturn" but already he was losing the confidence of voters, and soon after taking office became involved in a controversy that eventually cost him the mayoralty. He stood accused of corruption and ineptitude. He could not deal with the unemployment situation, his critics on the city council charged, because he allowed gangs and bootleggers to run their businesses without penalty, "while Detroiters starved in the streets." Eventually, a citywide referendum recalled Bowles in a special election in July.[35]

His replacement was Frank Murphy, a recorder court judge. Murphy found himself mayor of a city the government of which struggled between the extremes of the debate on state action to relieve the unemployed. On one side were the city industrialists led by Henry Ford. The depression was not the time for "Moscow inspired ideas," Ford argued; most of the unemployed were "people who refused to think and therefore refused to work diligently." Ford firmly believed that the business cycle would end the Depression and that if government interfered "people would not profit by the illness." For Ford, hard times demanded not state action, or municipal action for that matter, but faith in the business elite and the market. He represented many conservative leaders who viewed new ideas that led to greater state action as certain to "make the United States another Europe infected with the policies of socialism." Murphy sought to form a committee on unemployment that included Ford and other business leaders, but most of the industrialists withdrew when the committee recommended more federal involvement.[36]

On the other side were a growing number of radicals who not only sought more direct aid, but also regarded the communist party as the only party that truly cared for jobless. Also on this side were liberals who, though not communists, advocated the creation of a state-centered welfare program. Murphy responded initially by advocating a corporatist strategy. He organized the Mayors' Relief Committee to investigate unemployment in the fall of 1930. He began registration of the unemployed at the Free Employment Bureau and the Welfare Department, at which over 106,000 registered. The committee urged the city to convert closed factories into shelters for those facing eviction and place all available money into direct relief. Fisher Brothers and Studebaker donated space for lodging and meals. Through 1931, "over a million meals and over 300,000 nights lodging" came from the companies. The Employment Bureau, working at capacity, placed only 21,000 men, almost all in part-time positions that still left them indigent. The situation finally forced Murphy to change his position. By 1931, he had clearly shifted to advocating statist policy, in opposition to Detroit's business elite. He thus became one of the growing camp of mayors who, as part of Hoover's "essential public," abandoned the voluntarist vision for strong statist actions.[37]

Murphy supported several bills in the Michigan legislature, including unemployment insurance. The crisis had confirmed that unemployment "is neither the affair solely of manufactures nor of the unemployed, but the direct business of every citizen." As such, it required strong federal action. Unemployment insurance financed "partially or entirely" at the national level was the only practical or fair solution. Though cities such as Detroit would not always as now be prevented by near bankruptcy from providing relief, the policy ought to be made permanent. In the long term, Murphy argued, cyclical, seasonal, and technological unemployment was likely only to be worsened by increasing labor-saving machinery. Since industrialists were unwilling to endorse any type of secure insurance for the jobless and public works were never fully adequate, only a state-enforced, state-financed insurance plan could relieve the suffering of the jobless.[38]

While Murphy pushed for federal action, Detroit plunged deeper into destitution. The "City Welfare Department has been spending $2,000,000 a month," and yet a family of four received only $5 per week. Unable to stem the tide of the Depression and unaided by Washington, Detroit, like Milwaukee, witnessed several violent demonstrations, part of the national demonstrations of the Unemployed Council. The first came on March 6, 1930. Several thousand marched on city hall, where a clash with police left several injured and arrested. Murphy called for patience, arguing that the city "is doing all it can to relieve distress." He was also inclined to assign full blame for the violence, not to the demonstrators, but to the inaction of Herbert Hoover. "Sooner or later" Murphy said prophetically, "the federal government must do more to give relief or the radical elements of the country will rise up." Murphy, a liberal democrat, was motivated in this partly by his opposition the Communist Party, which grew stronger by the week as the crisis worsened. He saw this groundswell of radicalism as potential dangerous, locally and nationally. He thought strong state action in the form of redistributive democratic statist solutions, such as an Old Age Pension and Unemployment Insurance, would meet the basic needs of most of the unemployed, who were not organizers or even members of communist organizations. As long as those needs went unmet, the unemployed would demonstrate with the group they saw as most committed to their interests, the communists.

This threat was never greater than during the Ford Hunger March of March 7, 1932.[39] On that day, over 3,000 gathered to march on Ford Motor Company headquarters in Dearborn. The demonstration started peacefully, but when the marchers arrived on the border of Dearborn they met a small but aggressive Dearborn Police Department. The Dearborn police informed the demonstrators that they had no permit for the march. Undaunted, the workers pressed on and the police responded with tear gas and billy clubs. Eventually Detroit police arrived on the scene and both sides began shooting. Four were killed and over 100 injured. Industrialists feared these demonstrations were preludes to further communist action and might spark a revolution; Murphy feared that political stability was threatened. But in the event most of Detroit's workers did not follow up the march with participation in the communist party; instead they were energized to press for increased relief, and Murphy became even more vocal in calling for full state intervention.[40]

In November, partially in response to the Ford Hunger March and Murphy's continued public urging of a federal solution, Detroit overwhelmingly supported Franklin Roosevelt, the first ever Democratic nominee to carry the city. Murphy continued to advocate New Deal programs and the city supported Roosevelt's actions. Despite a worsening of the situation in early 1933 when several large Detroit banks collapsed, the city's workers, led by their mayor, joined others from all over the nation in turning from an anti-statist philosophy to one of democratic statism, with redistributive fiscal policy and recognition for workers at its core.[41]

Notes

1 Douglas Bukowski, *Big Bill Thompson, Chicago and the Politics of Image* (Urbana: University of Illinois Press, 1998); Herman Kogan and Lloyd Wendt, *Big Bill of Chicago* (Indianapolis: Bobbs-Merrill, 1953) 1-15; Harold Gosnell, *Machine Politics, Chicago Model* Chicago: University of Chicago Press, 1968. The focus of this chap[ter is on publics, as with the rest of the work,however, a more full discussion of discursive methods will need further research and development. This is a topic for researchers in the future, and will appear as part of a larger work forthcoming. John Bright, *Hizzoner Big Bill Thompson: An Idyll of Chicago* (New York: Jonathan Cape and Harrison Smith, 1930) 148-69.

2 *Chicago Tribune,* December 28, 1929, January 3, 1930; Mellon to Hoover November 15, 1929, Box 338, Presidential Papers, HHP; *New York Times,* December 29, 1929.

3 Bukowski, *Big Bill Thompson,* 88-90; *Chicago Tribune,* January 14, 27, 1930.

4 Budd to Hoover, September 16, 1930, Box 339, Presidential Papers, HHP; *Chicago Tribune,* October 2, 16, 18, 1930; Woods to Hoover October 1, 1930, Box 337, Presidential Papers, HHP.

5 Russel Sage Foundation statistical analysis of unemployment conditions, November 30, 1930 and March 30, 1931, Box 348, Presidential Papers, HHP. Grace Lee Maymor, *An Analysis of U.S. Census Figures on Unemployment in Chicago, 1930-31* (M.A. Thesis, University of Chicago, 1934) 12; Homer Hoyt, *One Hundred Years of Land Values in Chicago: The Relationship of the Growth of Chicago to the Rise in Its Land Values* (Chicago: University of Chicago Press, 1933) 267-73.

6 Horace Davis, *The Condition of Labor in the American Iron and Steel Industry* (New York: International Publishers, 1933) 102-10; "Business Tackles Relief for Jobless Through Association of Commerce" from *Chicago Commerce,* October 25, 1930, City Unemployment, Clipping File, Presidential Papers, HHP; Sanford Jacoby, *Emplying Bureaucracy: Managers, Unions, and the Transformation of Work in American Industry, 1900-1945* (New York: Columbia University Press, 1985) 200-20; Lizabeth Cohen, *Making A New Deal: Industrial Workers in Chicago, 1919-1939* (New York: Cambridge University Press, 1990) 240-9.

7 George Getz to Hoover, February 17, 1931, Box 338, Presidential Papers, HHP. *Chicago Tribune,* November 2, 15, 17, 23, 30, December 5, 10, 12, 13, 1930, January 6, 10, 11, 18, 30, 1931.

8 *Chicago Tribune,* October 19, 21, November 2, 9, 23, December 18, 21, 1930.

9 *Chicago Tribune,* October 14, November 9, 14, 1931; Croxton to Thompson, November 3, 1931, Box 339, Presidential Papers, HHP; PECE, Report on Unemployment in Chicago, December 30, 1931, Box 342, Presidential Papers, HHP.

10 Bukowski, *Big Bill Thompson,* 225-38; *Chicago Tribune,* November 7, 1931; PECE, Report on Unemployment Conditions, November 15, 1931, Box 344, Presidential Papers, HHP; Kathleen McCarthy, *Noblesse Oblige: Charity & Cultural Philanthropy in Chicago, 1849-1929* (Chicago: University of Chicago Press, 1982) 162-70.

11 *Chicago Tribune,* October 20, November1, December 1, 1931.

12 *Chicago Tribune,* November 1, 8, 12, 1931; Bukowski, *Big Bill Thompson,* 240-51, Alex Gottfried, *Boss Cermak of Chicago: A Study of Political Leadership* (Seattle: University of Washington Press, 1962) 172-9.

13 Reynolds to Hoover, December 12, 1931 and April 17, 1932, Box 351, Presidential Papers, HHP; *Chicago Tribune,* December 10, 1931, March 18, April 11, 1932; Gottfried, *Boss Cermak,* 213-18; Croxton to Reynolds, April 12, 1932, Box 351, Presidential Papers, HHP.

14 Gottfried, *Boss Cermak,* 199-220; Gosnell, *Machine Politics,* 8.

15 Gottfried, *Boss Cermak,* 208-12.

16 Gottfried, *Boss Cermak,* 214-19, *Chicago Herald Examiner,* May 8, 1931.

17 *Chicago Tribune,* March 19, 1932.

18 *Chicago Tribune,* April 7, May 11, 25, June 4, 12, 1932. Gottfried, *Boss Cermak,* 200-19; H.K. Barnard, *Anton the Martyr* (Chicago: Marlon Publishing, 1933) 67-73.

19 *Chicago Tribune,* April 8, 1932; Cermak to Hoover April 7, 1932, Box 351, Presidential Papers, HHP.

20 Gottfried, *Boss Cermak,* 3-15, 238-88; Barnard, *Anton the Martyr,* 15-27.

21 *Chicago Tribune,* May 11, 15, 17, 19, 1932; *New York Times,* May 19, 1932; "Mayor Cermak Visits Washington," *Illinois Municipal Review* (vol. XI, June 1932) 345-50. Gottfried, *Boss Cermak,* 271-8.

22 *Chicago Tribune,* July 11, August 1, 16, 1932.

23 *Milwaukee Journal,* October 10, 1929.

24 *Milwaukee Journal,* January 15, 1930; *Milwaukee Leader,* November 14, 1930, March 6, 1930; Ovid B. Blix, Assistant Secretary, City Service Commission, "Unemployment in Milwaukee-1930-1931." nd. Box 348, Presidential Papers, HHP.

25 Gadd, *History of Wisconsin,* 363-70; William Davidson, chair, The Unemployed Council to Hoan, June 21, 1930, Box 59, Hoan Papers.

26 Ibid; *Milwaukee Leader,* March 6, 7, 9, 1930; *Milwaukee Journal,* February 5, 1930.

27 Davidson to Hoan, June 21, 1930, Box 59, Hoan Papers.

28 Hoan to Woods, November 14, 1930, Box 349, Presidential Papers, HHP.

29 Blix, "Unemployment in Milwaukee."

30 Hoan to Woods, November 14, 1930, Box 349, Presidential Papers, HHP; Woods to Hoan, December 8, 1930, Box 351, Presidential Papers, HHP; Hoover to Hoan, December 13, 1930, Box 351, Presidential Papers, HHP; Hoan to Woods, December 20, 1930, Box 51 Hoan Papers.

31 "Report of Wisconsin Citizens' Committee on Employment," June 19, 1931, Box 351, Presidential Papers, HHP. Gladd, *History of Wisconsin,* 375-7; "Recommendations of Wisconsin Committee on Employment, 1930-1931," Box 6, W. Ellison Chalmers Papers, WRL. Hoan to D.D. Lescohier, December 1, 1930, Box 49, Hoan Papers; D.D. Lescohier to Hoan, December 10, 1930, Box 49, Hoan Papers.

32 Daniel Hoan and Frank Murphy, "Two Mayors Who Care About the Unemployed," *The Unemployed,* Spring 1931, 1-3, 28-33.

33 Frank B. Woodford and Arthur M. Woodford, *All Our Yesterdays: A Brief History of Detroit* (Detroit: Wayne State University Press, 1969, 310-29; B. J. Widick, *Detroit: City of Race and Class Violence* (Chicago: Quadrangle Books, 1972) 43-57; Sidney Glazer, *Detroit: A Study in Urban Development* (New York: Bookman Associates, 1965) 79-112.

34 Sidney Fine, *The Automobile Worker Under the Blue Eagle* (Ann Arbor: University of Michigan Press, 1963) 2-4; Widick, *Detroit,* 43.

35 *Detroit Free Press* covered the story daily throughout the controversy. See in particular June 15, July 1, July 22, 1930.

36 *Detroit News,* June 17, 1930, September 7, 1930, March 16, 1931; Glazer, *Detroit,* 99.

37 Widick, *Detroit,* 46-8; Daniel Hoan and Frank Murphy, "Two Mayors Who Care About the Unemployed," 29; Russell Sage Foundation, "Report on Unemployment in Several Large Cities" November 15, 1931, Box 348, Presidential Papers, HHP.

38 Hoan and Murphy, "Two mayors Who Care About the Unemployed," 30.

39 Ibid., *Detroit News,* March 6, 7, 10, 1930.

40 *Detroit News,* March 7, 8, 1932; Glazer, *Detroit,* 92-4; *New York Times,* March 8, 1932.

41 Murphy, speech before the city council, in *Detroit News,* November 10, 1932, Glazer, *Detroit,* 98; Woofdord, *All Our Yesterdays,* 315.

Chapter 9
Conclusion: Herbert Hoover and the Public Sphere

Jurgen Habermas' *The Transformation of the Public Sphere: An Inquiry into a Category of Bourgeois Society* offers highly suggestive strategies for understanding Hoover's discourse and his relief policies. Habermas defines the public sphere as the arena of rational critical debate first present in the bourgeois societies of the west during the enlightenment. This sphere existed outside government among private individuals, who communicated through the press and public opinion. In this sphere, poised between the state and civil society, people "engage the state on public matters of commodity exchange and social labor." Here public opinion forms, and actions by the state are assessed and criticized. If we apply this theory to Hoover, several questions arise. How did Hoover engage the public? Or, more specifically, what "public" or "publics" did Hoover see as critical to create or sway opinion in favor of his proposals? How did he attempt to manipulate or move public opinion?[1]

In the developing economy of the twenties a powerful public emerged: technical workers of the economy. This group consisted of engineers and new corporate organizational managers, and of intellectuals in the new social sciences such as Wesley Mitchell, Otto Mallory, John Dewey and Thorsten Veblen from the fields of sociology and economics. Also included in this group were knowledge-generating organizations such as The National Bureau of Economic Research and the Russell Sage Foundation. A closer look at the unemployment conference shows this public at work.

Hoover's "public of action" was not the public in general, nor the holders of "public opinion" he wished to sway. By "public of action" I mean the public(s) Hoover engaged to conduct rational critical debate, and then act. Hoover's corporatist strategy led him to select a public of action that would represent the key constituencies of his corporatist vision, and to focus that public toward voluntarist action. In other words, this public was not only to discuss the policy of the state, but also, because Hoover's voluntarism rested on anti-statist philosophy, to carry out that policy. The public Hoover coveted, then, was made up of elites from various sectors of society who already supported policies that limited state action. These elites came from the core corporatist areas of business, conservative labor unions, municipal government, and the social sciences. For example, Hoover courted the technocratic community of engineers who knew how to promote growth through efficiency. Toward this end, Hoover brought the engineering community together to study industrial waste and increased standardization. Such conferences formed a critical part of the construction of Hoover's "public," organized to promote a self-governing economic system in which both capital and labor cooperated in matters of efficiency, with higher production at a lower cost per unit. Management was attracted by the promise of maintaining wage levels and preserving the open shop. Thus, two areas of corporatist structure—engineers and managers—were in place. Of course labor resisted the open-shop movement, but because of its general weakness in 1921 and throughout the decade, the AFL, the nation's most powerful union, found itself capitulating to the voluntarist vision, the anti-statism of which it shared. Businesses saw a clear benefit in the effort to eliminate waste, standardize, and raise production. Large manufacturers saw in voluntarism the ability to consolidate power, and smaller producers saw wider possibilities for local or national market share. Working through key associations such as the National Association of Manufacturers (NAM), the Civic Federation, and the U.S. Chamber of Commerce, Hoover co-opted the associational leaders, and thus his policies were at least accepted, and at various times vigorously championed by, these particular interests within the sphere of corporate leadership.

C.H. Markum, President of the U.S. Chamber of Commerce, supported Hoover and his vision in 1921, and the institution continued to support him throughout the decade. Likewise, NAM doggedly supported Hoover's anti statist ideals, advocating especially such things as standardization. In the Depression, NAM outspokenly supported Hoover's resistance of progressive moves in the House of Representatives, particularly the Wagner and Costigan bills.

Associated with the engineers was another important part of the bourgeois public Hoover sought out, the new social sciences and, particularly, economists and sociologists, from whom he expected key information for the corporatist body pursuing policy. Two of these institutions were critical in promoting Hoover's vision, the NBER, and the Russell Sage Foundation. The NBER published all of the follow-up studies to the unemployment conference, on such various subjects as technological unemployment, seasonal unemployment, and labor relations; these were done primarily by Leo Wolman and Otto Mallory. Two sets of works encapsulate the thought of this segment of academia: the reports to the Unemployment Conference in 1921 and the culmination of a decade-long investigation by the President's Committee on Unemployment, *Recent Economic Changes* and *Recent Social Trends*. These two massive studies were the first comprehensive examination of the economic life of the country, and associated social changes, during a specific decade. Many of the authors who contributed to these studies were also members of the NBER and, as such, formed an academic alliance commissioned by Hoover; the studies therefore came with his endorsement. Their goal was to "report on recent...trends in the

United States with a view to...supply a basis for the formulation of large national policies looking to the next phase in the nation's development." The "public" in this case, then, was not the citizenry at large, but rather the narrow group of legislators and intellectuals who would use this information in its debate about future policy. Several reports in these volumes, such as Howard Odum's "Public Welfare" and Sydnor Walker's "Social Work," shed light on a changing notion of the term "public" in regard to relief and social work. The citizenry at large is regarded in these reports, as in the influential work of Wadill Catchings, not as vital participants in policy discussion, but rather, strictly as consumers.[2]

"Public welfare" appears in these reports within the category "social welfare." Social welfare is "both the product and process of that group of social achievements...designated by amelioration." It also designated a situation of deficiency requiring supplementary help. The goal of providing social welfare, then, "is to provide scientific and practical ways of attacking problems of inequality." Included in social welfare was the role municipal or state government played in relief. This was deemed "public welfare." Public welfare fell within the category of social welfare as an extension of private charitable efforts, of "private welfare."[3]

Although there remained differences between private and public relief administration, the term "public welfare" expanded its meaning throughout the decade and through the Hoover presidency. For example, some activities involving children and the aged moved from private to public welfare. In 1911, Mother's Aid had been instituted in only 2 states, Illinois and Wisconsin: by 1926, such aid had been enacted in 42 states. Old age pensions also expanded from Nevada and Montana (1923) and Wisconsin (1925) to 18 states by 1931. By then clearly, public welfare was expanding to include a range once exclusively left to the private sphere. This expansion reflected a more general transition from anti-statist to statist. As more states enacted legislation calling for governmental responsibility for the poor, the functions covered by public bodies also expanded. As unemployment became much more of a burden at the end of the decade, states expanded government involvement in that critical form of relief, extending social insurance to cover unemployment. So, under Hoover's watch as President, the idea of public relief or welfare expanded despite resistance at the federal level. When Congress began to debate expanded relief, it was clear that a growing segment of the national legislature saw public welfare as relief that should be expanded on the federal level.[4]

Habermas' work is so suggestive for historians because he brings to democratic theory a concern for the origins of the social conditions that allow for a full, rational debate by private citizens about public matters with some expectation of influencing policy. "Private people come together as a public...to engage them [public authorities] in a debate over the general rules governing relations in the basically privatized but publicly relevant sphere of commodity exchange and social labor," he wrote. In the period he described, from the 17th through the 20th century, the viability of the public sphere depended on the quality and quantity of discourse relating to the state and the market. Rational critical debate about these forces enabled the public to address matters of state and economy democratically. Habermas defined the quality of debate as a function of the kind of people, and the quantity as a function of the number of people, who participated in it. Over the period, Habermas claims, the quality of debate, originally determined by an educated, male, bourgeois, propertied elite, was changed by the growing quantity, by the expansion of news, associations, and public opinion.[5]

Importantly for our study, Habermas shows that rational critical debate became institutionalized as the general public entered into public discourse. However, as capitalist society changed, so too did the public sphere. As the corporatist institutions of society—labor, corporations, associations, etc.—grew, "power was taking place between the private bureaucracies, special interest associations, parties and public administration. The public, as such, is included only sporadically in this circuit of power." As societies grew technologically, and the private sphere became more isolated, the quality of discussion was more easily manipulated, while at the same time more sophisticated media increased available information, but to a public working longer days and isolated from meaningful discussion. Finally, Habermas argues that the public sphere died at the end of the 19th century, killed off by state penetration of civil society and mass consumer pleasures. This interpretation, however, is open to objections concerning race and gender, and does not take into account the continuing presence of several "publics" who represented the elite of the early twentieth century and were still able to critique policy concerning the state and the market. Hoover attempted to organize some of these publics and lead them to dominate discussion of policy, and later to preserve their dominance as alternative, subaltern, and growing publics pressed their way into the larger arena of discussion and challenged his control of the public sphere.[6]

Public discourse in the Hoover years, then, operated in two ways. Hoover relied on an "essential" public, an educated and industrial elite, sought out, assembled, and commissioned to provide discussion outside the legislative realm, but sanctioned, or organized, by him. The Unemployment Conference was a good example of this engineering of a public. Second, he relied on the press and general "public opinion" to pressure his essential publics to conform to his methods. Here, as throughout the decade, Hoover summoned leaders of business and labor to debate matters of "industrial self-government": raising productivity, settling disputes through arbitration, asking for labor peace and entering the wider discourse on unemployment, charity, and the place of the state in the area of relief. The leading associations involved, NAM, the U.S. Chamber of Commerce, and the Association of Railroad Managers, were in agreement with the only labor organization consulted regularly by Hoover, the conservative AFL. All these groups were opposed to more direct government intervention, albeit for different reasons.

In addition to these corporatist groups, Hoover included among his "essential" publics the academics who worked through emerging think tanks such as the NBER and the Russell Sage Foundation. These were to join the corporatist groups in another essential function of the "public" for Hoover—the promotion of public approval of his policies. This area of the public sphere is crucial in the work not only of Habermas, but of Walter Lippman as well. In discussing public opinion, we must understand its myriad general meanings as well as Hoover's use of it and the consequences for policy and, in a wider sense, democratic theory.[7]

Within the democratic social welfare state of the early twentieth century, public opinion was seen as working through institutions such as the legislature: "public opinion makes its desires known to the government, and the government makes its policies known to public opinion." In American democracy, a fixed party process ensures an institutionalized discussion of events, but public opinion has little actual influence on governing because, in the winner-take-all American system the majority party becomes the legitimized expression of public opinion and largely ignores voices of dissent. But if in fact the "public" is the general population and its "opinion" measured or perceived, and access to the sphere of rational critical debate is limited to a manufactured elite public whose ideas may not match those of the general public, then public opinion is ignored in favor of the controlled production of the constitutional apparatus manipulated to ensure a particular agenda. This in effect negates democratic openness. The question highlighted by Habermas' theory is to what degree, if at all, Hoover's corporatist manipulation of the public and the public sphere was a construction of the political economy which was in fact acceptable to the public until economic conditions shifted popular opinion. Does Hoover's careful staging of the processes of public reasoning in fact precisely exemplify the death—by state penetration of civil society—of the public sphere that Habermas recorded? We can answer this question only by examining alternative as well as mainstream publics, particularly in the early years of the decade.[8]

Hoover's corporatist vision of framing a public by aligning powerful interests to debate and devise policy suggests a key argument of John Dewey's in "The Public and Its Problems." Dewey argues that advancements in technology destroyed or, at a minimum, hindered face-to-face contact and dialogue among community members. The result was to facilitate "the rapid and easy articulation of opinion and information so as to generate constant and intricate interaction far beyond the limits of face to face communities." The consequence of this distance between citizen and state was that powerful interest groups and associations were able to make policy, leaving the "public…bewildered." Even though individual participation in voting was expanded and the rhetoric of the state was clearly individualist, citizens influenced policy only by voting and therefore to little effect.[9]

In this light, we may better understand Hoover's use of what he called public opinion. He promoted voluntarism by means of his status, rather than through any formal or legal enforcement mechanism. The key to his vision of the associative state was the cooperative effort of the corporatist elements of society—business and labor, and the state as facilitator, not regulator. Yet how then could Hoover persuade those who might not agree with him to cooperate? From the Unemployment Conference through his presidency, Hoover argued that the associative state must be enforced through the mobilization of public opinion concerning particular associations or individual leaders.

During and immediately after the Unemployment Conference, Hoover worked very hard with the press as well as the Conference committees to ensure that the recommendations made during the Conference were implemented. By and large, the major newspapers supported the Conference, and several aroused the expectation that cooperation among employers and a commitment to higher production by labor would pull the country out of recession. The news encouraged Hoover to think that "our policies are supported by public opinion." Voices for strong intervention were muted; Hoover's enforcement mechanism was in place. However, when prosperity returned in the summer 1922, though there was no real test of Hoover's method, he thought that prosperity at least partially owing to his framing of his vision of individualism and the virtuous state.

Thus, he addressed the coal situation in a similar way, as shown in Chapter 3. He formed committees to study the situation and make recommendations in an effort to sidetrack calls for nationalization or, at a minimum, strong regulation of the industry. The key to his plan of establishing cooperative effort in the industry was the publication and promotion of the recommendations of the Construction and Mining Committee of the Unemployment Conference. Hoover assumed that operators and miners could be brought to the table, agreements could be worked out between the union and operators, and disparities could be settled between union and non-union fields, all by the cohesive power of public opinion. The provisions of the 1922 agreements in the bituminous fields appeared to confirm Hoover's view. As shortages mounted and prices rose, the public did voice its displeasure and its desire for an agreement. For Hoover, this was evidence of his ability to use pressure from the public to influence employers. However, in the Depression, the tactic backfired, because the public was dismayed more by the state's than by employers' inaction. This hampered Hoover's efforts to use public opinion as a coercive tool and simultaneously opened the door to potential statist maneuvers that might cross the boundary into "dangerous regulations."

Moreover, Hoover's assumption that public pressure played a significant role in determining the outcome of the coal strike and the agreements of 1922 was inaccurate. While Congress threatened more strict regulations of the industry, Hoover continued to rely on informing the public as a means of influencing employers. Yet a lack of constructive measures to persuade employers to halt wage reductions and the clear sympathy in the country for miners made the strike of 1922 inevitable. Employers' actions leading up to the strike exposed the flaws in Hoover's theory of coercion through public opinion. First, public attitudes were impotent against an entrenched, well-organized employer class.

Second, the national organization of the coal industry made it virtually impossible for Hoover's tactics to work: the industry was threatened mainly by the disparities between unionized and non-unionized fields. Hoover did recognize this, but since he had no leverage with non-union employers, this disparity continued to plague the industry and frustrate his attempts to rationalize it.

Throughout the remainder of the decade, the coal industry continued to suffer from overproduction and tremendous labor strife. Hoover did nothing to solve the basic structural problems of glutted markets; instead he addressed transportation and spot prices, in the fervent belief that that was all that was required. In essence, Hoover protected what had become the key public for him, the coal owners, and showed this in his committee meetings and conferences. These discussions, taking place outside the realm of legislation, were conducted by private individuals addressing public concerns and assessing policy, but only within a narrow range of discourse that did not significantly challenge Hoover's anti-statist position.

The same approaches Hoover used in the coal situation he also attempted to apply to relief more generally. One of the cornerstones of Hoover's political economy and theory of the virtuous state rested on the primacy of municipal government and private charity as sources of relief, and the lack of federal intervention. This position was generally accepted, yet depending on the local unemployment situation and the politics of the mayor involved, it was challenged at times early in the decade and with more vigor during the crisis of 1929. Municipal leaders, then, were another critical public Hoover attempted to sway. If mayors responded positively to his voluntarist vision, Hoover would be able promote his corporatist vision nationally by showing mayors organizing in a similar fashion. This would reinforce public opinion in support of Hoover's vision. Understanding this, he worked very closely with Colonel Arthur Woods to pressure mayors to accept the proposals of the Unemployment Conference of 1921 as well as his later efforts during the Depression. In Chicago, Milwaukee, and Detroit, all three mayors, although of different parties and facing different internal political dynamics, showed that early in the decade the voluntarist paradigm was quite effective. They adhered to the broad outlines of Hoover's policies, and thus served as de facto supporters of Hoover's vision.

Though "Big Bill" Thompson of Chicago was critical of the Unemployment Conference, he railed against it more to make himself popular with labor than on ideological grounds. In fact, he worked within the voluntarist, corporatist framework, eventually setting up unemployment committees modeled on the Unemployment Conference. His Pageant of Progress was exactly the type of business/government cooperation Hoover was promoting. He left the massive burden of direct relief to private associations such as United Charities, who received no assistance, financially, from the city government. He established employment bureaus. These measures, although to a degree effective early in the decade, were ended by the recovery in March, after which Thompson could claim success in warding off unemployment, and popular support for his measures. The Depression, however, when he returned to his earlier policies, exposed the inadequacy of Thompson's machine politics and voluntarism.

In Milwaukee, Daniel Hoan showed that even a socialist could include voluntarism in the organization of relief. Hoan established innovative programs such as the Garden Homes Project, but also appointed the Committee of Twenty One to organize relief efforts along voluntarist lines. The committee made efforts to ensure building permits became available quickly and ran a free unemployment bureau. Hoan also, again in conformity with the Unemployment Conference, established limited public works projects, though as part of a constructive socialist vision. He accepted the broad idea of federally funded projects, yet in 1921-22 he clearly viewed municipal works as a prudent first step in the evolution of constructive socialist policy. His promotion of municipal ownership of harbors to combat exploitative rail rates was also part of his constructive socialist vision. These efforts, however, clearly rested within the bounds of Hoover's voluntarist vision.

Mayor Couzens in Detroit followed the ideology and methods of Hoover more closely than either Hoan or Thompson. He organized an unemployment conference in Detroit dominated by business leaders, and relied heavily on private charity for relief while the city promoted registration of the unemployed and public works. Couzens firmly believed that Hoover's assumptions about relief were correct, and the return of prosperity in 1922 convinced him that in fact the voluntarist model had provided sound strategies for handling the unemployed. Like Hoan and Thompson, Couzens provided examples for Hoover that the crux of his policy (that primary responsibility for relief rested with municipalities), and thus the key to maintaining the virtuous state, found support in the cities, and thus he became an important part of Hoover's essential public.

By the end of the decade, Hoover began to lose his ability to manipulate the essential publics of municipal leaders. In Chicago, Milwaukee, and Detroit, mayors moved away from reliance on private charity and local public bureaus of relief and petitioned for greater federal involvement. Hoover attempted to sway municipal leaders on several occasions, arguing that "local efforts of relief must be maintained" rather than "unwarranted and dangerous calls for the dole." Mayors Cermak, Murphy and Hoan all faced the growth of important and increasingly unhappy interest groups in their cities. As destitution, hunger, and poverty spread, these mayors shifted their focus from simple public works to active state intervention. In Detroit and Chicago, previously Republican Party strongholds, the election of 1932 ushered in Democratic regimes. Resistance to the ideal of the virtuous state and limited relief had triumphed.[10]

In the early New Deal years, the idea of associative efforts to solving the nation's ills was not completely overthrown; in fact it persisted through 1935. It most clearly expressed itself through the passing of the NRA. However, this came in an environment where the underlying assumptions about the language of relief and virtue had expanded. Hoover's vision and language was contested in the early Depression by publics he could no longer control. Essential publics of municipal leaders, intellectuals, labor, business leaders, and the national legislature, along with growing subaltern publics of women and blacks, put Hoover's vision of virtue and the state to the test. The popular unrest exhibited in the overwhelming victory of FDR did not completely overthrow the anti-statist impulse, but it did expand voluntarism to include more aggressive state action in organizing voluntary, cartelistic capitalism. Importantly, the advocates of more statist action were able by 1935 to move to a more clearly regulatory state, expanding the range of the role of the state in relief to include efforts such as Social Security and the Wagner Act. This expansion of the meaning of voluntarism and, by the end of the decade, the establishment of a clear regulatory philosophy, reflected a theoretical shift in the meaning of democracy. As Michael Sandel argued, there has been in the history of the United States two competing visions of liberty and virtue. On the one hand, Liberalism argues that government should play a dominant role in assuring "all citizens a decent level of income, housing and health" so that they may all exercise choice. On the other hand, republican theory rests on an idea of creating character in the citizenry so that it can develop "the qualities of character self-government requires." Hoover's language and philosophy clearly place him within this republican theory of liberty, and the contested nature of language about relief during the early depression foreshadowed a movement toward the liberal conception of liberty which to dominate American politics from the mid -thirties into the late 20th century. [11]

Now, in the late 20th century, after several years of expansion of poor laws such as AFDC, Medicare, and Medicaid, a growing conservative impulse reaching back to the republican ideal of liberty has re-emerged with policy ideas—such as the welfare reform of 1996—that hearken back to the same assumptions Hoover made about the virtuous state, liberty, and relief. Historians of policy and the state should pay serious attention to the underlying assumptions of policy makers in the areas of relief. Conceptual histories of words such as "welfare" reveal the persistence, over time, of the contestedness in language that translates into policy. This study represents the foundations of such a research agenda.

Notes

1 Habermas, *Transformation of the Public Sphere*, 48.

2 Howard Odum, "Public Welfare Activities," and Sydnor Walker, "Privately Supported Social Work," both appear in, Report of the President's Research Committee on Social Trends, *Recent Social Trends in the United States* (New York: McGraw Hill, 1933) 1224-73 and 1168-1223 respectively.

3 Odum, "Public Welfare" 1227; Walker, "Social Work," 1168, 1200-09, 1214-23.

4 Walker, "Social Work," 1199.

5 Habermas, *Transformation of the Public Sphere,* 62; see also, Calhoun, "Habermas and the Public Sphere," in Calhoun, *Habermas and the Public Sphere,* 1-50.

6 Michael Schudson, "Was There Ever A Public Sphere? If So, When? Reflections On the American Case," in Calhoun, *Habermas and the Public Sphere* 143-161. The article is very suggestive that the concept of the public sphere is useful for periods both before and after the 19th century. Peter Uwe Hohendahl, "The Public Sphere: Models and Boundaries," in Calhoun, *Habermas and the Public Sphere,* 99-108. Hohendahl also points out that limiting the idea of the public sphere to a specific time is unwise. He argues that "this theory must not rely on historical arguments but secure the conception in abstract philosophical terms." 101. Thus, from a theoretical point of view, the argument that the public sphere was killed off at the end of the 19th century does not apply in an absolute sense because the theoretical model is applicable to contemporary discussion of democratic theory.

7 Walter Lippman, *Public Opinion* (New York: Free Press, 1997)103-125.

8 Habermas, *Transformation of the Public Sphere,* 56; also 123-9; Walter Lippman, *Public Opinion* esp. 161-95.

9 John Dewey, *The Public and Its Problems* (Athens: Ohio University Press, 1954) 114. A public can be defined as a group that is indirectly or directly affected by the consequences of the acts affecting that group externally or internally. Dewey argues that "those indirectly affected {by policy} formed a public which took steps to conserve its interests by instituting composition and other means of pacification to localize the trouble." P17. The act of relief affects the unemployed and has indirect consequences for publics impacted by the policy- the poor themselves, social scientists who investigate policy, philanthropists and private charity organizations, municipal government, labor and corporate power. Thus, these are not merely interest groups, but vital publics that have interests they wish to protect.

10 Herbert Hoover to Croxton, June 23, 1932, Presidential Papers Box 214, HHP.

11 Alan Brinkley, "The New Deal and the Idea of the State," in Gary Gerstleand Steve Fraser, eds. *The Rise and Fall of the New Deal Order, 1930-1980* (Princeton: Princeton University Press, 1989) 85-121; Colin Gordon, *New Deals: Business, Labor, and Politics in America, 1920-1935* (Cambridge: Cambridge University Press, 1994) esp 204-79. Michael J. Sandel, *Democracy's Discontents: America in Search of a public Philosophy* (Cambridge: Harvard University Press, 1996) 4-8.

Bibliography and Primary Sources

There are several critical primary sources which require examination for the completion of the work. The Herbert Hoover Papers are quite extensive, with groups covering the unemployment conference and several industries, including coal and agriculture. The groups covering the presidential years include sections on the Reconstruction Finance Corporation and complete reports from the Departments of Commerce and Labor surveying conditions in the target cities. The James Davis Papers provide additional reports on these subjects as well as more extensive documents addressing the American Federation of Labor and issues of industrial courts, collective bargaining and several strikes which occurred during the period, particularly in the coal industry. The papers also highlight the tension between Hoover and Davis in making policy. In addition to these manuscript collections, the Department of Commerce Records (group 40-2) and Department of Labor Records (group 174-7), both in the National Archives, provide field reports and vital statistics for the period covered in the dissertation. Testimony given by Hoover to several congressional committees are particularly enlightening.

All of the mayors of the target cities have manuscript collections except William Thompson, mayor of Chicago from 1915-1923 and 1927-1931. Although this does present some difficulties, there are several biographies, city council reports, newspaper articles, city reports and papers within other collections to construct a useful narrative of his actions and decision making process to include him in the dissertation. William Dever, mayor between 1923 and 1927 has papers in the Chicago Historical Society. Daniel Hoan, mayor of Milwaukee from 1916-1940 has an extensive collection in the Milwaukee County Historical Society. This collection has considerable information on the relief crisis of 1921, the city's response, and a thorough section on the 1929-1933 period as well. In addition, the papers include correspondence with several socialist groups nationally and internationally, which assists in placing Hoan within the more conservative faction of the Socialist movement. James Couzens, mayor of Detroit from 1919-1922 and his successor, John Lodge, both have substantial manuscript collections in the Detroit Public Library, and Couzens also has papers in the Library of Congress covering his years in the Senate following the mayoral years.

Within the target cities there are several collections that focus on the actions of social welfare and relief agencies, organized labor, and employer associations throughout the period under consideration. For example, the Welfare Council Papers in the Chicago Historical Society provide rich information on the social welfare community's efforts, particularly during the 1921 relief crisis. The council was part of the umbrella organization United Charities and held its own unemployment conference in August 1921, with representatives of over 40 organizations, including Visiting Nurses, Chicago Commons, American Legion, and the Urban League. For the response to relief efforts from the organized labor perspective, the papers of John Fitzpatrick, president of the Chicago Federation of Labor, are particularly useful. This collection, also located in the Chicago Historical Society, includes correspondence and reports from the Welfare Council as well as the City Council on the matter of unemployment. Fitzpatrick was also a socialist and member of the Farmer Labor Party who advocated several alternative solutions to deal with unemployment different from organizations in the city as well as several critiques of Hoover's voluntarist approach. Selected papers of the Illinois Manufacturers Association, with holdings in the Chicago Historical Society as well as the Illinois State Historical Society in Springfield, provides useful documents on the open shop movement and various other subjects such as the coal situation and significant analysis during the depression years. Several individual companies also have collections which explore issues of company welfare and the business cycle, such as the Samuel Insull Papers at Loyola University and the papers of the Swift Company in the State Historical Society of Wisconsin.

Detroit and Milwaukee house similar types of collections, including the University Settlement House Papers in the Milwaukee County Historical Society, the United Charities of Milwaukee Papers in the State Historical Society of Wisconsin, and United Charities of Detroit in the Detroit Public Library. For actions of labor, the Wisconsin Federation of Labor Papers at the State Historical Society of Wisconsin and the Detroit Federation of Labor in the Detroit Public Library were used. For the national perspective, the microfilmed collections of Samuel Gompers and John L. Lewis are housed in Founders Library at Northern Illinois University. Several employers associations and industries of Milwaukee and Detroit will also be examined. In Milwaukee, collections of the Milwaukee Employers Association as well as several breweries in the city are housed in the Milwaukee County Historical Society. In Detroit, the papers of the Ford Motor Company proved excellent.

The response of the academic community as part of the growing professionalization of social investigation is critical to several chapters as well as the overall scope of the dissertation. A number of collections become important in this regard. Some of these collections are the John R. Commons Papers at the State Historical Society of Wisconsin, the William Burgess and Thorstein Veblin Papers at the University of Chicago, the Mary Van Kleek Papers at the University of Michigan, and the Wesley Mitchell Papers at Columbia University. One collection used in the concluding chapter to complement the work of Jurgen Habermas is the John Dewey collection at Southern Illinois University.

Additional Primary Sources:

Citizen's Committee on Unemployment and the Public Employment Office of Milwaukee. *Tenth Annual Report.* Milwaukee: Industrial Commission of Wisconsin, 1922.

Hoan, Daniel. *City Government: The Record of the Milwaukee Experiment.* Westport: Greenwood Press, 1974.

_____."Milwaukee Registers Progress." *National Municipal Review.* Vol. XII, No. 16 (1923).

_____. *The Failure of Regulation.* Chicago: The Socialist Party of America, 1914.

_____ and Frank Murphy. "Two Mayors Who Care About the Unemployed." *The Unemployed.* (Spring,1931).

Hoover, Herbert. *Addresses Upon the American Road. 1933-1960.* New York: Scribners, 1961.

_____. *American Ideals Versus the New Deal.* St. Clair Shores: Scholarly Press, 1972.

_____. *American Individualism.* Garden City: Doubleday, 1923.

_____. *Campaign Speeches of Herbert Hoover, 1932.* Garden City: Doubleday, 1933.

_____. *Herbert Hoover an American Epic.* H. Regnary, 1959.

_____. *Proclamations and Executive Orders March 4, 1929-March 4,1933.* Washington: U.S. Government Printing Office, 1974.

_____. *Public Papers of the Presidents of the United States: Herbert Hoover.*

Washington: U.S. Government Printing Office, 1976.

_____. *The Challenge to Liberty* West Branch: Herbert Hoover Presidential Library Association, 1989.

_____. *The Memoirs of Herbert Hoover: The Cabinet and the Presidency. 1920-1933* New York: Macmillan, 1952.

_____. *The Ordeal of Woodrow Wilson.* Baltimore: Johns Hopkins University Press, 1992.

Myers, William S. *The State Papers and Other Public Writings of Herbert Hoover.* Garden City: Doubleday, 1934.

Report of the President's Conference on Unemployment Washington: Government Printing Office, 1921.

_____, *Business Cycles and Unemployment.* Washington: U.S. Government Printing Office, 1923.

_____, *Recent Economic Changes in the United States.* New York: McGraw Hill, 1929.

Report of the United States Coal Commission. 5 volumes. Washington, D.C.: United States Government Printing Office, 1925.

President's Research Committee on Social Trends, *Recent Social Trends* New York: Whittlesey, 1934.

Thompson, William Hale. *Eight Years of Progress.* Chicago: City of Chicago, 1923.

Newspapers and Magazines:

Chicago Defender
Chicago Journal of Commerce
Chicago Tribune
Coal Age
Detroit Free Press
Detroit News
Illinois Municipal Review
Milwaukee Journal Sentinel
Milwaukee Leader
Nation
New York Post
New York Times
Washington Post
Washington Herald
Sacramento Union
Saturday Evening Post

Secondary Sources

Adams, Thomas Sewell. *Labor Problems: A Text Book.* New York: Macmillan, 1905.

Addams, Jane. Twenty *Years at Hull House.* New York: Macmillan, 1910.

Anderson, Howard C. *Herbert Hoover: A Study of Historical Revisionism.* Ph.D. Dissertation, Illinois State University, 1984.

Andrews, John Bertram, and John R. Commons, eds. *A Documentary History of American Industrial Society.* Cleveland: A.H. Clark, 1910.

Allen, Fredrick *Only Yesterday.* New York: Blue Ribbon Books, 1931.

Allswang, John W. *A House for All Peoples: Ethnic Politics in Chicago, 1890-1936.* Lexington: University of Kentucky Press, 1971.

Barber, William. *From New Era to New Deal: Herbert Hoover, The Economists, and American Economic Policy, 1921-1933.* Cambridge: Cambridge University Press, 1985.

Barnard, Harry. *Independent Man: The Life of Senator James Couzens*. New York: Scribners, 1958.

Barnard, H.K. *Anton the Martyr*. Chicago: Marlon Publishing, 1933.

Barret, James R. *Work and Community in the Jungle: Chicago's Packinghouse Workers, 1894-1922*. Urbana: University of Illinois Press, 1987.

Bate, Phyllis. *The Development of the Iron and Steel Industry of the Chicago Area, 1900 -1920*. Ph.D. Dissertation, University of Chicago, 1948.

Beard, Charles A. and Mary Beard. *The Rise of American Civilization* volume 2. New York: Macmillan, 1927.

Beasley, Norman. *Made in Detroit*. New York: Putnam, 1957.

Benjamin, Daniel. *U.S. and U.K. Unemployment Between the Wars: A Doleful Story*. London: Institute of Economic Affairs, 1992.

Berk, Gerald. "Corporate Liberalism Reconsidered: A Review Essay." *Journal of Policy History* 3(1991).

Berkowitz, Edward and Kim McQuaid. *Creating the Welfare State: The Political Economy of Twentieth Century Reform*. New York: Preager Publications, 1988.

Blatz, Perry K. *Democratic Miners: Work Labor relations in the Coal Industry, 1875 -1925*. Albany: State University of New York Press, 1994.

Bove, Paul A. *Mastering Discourse: The Politics on Intellectual Culture*. Durham: Duke University Press, 1992.

Bowen, Louise de Koven. *Growing Up With a City*. New York: Macmillan, 1926.

Bowman, John. *Capitalist Collective Action: Competition, Cooperation and Conflict in the Coal Industry*. Cambridge: Cambridge University Press, 1989.

Bright, John. *Hizzoner Big Bill Thompson: An Idyll of Chicago*. New York: Jonathan Cape and Harrison Smith, 1930.

Brinkley, Alan. "The New Deal and the Idea of the State." in Gary Gerstle and Steve Fraser, eds., *The Rise and Fall of the New Deal Order, 1930-1980*. Princeton: Princeton University Press, 1989.

Brissenden, Paul. *The I.W.W.; A Study of American Syndicalism*. New York: Columbia University Press, 1919.

Bukowski, Douglas. *Big Bill Thompson, Chicago and the Politics of Image*. Urbana: University of Illinois Press, 1998.

Burton, Clarence M. *History of Wayne County and the City of Detroit, Michigan*. Chicago: S.J. Clarke, 1930.

________. *The City of Detroit, Michigan, 1701-1922*. Detroit: S.J. Clarke, 1922.

Calhoun, Craig, eds. *Habermas and the Public Sphere*. Cambridge: MIT Press, 1992.

Cannon, Patrick. *The IWW*. New York: Merit, 1967.

Cantor, Milton. *The Divided Left: American Radicalism, 1900-1975*. New York: Hill and Wang, 1978.

Carver, J. *Principles of Political Economy*. Boston: Houghton Mifflin, 1919.

Catchings, Waddell and William Foster. *Money*. Boston: Houghton Mifflin, 1924.

Chambers, Simone. *Reasonable Democracy: Jurgen Habermas and the Politics of Discourse*. Ithica: Cornell University Press, 1996.

Chavis, John and William McNitt. *A Brief History of the Detroit Urban League*. Ann Arbor: Michigan Historical Collection, 1971.

Cohen, Lizabeth. *Making a New Deal: Industrial Workers in Chicago, 1919-1939*. Cambridge: Cambridge University Press, 1990.

Commons, John R. *Institutional Economics: Its Place in Political Economy*. Madison: University of Wisconsin Press, 1961.

_____. *Labor and Administration*. New York: A.M. Kelly, 1964.

_____. *Legal Foundations of Capitalism.* Madison: University of Wisconsin Press, 1957.
_____. *Myself, The Autobiography of John R. Commons.* Madison: University of Wisconsin Press, 1963.
_____. *Principles of Labor Legislation* New York: Macmillan, 1927.
_____. *The Distribution of Wealth* New York: Macmillan, 1905.
_____. *The Economics of Collective Action.* Madison: University of Wisconsin Press, 1970.
_____. *The History of Labour in the United States.* New York: Macmillan, 1918.
_____. *Trade Unionism and Labor Problems.* New York: A.M. Kelly, 1967.
_____, and Gerald G. Somers, eds. *Labor, Management, and Social Policy: Essays in the John R. Commons Tradition.* Madison: University of Wisconsin Press, 1963.
_____, and Sam A. Lewisohn, eds. *Can Business Prevent Unemployment.* New York: Alfred A. Knopf, 1925.
Cooper, Martha. *Analyzing Public Discourse.* Prospect Heights: Waveland Press, 1989.
Cooper, John M. *Pivotal Decades: The Ubited States, 1900-1920.* New York: W.W. Norton, 1990.
Cuff, Robert. "Herbert Hoover, the Ideology of Voluntarism and War Organization During the Great War." *Journal of American History* 64(September 1977).
Dancy, John C. *Sand Against the Wind: The Memoirs of John C. Dancy.* Detroit: Wayne State University Press, 1966.
Davis, Donald F. *Conspicuous Production: Automobiles and Elites in Detroit, 1899 -1933.* Philadelphia: Temple University Press, 1988.
Davis, Horace. *The Condition of Labor in the American Iron and Steel Industry.* New York: International Publishers, 1933.
Dewey, John. *The Public and Its Problems.* New York: H. Holt, 1927.
Dexter, Walter F. *Herbert Hoover and American Individualism, a Modern Interpretation of a National Ideal.* New York: Macmillan, 1932.
Douglas, Paul H. *American Apprenticeship and Industrial Education* New York: Columbia University Press, 1921.
_____. *Controlling Depressions.* New York: W.W. Norton & Co., 1935.
_____. *In the Fullness of Time: The Memoirs of Paul H. Douglas.* New York: Harcourt, Brace, Jovanovich, 1972.
_____. *Real Wages in the United States, 1890-1926.* New York: Macmillan, 1934.
_____. *Standards of Unemployment Insurance.* Chicago: University of Chicago Press, 1933.
_____. *The Problem of Unemployment.* New York: Macmillan, 1931.
_____. *The Worker in Modern Economic Society.* Chicago: University of Chicago Press, 1923.
_____. *Wages and the Family.* Chicago: University of Chicago Press, 1927.
Dubofsky, Melvin and Warren Van Tine. *John L. Lewis: A Biography.* Urbana: University of Illinois Press, 1986.
Epstein, Ralph. *The Automobile Industry, Its Economic and Commercial Development.* New York: A.W. Shaw, 1928.
Estleman, Loren D. *Edsel: A Novel of Detroit.* New York: Mysterious Press, 1995.
Ewen, Lynda A. *Corporate Power and Urban Crisis in Detroit.* Princeton, Princeton University Press, 1978.
Farr, James. *Political Innovation and Conceptual Change.* Cambridge: Cambridge University Press, 1989.
_____. *After Marx.* Cambridge: Cambridge University Press, 1984.
_____. *Discipline and History: Political Science in the United States.* Ann Arbor:

University of Michigan Press, 1993.

Fausold, Martin. *The Presidency of Herbert Clark Hoover.* Lawrence: University of Kansas Press, 1985.

Fearon, Peter. *The U.S. Economy, 1917-1945.* Manhattan: University of Kansas Press, 1987.

Fetter, Frank. *The Principles of Economics.* New York: Century, 1904.

Fine, Nathan. *Labor and Farmer Parties in the United States, 1828-1928.* New York: Rand School of Social Science, 1928.

Fine, Sidney. *The Automobile Worker Under the Blue Eagle.* Ann Arbor: University of Michigan Press, 1963.

Fishback, Price. *Soft Coal, Hard choices: The Economic Welfare of Bituminous Coal Miners, 1890-1930.* New York: Oxford University Press, 1992.

Foster, William. *The Great Steel Strike and Its Lessons.* New York: B.W. Huebsch, 1920.

Fott, David. *John Dewey: America's Philosopher of Democracy.* Lanham: Rowman & Littlefield, 1998.

Fragnoli, Raymond. *The Transformation of Reform: The Detroit Citizens League, 1912-1933.* Ph.D. Dissertation: University of Michigan, 1976.

Fraser, Nancy. "Rethinking the Public Sphere: A Contribution to the Critique of Actually Existing Democracy." In Craig Calhoun, ed. *Habermas and the Public Sphere.* Cambridge: MIT Press, 1992.

Fraser, Steve and Gary Gerstle eds. *The Rise and Fall of the New Deal Order, 1930 -1980.* Princeton: Princeton University Press, 1989.

Furner, Mary O. *Advocacy and Objectivity: A Crisis in the Professionalization of American Social Science, 1865-1905* (Lexington: University Press of Kentucky, 1975).

_____. and Barry Supple, eds. *The State and Economic Knowledge: The American and British Experiences.* Cambridge: Cambridge University Press, 1990.

_____. and Michael Lacy, eds. *The State and Social Investigation in Britain and the United States.* Washington: Woodrow Wilson Center Press, 1993.

Galbraith, John K. *The Great Crash, 1929.* Boston: Houghton Mifflin, 1972.

Gelfand, Mark I. *A Nation of Cities: The Federal Government and Urban America, 1933 -1965.* New York: Oxford University Press, 1975.

Glad, Paul. *The History of Wisconsin, Volume V: War, a New Era and Depression, 1914-1940.* Madison: State Historical Society of Wisconsin, 1990.

Glazer, Sidney. *Detroit: A Study in Urban Development.* New York: Bookman Associates, 1965.

Goodin, Robert E. *Reasons for Welfare: The Political Theory of the Welfare State.* Princeton: Princeton University Press, 1988.

Gordon, Colin. *New Deals: Business, Labor, and Politics in America, 1920-1935.* Cambridge: Cambridge University Press, 1994.

Gosnell, Harold. *Machine Politics, Chicago Model.* Chicago: University of Chicago Press,1968.

Gottfied, Alex. *Boss Cermak of Chicago: A Study of Political Leadership.* Seattle: University of Washington Press, 1962.

Gregory, John G. *History of Milwaukee Wisconsin.* Chicago: Clarke Publishing, 1931.

Grin, Carolyn. "The Unemployment Conference of 1921: An Experiment in National Cooperative Planning." *Mid-America* 55(April 1973).

Grossman, James R. *Land of Hope: Chicago, Black Southerners and the Great Migration.* Chicago: University of Chicago Press, 1989.

Habermas, Jurgen. *On the Logic of the Social Sciences.* Cambridge: MIT Press, 1988.

_____. *Structural Transformation of the Public Sphere: An Inquiry into a Category of Bourgeois Society.* Cambridge: MIT press, 1992.

_____. *The Habermas Reader.* Cambridge: Polity Press, 1996.

_____. *Theory and Practice.* Boston: Beacon Press, 1974.

Hansen, Alvin. *A Guide to Keynes* (New York: McGraw Hill, 1953).

_____. *Business-Cycle Theory, Its Development and Present Status.* Boston: Ginn, 1927.

_____. *Economic Policy and Full Employment.* New York: McGraw Hill, 1947.

_____. *Economic Stabilization in an Unbalanced World.* New York: Harcourt, 1932.

Harrison, Shelby. *American Foundations for Social Welfare.* New York: Russell Sage Foundation, 1946.

_____. *Public Employment Offices: Their Purpose, Structure and Methods.* New York: Russell Sage Foundation, 1924.

Harrod, R.F. *The Trade Cycle.* Oxford: Clarendon Press, 1936.

Hawley, Ellis. *Herbert Hoover, 1921-1928.* Iowa City: University of Iowa Press, 1981.

_____, "Herbert Hoover, the Commerce Secretariat and the Vision of an Associative State." *Journal of American History* 61(June 1974).

______. *The Great War and the Search for Modern Order: A History of the American People and Their Institutions, 1917-1933.* New York: St. Martin's Press, 1979.

Haywood, Bill. "Socialism, the Hope of the Working Class." *International Socialist Review.* (February 1912).

Hicks, John D. *Rehearsal for Disaster.* Gainesville: University of Florida Press, 1961.

Hofstadter, Richard. *The American Political Tradition and the Men Who Made It.* New York: Alfred A. Knopf, 1949.

Holub, Robert. *Jurgen Habermas: Critic in the Public Sphere.* New York: Routledge, 1991.

Hook, Sidney. *John Dewey: An Intellectual Portrait.* Amherst: Prometheus Books, 1995.

Houghteling, Leila. *The Income and Standard of living of Unskilled Laborers in Chicago.* Chicago: University of Chicago Press, 1927.

Hoy, Terry. *The Political Philosophy of John Dewey: Toward a Constructive Renewal.* Westport: Praeger, 1998.

Hoyt, Homer. *One Hundred Years of Land Values in Chicago: The Relationship of the Growth of Chicago to the Rise in Its Land Values.*
Chicago: University of Chicago Press, 1933.

Humphry, Jean M. *The Wisconsin University Settlement Milwaukee, Wisconsin, 1902-1931.* M.A. Thesis, Northern Illinois University, 1969.

Hunt, Edward Eyre. *What the Coal Commision Found.* Baltimore: The Williams and Williams Co., 1925.

Hurvitz, Haggai. *"The Meaning of Industrial Conflict in Some Ideologies of the Early 1920s: The AFL, Organized Employers and Herbert Hoover.* Ph.D. Dissertation, Cornell University, 1973.

Huthmacher, J. Joseph and Warren Susman, eds. *Herbert Hoover and the Crisis of American Capitalism.* Cambridge: Schenkman Publishing, 1973.

Jacoby, Sanford. *Employing Bureaucracy: Managers, Unions, and the Transformation of Work in American Industry, 1900-1945.* New York: Columbia University Press, 1985.

James, Marquis. *The Texaco Story: The First Fifty years, 1902-1952.* New York: Texaco Company, 1952.

Jennings, Edward. *Ethnicity and Class: Detroit's Polish Workers and the Organization of the United Automobile Workers.* Ph.D. Dissertation, Northern Illinois University, 1984.

Johnson, Julia E. *Government Ownership of Coal Mines.* New York: W.H. Wilson Co., 1923.
Jones, Barbara. *New Perspectives on Unemployment.* New Brunswick: Transaction Books, 1984.
Jones, Peter d'Alroy. *The Consumer Society: A History of American Capitalism.* Baltimore: Penguin Books, 1967.
Karl, Barry D. *The Uneasy State: The United States from 1915-1945.* Chicago: University of Chicago Press, 1983.
Katz, Michael B. *In the Shadow of the Poor House: A Social History of Welfare in America.* New York: Basic Books, 1986.
_____. *Poverty and Policy in American History.* New York: Academic Press, 1983.
_____. *The Undeserving Poor: From the War on Poverty to the War on Welfare.* New York: Pantheon, 1989.
_____ ed. *The Underclass Debate.* Princeton: Princeton University Press, 1993.
Keiser, John H., *John Fitzpatrick and progressive Unionism, 1915-1925.* Ph.D. Dissertation, Northwestern University, 1965.
Kendall, Willmoore and George Carey. *The Basic Symbols of the American Political Tradition.* Baton Rouge: Louisiana State University Press, 1970.
Keyssar, Alaxander. *Out of Work: The First Century of Unemployment in Massachusetts.* Cambridge: Cambridge University Press, 1986.
King, Willford. *Employment Hours and Earnings in Prosperity and Depression, United States, 1920-1922.* New York: National Bureau of Economic Research, 1923.
_____. *The Wealth and Income of the People of the United States.* New York: Macmillan, 1915.
_____. *Trends of Philanthropy: A Study in a Typical American City.* New York: National Bureau of Economic Research, 1928.
Kogan, Herman and Lloyd Wendt. *Big Bill of Chicago.* Indianapolis: Bobbs-Merill, 1953.
Korman, Gerd. *Industrialization, Immigrants, and Americanizers: The View from Milwaukee, 1866-1921.* Madison: State Historical Society of Wisconsin, 1967.
Lane, Winthrop D. *Civil War in West Virginia.* New York: Arnoand the New York Times, 1969.
Lankevich, George J. ed. *Milwaukee: A Chronological and Documentary History, 1673-1977.* Dobbs Ferry: Oceana, 1977.
Lavasseur, Emille. *Elements of Political Economy.* New York: Macmillan, 1905.
Layton, Edwin T. Jr. *The Revolt of the Engineers.* Cleveland: Case Western Reserve University Press, 1971.
Leavitt, Judith W. *The Healthiest City: Milwaukee and the Politics of Health Reform.* Princeton: Princeton University Press, 1982.
Legget, Walter W. *The Rise of Herbert Hoover.* New York: H.K. Fly Company, 1932.
Link, Arthur S. "What Happened to the Progressive Movement in the 1920s?" *American Historical Review* 64(July 1959) 833-51.
Lloyd, Craig. *Aggressive Introvert: A Study of Herbert Hoover and Public Relations Management 1912-1932.* Columbus: Ohio State University Press, 1973.
Lochbiler, Don. *Detroit's Coming of Age, 1873-1973.* Detroit: Wayne State University, 1973.
Lorant, John H. "Technological Change in American Manufacturing During the 1920s." *Journal of Economic History* 27(1967).
Lunt, Richard D. *Law and Order vs. the Miners of West Virginia, 1907-1933.* Hamden: Archer Books, 1975.
Lurie, H.L. "The Place of Federal Aid in Unemployment Relief." *Social Science Review.*

(December 1931).
Lustig, Jeffery. *Corporate Liberalism.* Berkley: University of California Press, 1982.
Macaulay, Frederick R. *Income in the United States, Its Amount and Distribution, 1909-1919.* New York: Harcourt, Brace and Company, 1921.
Malin, James C. *The United States After the World War.* New York: The Macmillan Co. 1930.
Martin, Elizabeth A. *Detroit and the Great Migration, 1916-1929.* Ann Arbor: Bentley Historical Library, University of Michigan, 1993.
Mayer, Harold M. *Chicago: Growth of a Metropolis.* Chicago: University of Chicago Press, 1969.
Maymor, Grace Lee. *An Analysis of U.S. Census Figures on Unemployment in Chicago, 1930-31.* M.A. Thesis: University of Chicago,1934.
McCarthy, Kathleen D. *Noblesse Oblige: Charity and Cultural Philanthropy in Chicago, 1849-1929.* Chicago: University of Chicago Press, 1982.
McCarthy, Thomas *The Critical Theory of Jurgen Habermas.* London: Hutchinson, 1978.
McDonald, James. *Socialism, Critical and Constructive.* New York: Cassell, 1924.
McDonald, Forrest. *Insull.* Chicago: University of Chicago Press, 1962.
McShane, Clay. *Technology and Reform: Street Railways and the Growth of Milwaukee, 1887-1900.* Madison: State Historical Society of Wisconsin, 1975.
Merriam, Charles. *Chicago: A More Intimate View of Urban Politics.* New York: Macmillan, 1929.
Miller, Sally. *Victor Berger and the Promise of Constructive Socialism, 1910-1920.* Westport: Greenwood Press, 1973.
Mitchell, Wesley C. *Business Cycles and Unemployment.* New York: National Bureau of Economic Research, 1923.
_____. *Business Cycles: The Problem and its Setting.* New York: National Bureau of Economic Research, 1927.
_____. *What Happens During Business Cycles.* New York: National Bureau of Economic Research, 1951.
Monkkonen, Eric. *Walking to Work: Tramps in America, 1790-1935.* Lincoln: University of Nebraska Press, 1984.
Montgomery, Royal E. *Industrial Relations in the Chicago Building Trades.* Chicago: University of Chicago Press, 1927.
Munslow, Alun. *Discourse and Culture: The Creation of America, 1870-1920.* London: Routledge, 1992.
Murray, Robert K. *Red Scare: A Study in National Hysteria, 1919-1920.* Minneapolis: University of Minnesota Press, 1955.
_____. *The Harding Era: Warren G. Harding and His Administration.* Minneapolis: University of Minnesota Press, 1969.
Nash, George H. *Herbert Hoover and Stanford University.* Stanford: Hoover Institution Press, 1988.
_____. *The Life of Herbert Hoover* Volumes 1and 2. New York: Norton, 1988.
Nash, Lee, ed. *Understanding Herbert Hoover: Ten Perspectives.* Stanford: Hoover Institution Press, 1987.
National Industrial Conference Board. *The Unemployment Problem.* New York: National Industrial Conference Board, 1921.
Nielsen, Kai. "Legitimation in Complex Societies: Some Habermasian Themes." *Annals of Scholarship.* 7(1990).
Noggle, Burle. "The Twenties: A New Historiographical Frontier." *Journal of American History* 53(September 1966).

Nosh, Michael. *Conflict and Accommodation: Coal Miners, Steel Workers, and Socialism, 1890-1920*. Westport: Greenwood Press, 1982.

Oestreicher, Richard J. *Solidarity and Fragmentation: Working People and Class Consciousness in Detroit, 1875-1900.* Urbana: University of Illinois Press, 1989.

Olson, James. *Saving Capitalism: The RFC and the New Deal, 1933-1940.* Princeton: Princeton University Press, 1988.

Orum, Anthony M. *City-Building in America.* Boulder: Westview Press, 1995.

Ozanne, Robert. *A Century of Labor-Management Relations at McCormick and International Harvester.* Madison: University of Wisconsin Press, 1967.

Palmer, Bryan D. *Descent into Discourse: The Reification of Language and the Writing of Social History*. Philadelphia: Temple University Press, 1990.

Parker, Glen L. *The Coal Industry: A Study in Social Control.* Washington, D.C.: American Council on Public Affairs, 1940.

Parrish, Michael. *Anxious Decades: America in Prosperity and Depression, 1920-1941.* New York: Norton, 1992.

Patterson, James T. *America's Struggle Against Poverty, 1900-1985.* Cambridge: Harvard University Press, 1986.

Peterson, Walter. *An Industrial Heritage: Allis-Chalmers Corporation*. Milwaukee: Milwaukee County Historical Society, 1978.

Philpott, Thomas L. *The Slum and the Ghetto: Immigrants, Blacks, and Reformers in Chicago, 1880-1930.* Belmont: Wadsworth publishing, 1991.

Piven, Francis Fox. *Regulating the Poor: The Functions of Public Welfare*. New York: Pantheon, 1988.

Rehg, William. *Insight and Solidarity: A Study of the Discourse Ethics of Jurgen Habermas.* Berkley: University of California Press, 1994.

Renshaw, Patrick. *The Wobblies: The Story of the IWW and Syndicalism in the United States*. Chicago: Ivan D. Dee, 1999.

Robinson, Edgar E. *Herbert Hoover, President of the United States.* Stanford: Hoover Institution Press, 1975.

Rorty, M.C. "How May Business Revival Be Forced?" *Harvard Business Review*. (April, 1932).

Rothbard, Murray, "Herbert Clark Hoover." *New Individualist Review* 4(Winter, 1966).

Ryan, Alan. *John Dewey and the High Tide of American Liberalism.* New York: Norton, 1995.

Sandel, Michael J. *Democracy's Discontent: America in Search of a Public Philosophy.* Cambridge: Harvard University Press, 1996.

Sautter, Udo. *Three Cheers for the Unemployed: Government and Unemployment Before the New Deal.* Cambridge: Cambridge University Press, 1991.

Schatz, Ronald. *The Electrical Workers: A History of Labor at General Electric and Westinghouse, 1923-1960*. Urbana: University of Illinois Press, 1983.

Schmidt, John R. *The Man Who Cleaned Up Chicago: A Political Biography of William Dever*. DeKalb, Northern Illinois University Press, 1989.

Schwarz, Jordan. *The Interregnum of Despair: Hoover, Congress and the Depression.* Urbana: University of Illinois Press, 1970.

_____. *The New Dealers: Power Politics in the Age of Roosevelt.* New York: Knopf, 1993.

_____. *The Speculator: Bernard Baruch in Washington, 1917-1965.* Chapel Hill: University of North Carolina Press, 1981.

Seckler, David. *Thorstein Veblen and the Institutionalists: A Study in the Social*

Philosophy of Economics. Boulder: University of Colorado Press, 1975.

Seltzer, Curtis. *Fire in the Hole: Miners and Managers in the American Coal Industry*. Lexington: University of Kentucky Press, 1985.

Simon, David R. *The Expansion of an Industrial City: Milwaukee, 1880-1910*. Published by the author, 1971.

Skinner, Quentin. *Machiavelli and Republicanism*. Cambridge: Cambridge University Press, 1990.

_____. *Philosophy in History: Essays on the Historiography of Philosophy*. Cambridge: Cambridge University Press, 1993.

_____. *The Foundations of Modern Political Thought*. Cambridge: Cambridge University Press, 1978.

_____, *The Return of Grand Theory in the Human Sciences* (Cambridge: Cambridge University Press, 1985).

Sklar, Martin J. *The Corporate Reconstruction of American Capitalism, 1890-1916: The Market, the Law and Politics*. New York: Cambridge University Press, 1988.

Sobel, Robert. *Herbert Hoover at the Onset of the Great Depression*. Philadelphia: Lip pincott, 1975.

Soule, George. *Prosperity Decade: From War to Depression, 1917-1929*. New York: Rinehart, 1947.

Spear, Allan. *Black Chicago: The making of a Negro Ghetto, 1890-1920*. Chicago: University of Chicago Press, 1967.

"Standards and Recommendations for the Relief and Prevention of Unemployment." *American Association of Labor Legislation*, (September 1921).

Still, Bayrd. *Milwaukee: The History of a City*. Madison: State Historical Society of Wisconsin, 1965.

Suffen, Arthur E. *The Coal Miners' Struggle for Industrial Status: A Study of the Evolution of Organized relations and Industrial Principles in the Coal Industry*. New York: Macmillan, 1926.

Taylor, Graham. *Chicago Commons through Forty Years*. Chicago: University of Chicago Press, 1936.

Thomas, Richard W. *Life for Us is What We Make It: Building Black Community in Detroit, 1915-1945*. Bloomington: Indiana University Press, 1992.

Thompson, Frederic. *The IWW.: Its First Fifty Years*. Chicago: University of Chicago Press, 1955.

Ticknor, Thomas J. *Motor City: The Impact of the Automobile Industry Upon Detroit, 1900-1975*. Ph.D. Dissertation, University of Michigan, 1978.

Trattner, Walter. *From Poor Law to Welfare State: A History of Social Welfare in America*. New York: The Free Press, 1986.

Trotter, Joe W. *Black Milwaukee: The Making of an Industrial Proletariat, 1915-45*. Urbana: University of Illinois Press, 1988.

Tugwell, Rexford. *Mr. Hoover's Economic Policy*. New York: John Day Co., 1932.

Tuttle, William M. *Race Riot: Chicago in the Red Summer of 1919*. New York: Atheneum, 1970.

Unger, Irwin. "The New Left and American History." *American Historical Review*. 72(July 1967).

United Mine Workers. *Government of Coal*. Clearfield PA., 1921.

Van Kleek, Mary, and Benjamin Selekman. *Employees Representation in Coal Mines: A Study of the Industrial Representation Plan of the Colorado Fuel and Iron Company*. New York: Russell Sage Foundation, 1924.

Van Kleek, Mary. "Toward a National Employment Service." *Survey*. (April, 1931).

Veblen, Thorstein. *The Engineers and the Price System*. New York: Viking, 1921.

_____. *The Theory of the Leisure Class: An Economic Study in the Evolution of Institutions*. Macmillian, 1899.

_____. *The Theory of Business Enterprise*. New York: Scribner's, 1932.

Vedder, Richard K. and Lowell E. Gallaway. *Out of Work: Unemployment and Government in Twentieth-Century America*. New York: Holmes & Meier, 1993.

Vexler, Robert L. Detroit*: A Chronological and Documentary History, 1701-1976*. Dobbs Ferry: Oceana, 1977.

Watkins, T.H. *The Great Depression: America in the 1930s*. Boston: Little Brown, 1993.

Warren, Harris G. *Herbert Hoover and the Great Depression*. New York: Norton, 1967.

Weems, Robert E. *From the Great Migration to the Great Depression: Black Milwaukee, 1915-1929*. M.A. Thesis, University of Wisconsin, 1982.

Weinstein, James. *The Corporate Ideal in the Liberal State, 1900-1918*. Boston: Beacon Press,1968.

_____. *The Decline of Socialism in the United States, 1912-1925*. New York: Vintage Books,1969.

Weinzweig, Irving. "The Unemployment Insurance Plan of the Amalgamated Clothing Workers of America." *The Unemployment Review*. (June, 1931).

Weis, Nancy J. *The National Urban League: 1910-1940*. New York: Oxford University Press, 1974.

Wells, Robert W. *This is Milwaukee*. Milwaukee: Renaissance Books, 1981.

Wendt, Lloyd, and Herman Kogan. *Big Bill of Chicago*. Indianapolis: Bobbs-Merrill, 1953.

Widick, B.J. *Detroit: City of Race and Class Violence*. Chicago: Quadrangle Books, 1975.

Wiebe, Robert. *Businessmen and Reform: A Study of the Progressive Movement*. Cambridge: Harvard University Press, 1962.

_____. *Self-Rule: A Cultural History of American Democracy* (Chicago: University of Chicago Press, 1995).

_____, *The Search for Order, 1877-1920*. New York: Hill and Wang, 1967.

Williams, Raymond. *Keywords: A Vocabulary of Culture and Society*. New York: Oxford University Press, 1976.

Williams, William A. *The Contours of American History*. Cleveland: World Publishing Co., 1961.

Wilson, Howard E. *Mary McDowell, Neighbor*. Chicago: Chicago University press, 1928.

Wilson, Joan Hoff. *American Business and Foreign Policy, 1920-1933*. Lexington: University Press of Kentucky, 1971.

_____. *Herbert Hoover, Forgotten Progressive*. Prospect Heights: Waveland Press, 1975.

Wolman, Leo. *Ebb and Flow in Trade Unionism*. New York: National Bureau of Economic Research, 1936.

_____. *The Clothing Workers of Chicago, 1910-1922*. Chicago: The Chicago Joint Board, Amalgamated Clothing Workers of America, 1922.

_____. *The Growth of American Trade Unions, 1880-1923*. New York: National Bureau of Economic Research, 1924.

Wood, Clement. *Herbert Clark Hoover: An American Tragedy*. New York: M. Swain, 1932.

Woodford, Frank B. and Arthur M. Woodford. *All Our Yesterdays: A Brief History of Detroit*. Detroit: Wayne State University Press, 1969.

Zorbaugh, Harvey W. *The Gold Coast and the Slum: A Sociological Study Chicago's Near North Side.* Chicago: University of Chicago Press, 1929.

Zunz, Olivier. *The Changing Face of Inequality: Urbanization, Industrial Development, and Immigrants in Detroit, 1880-1920.* Chicago: University of Chicago Press, 1982.

Index

www.ingramcontent.com/pod-product-compliance
Lightning Source LLC
LaVergne TN
LVHW102006210926
848483LV00009B/78
* 9 7 8 0 7 6 1 8 3 2 3 4 8 *